Dave Carrigan

May 2020

Becoming a No-Fail Mission
The Origins of Search and Rescue in Canada

James Pierotti

ISBN: 978-1-4834-8663-5 (sc)
ISBN: 978-1-4834-8664-2 (e)

Lulu Publishing Services rev. date: 09/25/2018

This study is dedicated to all the search and rescue professionals who did not make it home from their mission, and to their families that suffered. This book aims to explore an essential service in which some military people choose risk and danger *that others may live.*

Contents

List of Figures and Tables

Abstract

The Royal Canadian Air Force's (RCAF's) involvement with the search and rescue (SAR) mandate in Canada dates to 1947. The RCAF's Air Sea Rescue (ASR) predecessor capability from the Second World War dates back to 1942. How and why did the RCAF become involved with both of those capabilities, and is there historical rationale for the continued involvement of the RCAF in the domestic SAR service today? As the Canadian government has pondered civilian contract options for the delivery of SAR in recent years, the rationale behind assigning the SAR service to the RCAF in the first place becomes fundamentally important to future decisions.

Prior to the Second World War, a SAR service was virtually non-existent, so this book will outline the very limited Canadian pre-war rescue services and follow the tumultuous developments in Canadian rescue services for the first 25 years. This book uses previously unexamined RCAF and other governmental primary-source documentation to outline the major developments in the Canadian rescue system from 1939 to 1964, including the long-overdue formation of the Canadian Coast Guard in 1962. A comprehensive report conducted in 1964 on the SAR organization stated that the rescue service had achieved maturity, and this report bookends the evolution from negligible aviation- and maritime-rescue capability to a stable SAR organization that is remarkably similar to the one still in use today.

The overall argument offered is that the factors behind the RCAF involvement in military and domestic SAR were critical to the development of the rescue service, and history suggests that Canada needs to understand the rationale behind the RCAF providing the national SAR service in order to make informed decisions on the SAR organization of the future. Amplified with operational examples of the rescue system in action, this previously untold history aims to further the debate on the use of military resources for domestic responsibilities.

Preface

"We are declaring an emergency. …We have to land immediately."[1] Those were the last words to Halifax air traffic control from Swiss Air 111, a Boeing MD-11 aircraft full of people on its way to Geneva, Switzerland, from New York City on 2 September 1998. Near the quaint and quiet town of Peggy's Cove, Nova Scotia, the aircraft plummeted into the sea six minutes after declaring an emergency, and it hit the water so hard that buildings 15 kilometres away were shaken. It was a horrific accident that claimed 229 lives.

Even as the accident was taking place, Canada's SAR organization was responding to the radio communications from the doomed flight with resources in the form of a Labrador helicopter and Hercules aircraft (from Greenwood, Nova Scotia, approximately 70 nautical miles from the accident site) and Canadian Coast Guard vessels in the area. However, if anyone had survived the aircraft crash, many more resources would have been required. Canada's SAR system is very capable when it comes to aircraft crashes with a few poor souls on board, but any accident with hundreds of people on board would require many resources from all levels of government to prevent drowning or hypothermic deaths.

Even without the dearly hoped-for survivors, this emergency required support from all levels of Canadian government and the local communities to provide enough resources for the tragedy's consequence-management efforts. In the initial stages, however, and with all due respect to the men and women who responded from the Canadian Coast Guard, Canadian military resources primarily led the large and necessary response. The

---

[1] The Canadian Encyclopedia, "Swiss Air 111 Tragedy," 14 September 1998, http://www.thecanadianencyclopedia.ca/en/article/swissair-111-tragedy/ (accessed 25 April 2018).

rescue coordination centre (RCC) in Halifax, an Air Force unit, was the lead organization for coordination. Canadian Army personnel in Trenton, Ontario, prepared and loaded major air disaster equipment onto a tactical airlift CC-130 Hercules, based on an RCC request. Navy assets from Halifax put to sea to coordinate overall search efforts in the area as part of the major-disaster response of the SAR service for a large incident. A more well-known fact, aircraft from Canada's Air Force flew over the area in the fruitless search for survivors. As part of the Air Force response, 413 Transport and Rescue Squadron in Greenwood, Nova Scotia, called out all available squadron personnel to assist in the rescue or recovery efforts.

The morning after the crash, I was one of the aircrew called in by 413 Squadron to fly over the impact area to provide an aerial overview of the situation for the onboard navy captain responsible for the on-scene maritime vessel resources. I was an experienced air navigator on the CC-130 Hercules at the time, but the Swiss Air tragedy was my first SAR mission, as I had just arrived at the squadron from a tactical airlift background in Trenton, Ontario. That flight was a pivotal moment in my life, as I had never before been part of a capability so meaningful to the Canadian public and with so much scrutiny on how well we all did our jobs. The beehive of activity around me had but one purpose: to provide the best possible response to the Swiss Air crisis, with individuals coming together as a large and coordinated team. Even though the life and death of survivors are not always influenced by the SAR mission response, as those poor souls on Swiss Air 111 prove, every person responding to emergencies can make a real difference to the families, the other responders, and the public. That day, I was able to make a difference in my own way for the people who were onboard the Hercules aircraft with me, by plotting the locations of all the vessels and debris we spotted on a map that was later used by the navy captain to develop his complete awareness of the disaster area. Despite my small role in the assistance to the massive tragedy, I knew then that I had found my calling, and I have proudly remained involved in Canada's SAR organization ever since.

Many years later, I found myself looking for a book-length research topic while working on a master's degree, and I recalled my amazement at the large and immediate response to the Swiss Air tragedy by the Canadian military. The military may seem like an obvious choice to handle a large crisis like Swiss Air 111, but the reason it was called upon immediately was because the RCAF is operationally responsible for the domestic SAR organization in Canada. Calling out RCAF resources was, and remains, standard procedure for daily SAR operations. This responsibility begs several questions: How did it come about that the RCAF became responsible for everyday domestic SAR in Canada? Why was the Air Force also assigned responsibility for maritime emergencies? Are those reasons still valid today?

Research provided answers to those questions, and evidence and arguments will be provided in due course, but not with a progression of events that I expected. Surprisingly, I found that the RCAF had not wanted the SAR role, and indeed, it had tried several times to be rid of it. I had originally believed that the Air Force volunteered for the role, but I found that the RCAF was reluctant to rescue until 1959. Between 1959 and 1964, however, strains to the Canadian SAR service had become critical, and both the government and the RCAF made significant changes to improve the service. By 1964, the reasons for RCAF involvement in SAR had become deeply rooted and you, the reader, will be provided with evidence to assess whether the historical rationale behind the RCAF's responsibility for SAR remains valid today.

In the process of uncovering SAR history in Canada, through the Second World War and into the Cold War, I came to believe that the narrative surrounding Canada's rescue development is a highly interesting story that has continued applicability today. The story will primarily cover the developments from the perspective of the RCAF, but the Royal Canadian Navy's (RCN's) important role in rescue development will be outlined as well as the little-known role of the Canadian Army in support of ground search teams. Near the end of the 25 years covered in the course of this book, the long-awaited development of the Canadian Coast Guard became a key contributor within the overall SAR organization, as it formalized a partnership with the RCAF that has been highly successful ever since. The RCAF and the Canadian Coast Guard conduct daily SAR missions, but the role of the other military environments[2] is also important in any

---

[2] Since the unification of Canada's three services into the Canadian Armed Forces on 1 February 1968, maritime, land and air forces are referred to as "environments."

large disaster, as proven by the involvement of the other environments in the Swiss Air tragedy.

The domestic SAR service of today is but one part of a larger capability, from searching for lost people in Canada to combat rescue in a deployed military operation. All parts of the larger capability will be discussed in due course, but the focus of this book will be on the federal SAR organization that exists in Canada to provide SAR services to people involved in domestic aeronautical and maritime emergencies. The SAR service responds primarily to aircraft and vessel emergencies that occur anywhere over Canadian territory and the Great Lakes as well as seas that have been assigned to Canada for SAR purposes. Deploying SAR services to support military forces overseas will be discussed, but it will become clear that the military aspect of SAR has not been a significant concern for the RCAF since the Second World War.

Due to a lack of military combat-rescue focus even during and then after the Second World War, the RCAF accidentally became expert in domestic-rescue requirements. In the process of developing expertise, a separation developed between the RCAF and the police for SAR response over Canadian soil and waters. The police, either Royal Canadian Mounted Police (RCMP) or local police forces, became responsible for missing persons and maritime emergencies that occur in lakes other than the Great Lakes, while the RCAF became responsible for aeronautical emergencies of civilian or military aircraft anywhere over Canadian territory and areas of the ocean internationally assigned to Canada. Shortly after those policies developed, the RCAF became responsible for maritime emergencies in Canada's Great Lakes and oceanic areas assigned by the international community. In summary, lost people or community emergencies are the responsibility of the police of jurisdiction or other provincial authorities, while the RCAF's role is primarily for aeronautical and maritime emergencies; although, the RCAF can be requested to assist with provincial or police missions.

This book explains how and why those policies came about. The first chapter starts with a description of the state of rescue in 1939, the beginning of our story, and then it outlines the current system to clarify the components of Canadian rescue that were created by 1964, which will be the end of this story. The first chapter also provides an overview of the major themes woven throughout all the chapters to set the stage for what follows.

The second and third chapters describe the ASR capability that was developed during the Second World War: a combat-rescue system deemed essential to fight a war on and over Canadian territories and waters in the event of invasion. Later chapters cover the post-war developments of the SAR service in Canada from a high-level overview and in a chronological order. The history provided ends in 1964, but it will be made clear that there is surprisingly little difference between the basic structure of the SAR organization of that time and the one today.

The main purpose of this book is to describe why the RCAF was given responsibility for domestic SAR and how the system developed into what is recognized today. What this book will not do is describe the myriad of aircraft, units, and leadership changes along the way. There are other books that describe the details of aircraft, units, and people as they were moved and changed over the years described in this book, and those details are not repeated here. Despite the high-level approach, included are stories of actual rescues, as they clarify aspects of the SAR organization and were, in some cases, critically important to subsequent developments. Therefore, specific rescue examples taken from primary sources have been used throughout to offer insight into how the rescue system was operationally used. Some well-known SAR missions may have been left out, and if so, they were omitted due to my own error or because there did not appear to be a correlation with key features of Canadian rescue development.

One oddity that is used throughout is the use of the word aircraft. An aircraft can mean all kinds of heavier-than-air craft, but in this book, aircraft has only been used to describe fixed-wing powered aircraft that land on wheels, and not seaplanes or helicopters. This rather limited definition has been used in order to be clear when the resource described is actually a helicopter or a seaplane that lands or takes off on water, and it will become evident that the differentiation is important in the post-war environment. In this book, specific makes and models of all airframes are unimportant to this narrative. The importance of airframes to the discussion is the capabilities that they provide to rescue services in general, and that is why the discussion has been simplified to the three general terms of aircraft, seaplanes, and helicopters.

Ultimately, this is a story about the people of the RCAF and how they dealt with life-and-death rescue matters during and after the Second World War. It was exciting to research, and it is equally exciting to be able to tell these little-known details and argue for the continued relevancy of SAR history to the contemporary environment. People lost their lives when rescue services were not available before the Second World War, and even the creation of rescue services during and after the war could not possibly save all lives or prevent the rescuers from losing their own. I have attempted to do justice to all of those people involved in the dramatic events that defined SAR progression, and I have tried to provide a balanced approach to developments that, especially in the 1950s, can be easy to criticize. The lack of government funding for the RCAF's SAR organization and the very long time it took for the Department of Transport (DoT) to own up to its responsibilities in domestic transportation rescue in the form of a coast guard are two examples of areas where one can draw harsh judgement. However, the times were different, and one cannot always apply current judgement on past decisions. For maritime rescue, it took a very long time before the community at sea demanded the same level of service as the aviation community, which is but one of the nuances that deeply affected post-war rescue development. In any event, the changes of the early 1960s were highly enlightened in comparison to the decade prior, and the changes ensured that SAR in Canada received the lasting priority it still deserves.

Throughout my journey with this topic, I struggled with turning my research into effective writing. I was greatly assisted in this process by Doctors Randall Wakelam and Steve Lukits. Their patience, dedication, and guidance were essential to my long-awaited understanding of how to create a thesis-driven argument without getting lost in historical narrative, which I did a lot. It was important that they had their "hands on the tiller," as a mariner would say, because I sure did not know where I was going for quite some time. Once I had my argument solidified, Lisa Moulton pored over the manuscript and taught me the finer points of sentence structure and formatting. Without the assistance of these three talented people, my ideas could not have become a book.

Majors Gillian Parker and Bill March were very helpful to me as I was conducting research. Gillian gave me access to a historical file in the

Canadian Joint Operations Command (CJOC) that proved very useful in understanding how the RCAF came to believe that it volunteered for the SAR role. Bill helped me locate books in the RCAF Aerospace Warfare Centre that contained pertinent information I never would have found otherwise. I would also like to express deep thanks to Major Mathias Joost at the Directorate of History and Heritage. Mathias is a fount of knowledge; he, too, pointed me towards sources I did not know existed, and he even conducted research on my behalf between visits. I will always be grateful for the essential research assistance of all three of these remarkable people.

Above all, I wish to acknowledge the efforts of my wife, Kelly. She read this manuscript several times and has provided me with an unflinching assessment of sections that had gone astray. Kelly and our daughter had to work around my meetings, research, and full-time work. They were very understanding of the long hours needed for this project, and the journey would not have been as rewarding and enjoyable without their patience and support.

I hope this book is worthy of the efforts of all of those people who provided help along the way of discovering how the SAR system was created. Although the current system is not perfect and not all missions reflect positively on those involved, there is much to be proud of in the Canadian SAR organization and the RCAF's involvement within it. It is my hope that this book sheds light on why the military can bring a lot of value to both daily SAR missions and large crises like the Swiss Air tragedy. It is also my hope that this book becomes useful in discussions on who will provide SAR services to Canadians in the future. SAR is serious business, and lives depend on Canada's ability to treat the responsibility as, in military parlance, a no-fail mission.

List of Abbreviations

AFHQ	Air Force Headquarters
AOC	air officer commanding
ASR	air sea rescue
ASRO	air sea rescue officer
ATC	Air Transport Command
CAP	Canadian Air Publication
CAS	Chief of the Air Staff
CJOC	Canadian Joint Operations Command
CO	commanding officer
DND	Department of National Defence
DHH	Directorate of History and Heritage
DoT	Department of Transport
EAC	Eastern Air Command
HF/DF	high frequency direction finding
HQ	headquarters
ICAO	International Civil Aviation Organization
ICSAR	Interdepartmental Committee on Search and Rescue
IMCO	Intergovernmental Maritime Consultative Organization
IMO	International Maritime Organization
JRCC	joint rescue coordination centre
LAC	Library and Archives Canada
NATO	North Atlantic Treaty Organization
NWAC	North West Air Command
NWSR	Northwest Staging Route
Op	operation
RAF	Royal Air Force

RCAF	Royal Canadian Air Force
RCC	rescue coordination centre
RCMP	Royal Canadian Mounted Police
RCN	Royal Canadian Navy
RN	Royal Navy
SAR	search and rescue
TCA	Trans Canada Airlines
UK	United Kingdom
US	United States
USAF	United States Air Force
WAC	Western Air Command

RCAF Ranks

In descending order
(Current RCAF equivalents listed in parentheses)

Air Officers (General Officers)

A/M   Air Marshal, Chief of the Air Staff (Lieutenant-General, Commander RCAF – LGen, Comd RCAF)
A/V/M   Air Vice-Marshal (Major-General – MGen)
A/C   Air Commodore (Brigadier-General – BGen)

Senior Officers

G/C   Group Captain (Colonel – Col)
W/C   Wing Commander (Lieutenant-Colonel – LCol)
S/L   Squadron Leader (Major – Maj)

Junior Officers

F/L   Flight Lieutenant (Captain – Capt)
F/O   Flying Officer (Lieutenant – Lt)
P/O   Pilot Officer (2nd Lieutenant – 2Lt)
F/C   Flight Cadet (Officer Cadet – OCdt)

Non-Commissioned Personnel

WO 1   Warrant Officer Class 1 (Chief Warrant Officer – CWO)
WO 2   Warrant Officer Class 2 (Master Warrant Officer – MWO)
F/Sgt   Flight Sergeant (Warrant Officer – WO)
Sgt   Sergeant (Sergeant – Sgt)
Cpl   Corporal (Master Corporal – MCpl)
LAC   Leading Aircraftman (Corporal – Cpl)
AC 1   Aircraftman Class 1 (Aviator, trained – Avr (T))
AC 2   Aircraftman Class 2 (Aviator, basic – Avr (B))

Chapter 1: The Beginning and the End

Search and rescue is part of the fabric of modern society. If a Canadian goes missing in the woods, we call the police, and then we can call an ambulance for the injured once they are located. Within our cities and towns, we can call the local fire department for urban rescue. Similarly, if someone on an aircraft or a vessel at sea is in danger, we call an RCC. If the distress is real, we know that someone is going to head out to try and save the lives at risk, no matter the weather. It has become an expectation.

This book is about SAR services, specifically for aviation and maritime emergencies, and the fact that they are a relatively new phenomenon. In 1939, no matter what the emergency, the only real recourse in Canada was to call the police and hope they could arrange for someone to come and provide assistance. There were some emergency marine services in the world, but pre-war rescue services in Canada were highly limited. Canadians had to be more self-sufficient in those days.

The Second World War was a fundamental turning point for many parts of today's society, and rescue was no less changed by war. The German Luftwaffe and the British Royal Air Force (RAF) learned the hard way that rescuing aviators from the sea could turn the tide in an air-superiority battle, as will be outlined by a lesson learned during the Battle of Britain in 1940. The RCAF took note and started developing a rescue system in 1942, which closely resembled the British ASR service and was called by the same name. By the end of the war, the RCAF had developed a sound service to rescue aviators, and it was very open about assisting civilian mariners when a call for help was received. Following the war, ASR was renamed SAR to acknowledge that post-war rescues were no longer limited to saving aircrew from the sea, as planes crashed on land as well.

For reasons that will be explained in detail later, aviation SAR in

Canada became the operational responsibility of the RCAF in June 1947, and three years afterwards, the government added maritime SAR to RCAF responsibilities.[3] Since that time, RCAF SAR aircraft have responded to aviation and maritime emergencies from the Atlantic to the Pacific, and to the North Pole. In 1962, the Canadian Coast Guard was formed; it formalized a robust maritime-rescue component that complemented the RCAF's capable aviation component of rescue. Today, the RCAF and the Canadian Coast Guard are the public faces of the well-renowned SAR capability that has become an essential service for aviators and mariners operating in Canada.

For RCAF personnel who currently provide the rescue service, generally speaking, the history of SAR is hardly important. How the service came about appears contextual and irrelevant compared to real-world problems such as aircraft availability and effective search procedures. I know of what I speak, as I was one of those with limited time or effort for critical thought on the evolution of SAR in Canada, as I did not believe it mattered. However, there have been many discussions recently on the privatization of the SAR service in Canada and the United Kingdom (UK), and if big changes like privatization are to be seriously considered, then history matters quite a bit. As RCAF SAR is my military area of expertise and it was under discussion for transfer to the private sector, I wanted to understand the history and the true rationale for RCAF involvement in the SAR role at the beginning of the mandate to see if it made sense for the RCAF to give up the role.

The first high-level discussion on the privatization of the SAR service in Canada took place in 2011 by the Harper Government. The discussion ended quietly, as it was suspected that the RCAF would "fight any such move" to take away a non-military mandate.[4] At least, this was the suggestion by a *National Post* article that argued the RCAF would never

---

[3] LCol Clinton Mowbray, "Lessons Forgotten? A Historical Examination of the RCAF Search and Rescue Organization" (directed research project, Canadian Forces College, Toronto, ON, 2010), 110.

[4] David Pugliese, "Ottawa May Privatize Search-and-Rescue Projects," *Postmedia News*, 21 July 2011, http://news.nationalpost.com/news/canada/ottawa-may-privatize-search-and-rescue-projects (accessed 25 April 2018).

voluntarily give up the SAR mandate. Why the RCAF would take that stance was largely ignored, possibly because the rationale for the RCAF role in SAR was never clarified in the first place, but the seed of privatization in Canada had been sown.

To some extent, the privatization of SAR services was a consideration in Canada because one of our closest allies has now done it: in 2013, the UK announced that it was proceeding with contract services for aviation and maritime rescue starting in 2016.[5] The situation in the UK had different factors, as it retained a combat-rescue capability within the military, but the rescue world has been watching closely to see if there are significant benefits or drawbacks to using contract services for domestic rescue. By contrast, Canada does not maintain an air combat-rescue capability, so privatization would likely remove all aviation rescue services from the military. This is a change that could have other ramifications across Canadian society, such as the current RCAF support to provinces and police services, which is why a full understanding of the development of the SAR service in Canada has become a timely and important topic: so that any future decision on the provider of SAR services will include a thorough look at available primary-source evidence.

In April 2016, the topic again became current with the revelation that the Liberal Government was considering privatizing SAR in Canada as part of its defence planning review, and there was a suspicion that the RCAF would again fight to keep the SAR mandate.[6] Privatization is no longer under consideration by Prime Minister Justin Trudeau's Government, but the subject raises interesting questions on why the RCAF seems to consider domestic SAR a military role. Had the RCAF always viewed the SAR mandate as an important military role? Had the RCAF actively sought the SAR mandate? Are there historical factors that suggest an importance

---

[5] Stephen Morris, "British Search and Rescue Services to be Run by US Company," *The Guardian*, 26 March 2013, http://www.theguardian.com/uk/2013/mar/26/uk-search-and-rescue-bristow (accessed 25 April 2018).

[6] Lee Berthiaume, "Liberals Considering Privatizing Search and Rescue Operations as Part of Canadian Forces Review," *National Post*, 11 April 2016, http://news.nationalpost.com/news/canada/liberals-considering-privatizing-search-and-rescue-operations-as-part-of-canadian-forces-review (accessed 25 April 2018).

of the RCAF's continued role in rescue delivery? These fundamental questions could not be answered with the existing literature on Canadian rescue history, and answers are absolutely needed to make credible decisions on future rescue services in this country. There will be considerable new evidence offered in due course to answer the above questions, but for now, this chapter provides a very broad overview of the existing knowledge of the Canadian SAR service as well as the argument and themes that will be used to support the rest of the book.

The two most applicable works on Canadian SAR history are the Para Rescue Association's *That Others May Live* and Canadian Lieutenant-Colonel G. Y. Smith's (Retired) *Seek and Save*. *That Others May Live* contains considerable detail about the wartime development of the rescue capability, but details are provided strictly from a parachute-rescue specialist's perspective, as the book aims to deliver a history of this particular personnel trade within the RCAF.[7] *Seek and Save* tells the story of 103 Rescue Unit, the only original rescue squadron still in service today and which Smith commanded in the late 1980s.[8] Smith's book is one of many SAR-squadron histories available, but all the other histories examined have much less detail of the overall SAR organization through the decades. Smith does an admirable job of outlining the history of 103 Rescue Unit from its inception in 1947 through the time frame of consideration here and provides valuable contextual information of an RCAF unit operating on the East Coast.

In their discussion on why the Air Force was assigned the SAR responsibility, these two books offer a hypothesis of a loyal RCAF, volunteering the most cost-effective solution to a penny-pinching government.[9] However, the sources do not adequately answer the questions of why the RCAF volunteered for the SAR mandate and how a wartime system was transformed into the civilian service still provided by the RCAF today. There is good reason for the lack of complete answers, as both of those ed-

---

[7] The Para Rescue Association of Canada, *That Others May Live: 50 Years of Para Rescue in Canada* (Astra: The Para Rescue Association of Canada, 1994).

[8] G. Y. Smith, *Seek and Save: The History of 103 Rescue Unit* (Erin, ON: The Boston Mills Press, 1990).

[9] Ibid., 11; and The Para Rescue Association, *That Others May Live*, 31.

ucational works focus on a specific aspect of the rescue service in Canada, unlike this book that examines the overall development of the SAR system. Those two books needed to know enough of the development to tell their story, and the volunteering hypothesis was reasonable.

In the research for this book, I came to believe that the source of the volunteering hypothesis was uncovered. CJOC, in the nation's capital, holds a thin file of historical documents, dating back to 1946, that military officers have kept for its importance to understanding key developments in the SAR service provided by the RCAF. One of the documents relates the minutes of a Cabinet Defence Committee meeting from 10 January 1946 in which "the Chief of the Air Staff expressed the opinion that an adequate peacetime [air, sea, and land rescue] service could be provided by the RCAF in co-operation with the Navy, Transport, and RCMP and that no substantial increase in RCAF post-war establishment would be involved."[10]

Further research suggests that the quote above, which reasonably can be taken as volunteering for SAR, was a result of earlier pressure from the Cabinet for either the Air Force or the Navy to lead a SAR organization. In that context, the Chief of the Air Staff's statement meant that, of the two services that would have to lead SAR, it made more sense for the RCAF to lead the effort. While the nuance might seem unimportant, a non-volunteering RCAF explains much of the evidence around the developments of the overall SAR organization after the war, and it suggests that a new look at early SAR history in Canada can offer useful insight.

The aims of this book are to identify under what circumstances the RCAF acquired operational responsibility for the aviation and maritime SAR system in Canada as well as to outline how and why the RCAF developed the 1964 version of rescue, recognizable today. This book offers understanding of the origins of formal aviation and maritime SAR in Canada, and it closes much of the gap in knowledge that currently exists about the RCAF's first 25 years of ASR and SAR development in Canada.

It will be argued throughout that the RCAF and the Canadian

---

[10] CJOC Historical Files, "Cabinet Defence Committee Minutes for 10 January 1946," 2.

government proved reluctant to develop air- and sea-rescue systems until public pressure resulted in the DoT's new Canadian Coast Guard provision of financial and operational assistance starting in 1962. It will be shown that the RCAF desperately required assistance to deliver domestic SAR by the end of the 1950s, and when government assistance was planned beginning in 1959 with DoT resources, the RCAF ceased its resistance. Evidence provided after 1962 will be used to describe how the Canadian Coast Guard and RCAF delineated responsibility so that you, the reader, can assess whether the historical context is still relevant to the current discussion on who should provide SAR services. By the time all evidence is provided, and despite any resistance displayed by the RCAF throughout the process, there should be no doubt that the RCAF was solely responsible for successfully developing and delivering SAR services before 1962.

After delving into the limited history of pre-war SAR in Canada, it will be necessary to present an overview of Canada's current rescue system in order to highlight the eventual end state of the SAR organization. It is also useful to offer three themes that are applicable to all time frames of this study. These themes will subsequently be used to provide a framework for conclusions that will integrate the events of each chapter into the wider Canadian and international environment. Despite the 25 years the SAR system took to develop, the narrative surrounding the evolution of the SAR system in Canada is an impressive story of dedicated professionals who built a robust rescue system from the ground up, with a minimal amount of personnel, money, equipment, and government support. Compared to the system in place by 1964, the pre-war rescue services will appear pathetic.

Pre-war Canadian Rescue Capabilities

Rescue services in Canada, prior to the war, were haphazard, and the RCAF did not have any mandated role in providing them. "Calls for help could be received by the RCMP, the Navy, the Army, the Air Force, Municipal Police and commercial or civilian organizations."[11] There was negligible rescue regulation at the national and international levels, and the

---

[11] The Para Rescue Association, *That Others May Live*, 10.

scarcity of documented guidance highlights the lack of a national rescue policy.[12] At sea, volunteers of the Canadian Lifesaving Service provided a limited rescue service to mariners of Canadian oceanic areas and the Great Lakes; although by 1939, it was greatly diminished from its heyday in 1915 when there had been 40 stations across the nation.[13] On land, whether it was for response to a crashed aircraft or for any kind of public assistance, known at that time as "mercy flights," the RCMP coordinated rescue assistance using resources from any available organization.[14] Simply stated, there was no Canadian rescue system.

The lack of formal rescue policy or procedures meant that the RCMP was more likely to receive calls for help from the public than military organizations. The RCAF was still reeling from budget cuts of the Great Depression era earlier in the 1930s, so it was not inclined to volunteer for extra duties.[15] Combined with a lack of requirement for aviation rescue in those early days, there was little need for rescue services provided by aircraft or seaplanes. However, it is a good time to explain how assistance to public emergencies was, and still is, provided. Namely, the public is assisted through a type of activity the RCAF calls a humanitarian mission.

A humanitarian mission is one where the mandate for the response exists with the police of jurisdiction or provincial/territorial authorities, but the lead organization believes its resources are insufficient for the rescue at hand and makes a request to the applicable military RCC for federal

---

[12] A detailed search was made for documentation critical of rescue services in the late 1930s in RCMP and DoT files, but nothing was found.

[13] Clayton Evans, *Rescue at Sea: An International History of Lifesaving, Coastal Rescue Craft and Organisations* (London: Conway Maritime Press, 2003), 209.

[14] LAC, RG24-D-1-c, Vol. 8164 File Part 1-2, 1700-27 SUB 1, Organization and Administration – Air, Sea, Search and Rescue Services, Interdepartmental Committee on SAR, Vol. 1, prepared by Chairman S/L R. J. Lehman, 30 November 1945, "Minutes of Meeting 4 of the Interdepartmental Committee on Post-war Air Sea Rescue."

[15] W. A. B. Douglas, *The Official History of the Royal Canadian Air Force, Vol. 2, The Creation of a National Air Force* (Canada: University of Toronto Press, 1980), 89.

assistance.[16] Examples of humanitarian missions are requests to search for missing persons; requests to transport critically ill people when civilian aircraft or vessels cannot conduct the mission quickly enough; or requests to transfer urgently required emergency supplies, like medicine, to remote locations.[17]

Throughout this book, the term "humanitarian" will be used to describe requests for federal SAR assistance from the provinces, territories, or police. Throughout the time frame covered here, the most common term used was "mercy flights," which described missions when RCAF or civilian aircraft transported ill persons or critically required food or medicine. However, some missions were categorized as "missing persons" missions, "RCMP assistance," or simply "other."[18] None of these mission descriptions were part of the formal SAR mandate that developed for aeronautical and maritime SAR, so the term humanitarian to describe all such use of SAR resources will simplify the discussion.

There are no detailed records of humanitarian flights within five years prior to the war, but there is a report by J. A. Wilson, the Controller of Civil Aviation, written in 1934. For the period 1932–1934, one airline operating in north-west Canada, Canadian Airways, stated that a staggering 167 humanitarian flights had been conducted to help Canadians in remote locations, and other airlines in Canada added another 35 flights to the total.[19] There is little or no documentation on why humanitarian flights were largely conducted by civilian airlines, but educated guesses can be made.

First, there were far fewer government services available to Canadians before the war, and expectations were lower. This will become very clear in

---

[16] National Defence and Fisheries and Oceans Canada, *CAMSAR, Canadian Aeronautical and Maritime Search and Rescue Manual, Combined Edition – Volumes I, II, and III*, Supplement to the IAMSAR Manual, B-GA-209-001/FP-001, effective date 30 September 2014, CAMSAR II, Chapter 3.04.

[17] DHH 79/631, RCAF Search and Rescue Operation 1947–1970, DIS Files 1–14, SAR Ops 1955, File 9, 15 February 1956, "Royal Canadian Air Force Release No. 8634."

[18] DHH, 79/631, "Royal Canadian Air Force Release No. 8634."

[19] LAC, RG24-E-1-c, Vol. 18113, Search and Rescue Policy, SAR – Organization and Administration, Report to the Chief of the General Staff from Controller of Aviation, J. A. Wilson, 30 April 1934, "Flights of Mercy."

the discussion on the post-war era, when comparisons were made between rescue services for military and civilian aircraft and struggles ensued to meet new Canadian expectations with massive wartime debt and limited financial resources after the Second World War. In the pre-war era, it appeared that the costs of humanitarian flights were downloaded to communities or individuals. With little expectation of federal assistance, contracted services were the only real option.

Second, these early days of aviation were well known to be times of trial and error. Pilots pushed the safety envelope of flight, partly because there were no regulations and partly because no one really knew what the limits of weather and aircraft were. Risk was inherent in flying, and even the passengers who flew in those days must have known the risks involved in taking to the skies in the frail machines of the 1930s. Stories of derring-do and bravery exist among the histories of civilian pilots and military pilots, which strongly suggests that the cultures of these airmen were remarkably similar. Indeed, the accounts of the humanitarian flights conducted by the airlines between 1932 and 1934 are hair-raising tales of bravery by the dozen. War would later differentiate the safety culture of civilian aviation from the military risk taking that was emphasized by desperate wartime need, but in the time before the war, there was little difference between aviation disciplines. Without additional benefits to be achieved with using the RCAF to fly humanitarian missions, it made sense to use commercially available options for time-sensitive assistance flights.

As few rules existed in those days, it was up to the pilot to determine the viability of the commercial-flight opportunity based on their judgement and experience. One pilot stands out above all others in the judgement and conduct of these commercially provided humanitarian flights in the 1930s: Mr. Wilfrid R. "Wop" May, a pilot who had a clear love of aviation.[20] He flew the most humanitarian missions, 24 total, compared to the next most-prolific pilot on the list, a Mr. Schads, with 14 such flights. "Wop" May is worth introducing now, as he becomes an important part of this story in 1944, and he is still considered an important historical figure in the RCAF and specifically within the SAR community.

---

[20] Ibid.

He first became famous during the Great War as a novice pilot who tangled with the deadly German fighter ace, Manfred von Richthofen, more commonly known as the Red Baron. After that stunning introduction to aerial combat, May went on to become a well-known fighter ace during the last year of the Great War on the Sopwith Camel aircraft. He later became one of Canada's most famous bush pilots, a transport airlines pilot, and a civilian pilot instructor of considerable renown. Part of May's enduring appeal today is the resourcefulness of his character that still resonates with aircrew in the SAR role. There is a story about him "being stranded in a remote northern area with a fractured wooden propeller [on his aircraft]. He shot a moose; boiled its hooves to make glue; used its sinews for wrappings and flew on to make history."[21] With pilots like May available to conduct humanitarian flights for distressed Canadians or their communities, there was less pressure for the RCAF to become involved in flights to help the Canadian public. Humanitarian flights were not a major source of Air Force activity before the Second World War.

The RCAF may not have been greatly involved in humanitarian flights, but it did have a limited rescue presence in the maritime domain. The RCAF of 1939 flew seaplanes at five units across the country, and to support the seaplanes, the RCAF had acquired 88 various marine vessels to tow the planes, service them, and to assist with rescue of aircrew from the RCAF seaplanes.[22] Four of these vessels were high-speed rescue craft, capable of 35 knots for prolonged distances.[23] There were two of these vessels on each coast, and they were available for rescue work under the command of the station where the vessels and the seaplanes were based.[24] The seaplane locations were Dartmouth, Nova Scotia; Rockcliffe, Ontario; Trenton, Ontario; Winnipeg, Manitoba; and Vancouver, British Columbia. Before

---

[21] The Para Rescue Association, *That Others May Live*, 11.

[22] J. E. Vernon, "RCAF Marine Craft," in *4ᵗʰ Annual Air Force Historical Conference: 80 Years of Maritime Aviation in Canada* (12 Wing, Shearwater, NS: 24–25 August 1998), 103 and 106.

[23] Geoff D. Pilborough, *The Royal Canadian Air Force Marine Squadrons, Vol. 1, 1935–1945* (Edmonton: Canimpex, 1996), 62.

[24] Hugh A. Halliday, "The Role of the Boats: Air Force Part 46," *Legion Magazine* (30 August 2011).

the war, the use of these aircraft for rescue missions was uncommon and completely unregulated.

One example of the kind of ad hoc rescue efforts that were conducted before the war occurred on 21 September 1939. Sergeant (Sgt) Jones Francis Doe was flying as observer in a seaplane flown by Sgt J. K. Hay, when the pilot lost consciousness during a search for a civilian "who had been adrift on a disabled motor boat for several days." Sgt Doe spotted the civilian sailor, landed safely, conducted the rescue, and then returned to Trenton "with no knowledge whatever of an aircraft."[25] It was a very admirable act, but an untrained person landing a seaplane far from shore and taking off again could easily have resulted in the loss of lives of rescuers and rescuees instead of the happy result from this particular example. Clearly, risk management was not yet a significant concern for the RCAF, but it would have to become so if the RCAF was to learn to weigh the benefit of risky missions against the potential cost of personnel and resources. Risk management would eventually create a separation between military and civilian aviation cultures.

Civilian airlines had already started an interesting transition in the late 1930s towards an era of passenger safety, contrary to the military's continued risk taking. Canadian Airways, most well known for bush flying, started an experimental scheduled-flight service between Winnipeg, Manitoba, and Red Lake, Ontario. Canadian Airways bid for a contract to set up further scheduled routes for the government, but instead, the Canadian government chose to establish its own airline, Trans Canada Airlines (TCA). The first pilot hired for TCA was Z. Lewis Leigh in August 1937.[26] Leigh is another key player in the later development of the SAR organization, and his background in civil aviation and scheduled airline transport is important to track the diverging interests of civilian and military flying. The companies Leigh worked for before the war were in the business of transporting passengers and equipment, and making money.

[25] LAC, RG24, Vol. 20597, CAS File 63-1-1 Vol. 1 – "Honours, Decorations and Awards" – Period October 1940 to November 1940, 13 August 1942, "Recommendation for Honours and Rewards."

[26] Z. Lewis Leigh, *And I Shall Fly: The Flying Memoirs of Z. Lewis Leigh* (Toronto: Canav Books, 1985), 99.

Precision in timing and managing risk were key elements of transport airline growth, and Leigh led this effort by training new pilots to the point that TCA was able to start scheduled night-time passenger service between cities in April 1938.[27] As Leigh would later join the RCAF, some of the safety and professionalism that was developing in the civilian airline industry would later be incorporated into aspects of military flying. In the interim, however, the limited number of rescue missions by the RCAF would continue to accept considerable risk.

Despite the RCAF's ability to perform maritime rescue, it was rarely called upon for such work because the RCMP or Canadian Lifesaving Service normally responded to maritime emergencies.[28] In 1938, however, the RCMP handed over nine counter-rum-runner vessels to the RCAF as part of an overall programme to boost resources within the RCAF and RCN for war, and these vessels augmented the military-rescue capability at the seaplane units.[29] What little rescue capability the RCAF had at the beginning of the war was for rescuing aircrew from crashed seaplanes, which were normally flying close to their home station. However, when the RCMP handed over fast rescue vessels to the RCAF, it also meant that the RCMP had so few maritime resources left at its disposal that it could no longer perform maritime rescue for Canadians after the Second World War began. A vacuum of Canadian civilian-rescue capability was created that would be felt even in the United States (US).

As previously noted, there was a limited rescue capability from Trenton, Ontario, using RCAF aircraft if available. However, that was hardly sufficient for Lake Ontario, let alone the other Great Lakes, even during the war. The Americans were forced to take on that responsibility, and they

---

[27] Leigh, *And I Shall Fly*, 104.

[28] LAC, RG24, Vol. 8164, File Part 1-2, 1700-27 SUB 1, Memorandum for Cabinet Defence Committee, from E. W. T. Gill, Secretary, Cabinet Defence Committee, 8 January 1946, "Air, Sea, Land Rescue Services: Special Peacetime Functions of Armed Services."

[29] Ibid.

would later expand their coast guard in the Great Lakes throughout the Second World War.[30]

The lack of a civilian, domestic-rescue service was but one aspect of a Canadian lack of capability that had significant potential to affect relations with the US. At the beginning of the war, as the RCAF official history points out, both the Canadian government and the RCAF were well aware that the US was planning for an eventual war with Japan. The RCAF had deep concern that the Americans would use Canadian territory as they saw fit to defend against a Japanese threat to North America, unless Canada had an acceptable force at the ready.[31] The RCAF would require aircraft, manpower, and stations within Canada to prove to the Americans that Canada could cope with its own defence responsibilities.[32] Any deficiency that was noticeable to the Americans, as both aviation and maritime rescue were examples, was a potential source of sovereignty concern for Canadian territory and its waters. Close ties between American and Canadian air forces would be needed to avoid unnecessary American encroachment in Canadian areas of responsibility and sovereignty, over Canadian territory and its waters.

As the threat increased from both Germany and Japan, Canada realized that some amount of encroachment would prove necessary. In July 1940, an American government document titled "A Programme for Immediate Canadian Action" was drafted that warned that the US would intervene "at once if Canada is attacked or threatened—particularly if she is not sure of Canada's strategy and strength."[33] Following that document, a meeting between Canadian Prime Minister Mackenzie King and American President Franklin Roosevelt took place in Ogdensburg, New York, on 17 August 1940, to establish a Permanent Joint Board on Defense to ensure that Canada was involved in overall planning for the defence of

---

[30] Thomas P. Ostram, *The United States Coast Guard in World War II: A History of Domestic and Overseas Actions* (North Carolina: McFarland & Co. Inc., 2009), 25.

[31] Douglas, *Official History of the Royal Canadian Air Force*, 127 and 132.

[32] Ibid., 130.

[33] Donald Barry and Duane Bratt, "Defence Against Help: Explaining Canada–U.S. Security Relations," *American Review of Canadian Studies* (2007): 70.

the eastern seaboard of North America.[34] Canada was protected by large oceans, but if an enemy proved to be strong enough to reach across an ocean to strike Canada, America would be needed to prevent a successful invasion of Canadian soil.

The concept that describes Canada's 1940 security predicament would later become called "defence against help," a concept stemming from the Ogdensburg meeting where Roosevelt pledged to protect Canada if it were attacked, "while King promised only that the country [Canada] would not become a strategic liability; he did not commit the Canadian government beyond the defense of its own territory."[35] Canada needed to avoid too much help in order to maintain sovereignty, balanced against the need for a friend in battle. This balance would become a big part of a Canadian security shift towards an American orbit of influence during and after the Second World War, which is explained in more detail later.

Another important aspect of the pre-war RCAF was its well-established role in Canadian domestic air operations. The RCAF had demonstrated success in a wide range of non-military functions such as aerial photography and agricultural experiments during the interwar period, and this success was supported by the Chief of Staff Major General J. H. MacBrian in 1927.[36] As a result of the general's support, the RCAF "continued to operate as principal air arm of federal civil power until the mid-1930s."[37] There was a long-standing understanding within Canada that aircraft and personnel resources were too limited not to have synergy between the limited numbers of military aircraft and the growing domestic air requirements for a growing nation. Although the RCAF supported civilian air requirements, that support did not extend to rescue.

In fact, rescue in Canadian waters was an overlooked aspect of wartime planning, and that is a direct result of limited international scrutiny

[34] Richard Strauss, "The Diplomatic Negotiations Leading to the Establishment of American Bases in Newfoundland: June 1940 – April 1941," Memorial University of Newfoundland, March 1972, 24.

[35] Barry and Bratt, "Defence Against Help," 64.

[36] Larry Milberry, *Canada's Air Force: At War and At Peace, Volume 1* (Toronto: CANAV Books, 2000), 60.

[37] Ibid.

of rescue at sea in the lead-up to war. The last major international pre-war meeting on maritime transportation issues was the 1929 International Convention for the Safety of Life at Sea.[38] There was, and still is, regulation imposed on life-saving actions required of mariners, but prior to the war, none of these regulations extended to rescue requirements at the national level. The RCN was responsible for the limited marine service available in Canada at that time, but funding it was never made a priority.[39]

The most pressing problem in the domain of maritime rescue was providing sufficient rescue coverage, given the limited number of volunteer personnel and government vessels, paid for by the RCN despite a limited budget for such activities.[40] The Canadian Lifesaving Service went largely neglected, again as a result of lingering Great Depression budget cuts. One exception to public concern over the lack of any rescue vessel occurred on the west coast of Vancouver Island during the winter of 1938–39, an area notable for many shipwrecks.[41] Repeated requests were made for an RCN ship to provide winter rescue coverage in case mariners needed help in the dangerous area, but the response to this concern was that finances were tight and nothing could be done.[42] The public outcry was small enough that it was ignored in the larger concern of preparing for war, as sporadic responses to preventative rescue requests were acceptable given the international developments of the day. Once the war started, the RCN would neglect the inshore rescue requirement altogether, as it focused its efforts on the deep-sea battle.[43]

Prior to war, all Canadian organizations had to deal with emergencies on a case-by-case basis, and this would prove insufficient for combat operations in the years to follow. The government capabilities that did exist were limited in the maritime domain and were nearly non-existent for

---

[38] IMO, *International Convention for the Safety of Life at Sea* (London: 31 May 1929).

[39] Evans, *Rescue at Sea*, 208.

[40] Ibid.

[41] LAC, RG12 Vol. 2554, File No. 7800-1, Life-Saving Search and Rescue – General, Letter from the Supervisor of Nautical Services, 13 December 1938, "Life Saving Patrol West Coast Vancouver Island – Winter 1938–39."

[42] Ibid.

[43] Evans, *Rescue at Sea*, 208.

aviation and humanitarian emergencies, the latter largely the purview of civilian airlines. There were significant deficiencies in the area of maritime rescue in Canada, and financial pressures limited the government response to calls for increases. The evidence shows that the RCAF did not provide Canadian rescue capabilities at the beginning of the war, nor was there any other effective rescue system available to the Canadian public.

Overview of Rescue Systems

By the end of the Second World War, the lack of rescue in Canada was resolved for military services, and civilian-rescue services were not far behind. Further post-war developments would significantly change and refine the organization into what is recognized today, but the analysis of the growth and development of Canadian rescue systems requires a standard for comparison. The standard for comparison in the war years will be the British and American rescue services, while the post-war comparison will be against Canada's contemporary rescue organization.

At its simplest, the development of rescue systems was based on the requirement to send out a vessel or aircraft to save someone's life. Transforming that simple capability to a national or internationally co-ordinated system, however, was very complex. As discussed, there have been two major types of rescue systems: ASR and SAR. The ASR system created in the Second World War was intended as a combat-oriented means of rescuing downed aircrew, and ASR systems grew and matured in response to the expansion of combat operations worldwide. The SAR system created after the war was a necessary response to a new international climate where the safety of passengers was critical to the post-war growth of civil aviation and maritime transportation. These two types of systems need to be analysed differently because SAR development started where ASR development stopped, at least in Canada.

Before the Second World War, there were no ASR systems among air forces in Canada, the UK, and the US. If an aircraft was in trouble, it was incumbent upon the air station from where it was based to provide assistance.[44] When an aircraft radioed its home station and declared an emergency, station operational personnel would follow a checklist and send any available resources to assist, often without considering the operational repercussions of changing missions for aircraft.[45] This approach was largely effective prior to the war because military aircraft usually flew close to the station where boats or vehicles could reach crashes, and operational requirements were secondary to aircrew lives. As well, most accidents took place during the dangerous phases of take-off and landing compared to the relatively benign environment of en route training away from the station. As soon as combat became involved, such as long-range bombing raids and convoy patrols, this procedure-based response to rescues became wholly inadequate.[46] The en route portion of the mission became the most dangerous aspect of the flight due to enemy fire, and thus, crashes were far more likely away from the station. The change from training to combat operations made the existing rescue system nearly useless.

As Canada was an important partner with UK and US military forces, Canadian ASR development during the Second World War can be directly compared to allied ASR development. In the post-war era, Canadian developments will be compared against the current Canadian system. One could argue that a better comparison for the RCAF's post-war developments might be the UK or US rescue systems, but Canada chose a different path for SAR development after the war that makes comparison with allied countries surprisingly inappropriate. Both the UK and US maintained a combat-rescue capability after the Second World War, while Canada did not, and that meant that the rationale for rescue services residing with a military organization in those countries was fairly obvious. As well, the UK and US had existing domestic-rescue organizations prior to the war that remained intact throughout and after the war. By contrast, Canada's lack of an existing rescue service required a completely domestic civilian-focused

---

[44] George Galdorisi and Tom Phillips, *Leave No Man Behind: The Saga of Combat Search and Rescue* (Minneapolis: Zenith Press, 2008), 30.

[45] LAC, RG24-E-1-b, Vol. 3410, 466-1-3, Air/Sea Rescue Services – Minutes of RAF Monthly Air/Sea Rescue Meeting – Policy, File 464-3-3 Vol. 2, July 1942, "Air Sea Rescue." The major's signature is illegible and a day of the month was not provided.

[46] Galdorisi and Phillips, *Leave No Man Behind*, 30.

SAR capability that could have been provided by a civil organization. Even now, Canadian SAR policy is almost exclusively a civilian-oriented domestic responsibility instead of a capability that can rescue Canadians at home as well as military members crashed or lost during deployed military operations.[47] RCAF doctrine currently includes the potential use of SAR forces in times of war, so military rescue is formalized in policy, but the practical reality is that Canada only uses SAR forces for domestic-rescue missions.[48]

It is helpful to understand the highly effective Canadian SAR system of today to understand all rescue developments in Canada and because the similarity of the 1964 version to today makes for a satisfying ending to this story. A brief overview will show the organization, the resources assigned to the SAR mandate in 2014 (a recent year with very typical SAR-response numbers), and how often those resources were used in order to put into context the developments described within this book. As depicted in Figure 1, the current SAR system in Canada is organized into three SAR regions: Halifax, Trenton, and Victoria, and each region has one RCC named after the physical location of the centre.[49] Together, the three RCCs are responsible for aeronautical and maritime SAR in Canada, and they provide the SAR command and control by investigating incidents, assigning appropriate aircraft and vessels to search, and coordinating the rescue of people in distress.

---

[47] Royal Canadian Air Force, B-GA-404-000/FP-001, *Canadian Forces Aerospace Move Doctrine* (Astra: Canadian Forces Aerospace Warfare Centre, 2011), 39.

[48] Ibid., Chapter 3. Note that the RCAF deployed SAR forces for Operation Jaguar to assist Jamaica with its domestic rescue in 2011.

[49] Circa 2002, the name was changed to Joint Rescue Coordination Centre (JRCC) to capture the reality that the Canadian RCCs are responsible for both aeronautical and maritime SAR, which fits into the joint concept of North Atlantic Treaty Organization (NATO) military doctrine. The centres will be referred to as RCCs in this book to avoid confusion.

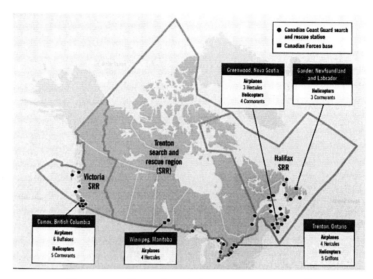

Figure 1. Canadian SAR Regions 2015[50]

There is one Maritime Rescue Sub-Centre in Quebec City, as of 2017, that assists SAR delivery in the St. Lawrence Seaway, and it reports to Halifax or Trenton RCC, depending on the location of the distress. Historically, examples of these sub-centres were used for aviation rescue and not maritime rescue, specifically in the prairies, but the presence of these small units for aviation- or maritime-only rescue did not have a significant impact on the overall development of the SAR system. Sub-centres will not be further discussed, as they had a negligible effect on overall developments of the Canadian SAR system.

The three RCCs responded to 9,172 SAR incidents in 2014, and these cases were initiated based on information suggesting there was a distress with an aircraft anywhere in Canada's area or a distress with a marine vessel in the oceans or Great Lakes of Canada's internationally assigned area of responsibility.[51] Aircraft distress situations accounted for 24.9 per cent

[50] Michael Ferguson, "Report of the Auditor General of Canada – Spring 2013" (Office of the Auditor General, 2013), Exhibit 7.3.
[51] Canadian Armed Forces and Canadian Coast Guard, *Federal Search and Rescue Operational Governance Committee Annual Report 2014* (Ottawa: CJOC, March 2015), iii.

of RCC activity in 2014, and marine distress situations accounted for 55.7 per cent of activity.[52] The remaining 19.4 per cent of RCC activity was in response to humanitarian missions when federal resources were needed to assist in rescue missions in provincial areas of responsibility.

The SAR mandate requires aircraft and vessels to respond to distress situations, and the RCAF and Canadian Coast Guard provide those resources today. The RCAF has a total of 39 SAR aircraft and helicopters available to provide four primary standby aircraft and four primary standby helicopters from five bases fairly evenly spread across the country.[53] While there are no SAR resources stationed in Canada's northern areas, the number of SAR missions has not justified northern basing of additional resources since the early 1950s. In 2014, those standby resources stationed in high-density areas responded to 655 missions and flew 2,420 hours. Put another way, the aircraft flew 3.8 hours per incident that required RCAF assistance provided by the RCCs.[54]

Additionally, the RCCs have the ability to coordinate the tasking of other military resources when there is an insufficient number of primary SAR aircraft for the task at hand. Other Canadian Armed Forces resources, such as RCN ships or non-SAR RCAF aircraft, were tasked 356 times in 2014. The Canadian Army was available to assist as required, but in recent times it has only been called upon to assist with large incidents such as Swiss Air 111. The total hours flown by non-SAR RCAF aircraft on SAR missions was very small at only 78 hours, while the hours logged by RCN ships were not available.[55] The inclusion of other RCAF aircraft into the conduct of SAR missions is particularly relevant to the story of SAR development in Canada, as RCC tasking of non-SAR military aircraft has historically affected other RCAF missions. In the early post-war period, the use of all RCAF aircraft for SAR missions was important for both civilian emergencies and the many military aircraft crashes that occurred in that era. Military aircraft crashes over Canada are now non-existent as

---

[52] Ibid., 22.

[53] Ibid., 2.

[54] Ibid., 22.

[55] Ibid., 20. The flight hours were provided by the Senior Staff Officer SAR for 1 Cdn Air Div, LCol Bryn Elliott, on 20 November 2015.

a regular source of SAR activity, but the frequency of all types of aviation crashes resulted in the SAR mandate spreading into all aspects of RCAF operations in the 1950s, which was a source of frustration for commanders and staff trying to manage other RCAF missions.

For the maritime component of SAR, the Canadian Coast Guard has 66 stations across the country where there are SAR-equipped marine vessels available on 30-minute notice at all times.[56] These vessels form the essential maritime component of the rescue system. In 2014, the Canadian Coast Guard provided crews and vessels to 3,881 SAR missions.[57] Compared to the RCAF use of resources for SAR activities, the Canadian Coast Guard sends out resources roughly four times more often. Undoubtedly, the Canadian Coast Guard is a critical component of the SAR framework in Canada, necessary for providing rescue expertise in the maritime domain. This component, however, did not exist until 1962. As the maritime mandate has changed little since 1950 and there were few or no immediately available rescue vessels on standby in the 1950s, the current fleet of numerous and effective resources contrasts greatly with the few resources and many difficulties that the RCAF encountered in 1950s maritime rescue.

In examining the evolution of rescue systems, developments will be assessed using three proposed characteristics of a national rescue system. These characteristics are:

- **National standards for aviation and maritime rescues in Canada** are the need to respond with the same level of service to all parts of the country for the particular incident type, aviation or marine, and not just in an area where there happens to be a rescue aircraft or vessel.
- **Available resources for all rescue mission types** refers to aircraft (seaplanes in the early years), helicopters, and a wide variety of maritime vessels all in well-placed locations to meet any emergency over Canadian territory or in Canada's oceanic and Great Lake areas. This range of rescue resources is common to most rescue

---

[56] Ibid., 4.
[57] Ibid., 20.

systems worldwide, and they often are used concurrently to complete a successful rescue.

- **Formalized policy for investigation and response in both military- and civilian-rescue missions** is used to identify that an organization has been mandated to take information from military and/or civilian individuals reporting an aviation or maritime incident and that elements of that organization, or another, are mandated to respond.

To make the system development clear throughout this study, shaded tables are presented here and then at the end of each chapter to highlight major developmental changes. The major changes described are policy changes at the RCAF and Canadian-government levels as well as resource changes across the country. The tables are intended to summarize the various changes throughout the developmental period in discussion. Another tool to assist in understanding these changes is the occasional addition of maps, the few that were found, to show the distribution of rescue resources within Canada.

As clearly shown, the state of rescue in Canada in 1939 was nearly non-existent, and it is, therefore, represented in Table 1 with significant deficiencies when compared to the national SAR system of today. Dark shading of boxed information means that resources or specific policies were deficient enough as to have a negative effect on that particular characteristic of the SAR system, and these deficiencies are briefly outlined within the table. Light shading identifies that there are deficiencies in either the policies or the resources, but that elements of the specific characteristic were partially meeting the requirement. No shading identifies that the resources or policies satisfactorily meet the particular characteristic. Within the three characteristics—national standards for aviation and maritime rescues, available resources such as aircraft and vessels on standby for rescue missions, and a formalized policy for military and civilian rescues—there are two columns that provide the aviation and maritime groupings of these characteristics. It will be seen that developments in these characteristics did not progress in a linear fashion.

Characteristic	Aviation	Maritime
National Standards	**Aviation rescues**. None	**Maritime rescues**. None
Available Resources	**Aircraft**. None	**Vessels**. Four RCAF vessels and a few Canadian Lifesaving Service and RCMP resources, but many areas went without
Formalized Policy	**Military rescues**. A station expectation for seaplane operations only	**Civilian rescues**. Limited policy existed with the RCN, responsible for the Canadian Lifesaving Service, but mostly neglected

Table 1. Canadian Rescue in 1939

The current SAR system, as depicted in Table 2, meets all the proposed characteristics of a national aviation-and-maritime-rescue system and is presented alongside Table 1 as examples of how the system will be explained. There are remarkable similarities between Table 2 (current system) and Table 8 (the 1964 system). By the standards presented here, the table remained un-shaded and meeting international standards from 1964 to today.

Characteristic	Aviation	Maritime
National Standards	**Aviation rescues.** Required by International Civil Aviation Organization (ICAO) and ordered by the government	**Maritime rescues.** Required by International Maritime Organization (IMO) and ordered by the government
Available Resources	**Aircraft** (and Helicopters). Provided by the RCAF at five locations	**Vessels.** Provided by the Canadian Coast Guard at 66 locations and supplemented by any available government ship
Formalized Policy	**Military rescues.** Required by NATO and provided by all environments of the military	**Civilian rescues.** Required by ICAO/IMO and provided by the RCAF and the Canadian Coast Guard

Table 2. Current System Overview

The three characteristics evolved unevenly over time. The specific characteristics of national standards for maritime rescues, available vessels for emergencies in ocean areas, and a formalized policy for civilian rescues are shown to be clear problem areas as we progress through SAR history. However, the importance of the time frame covered in this study is that these three characteristics were all ordered resolved by 1959 and were in practical and effective use by 1964. All changes since then have simply refined an already effective system.

A SUMMARY OF THEMES

In the process of organizing this book, it became evident that there are three themes woven through all aspects of the development of Canada's rescue system. They are a Canadian national requirement to develop and maintain sovereignty, international pressure on Canada to develop rescue systems, and government direction to conduct SAR at the lowest cost. These themes affected government and RCAF decision making as well as relevant public policy, throughout the development of both wartime and peacetime rescue systems.

Canadian sovereignty was front and centre for the military during the Second World War, and it remained important to decisions made after the war. Canada was caught between a long-standing colonial relationship with the UK and an understanding that the future required a far closer association with the US. However, it will become clear that there were events during and after the war when Canada had deep concern over American encroachment into Canadian territory, and the RCAF, at times, took action to minimize the American tendency to be involved in Canadian SAR. Sovereignty in Canada was strengthened by the existence of a well-developed rescue system.

International pressure came from Allied forces throughout the war, as interoperability was needed among the air forces to maintain the morale of aviators conducting missions in harm's way and to develop critical transatlantic flight procedures. By 1944, post-war planning had begun among the Allies, and initial discussions took place on aviation policy and regulations, which in turn drove post-war SAR development. After the war, the newly instituted ICAO applied pressure on all nations to standardize SAR capability from an aviation perspective. In 1948, the United Nations created the Intergovernmental Maritime Consultative Organization (IMCO), which was renamed IMO in 1982, and this organization formalized a requirement for nations to provide maritime SAR.[58] The international requirements overrode Canadian resistance to developing a national rescue system.

Finally, there was continual pressure in Ottawa to harmonize resource allocation to accomplish all government-mandated tasks with the minimum number of people, the least amount of equipment, and the lowest possible cost. This is much less evident throughout the war, but there were some surprising efforts at resource rationalization even during the war years. Afterwards, the government decided to accept the new responsibility for SAR with all existing departmental resources used in cooperation.

---

[58] IMO, "Brief History of IMO," copyright 2015, http://www.imo.org/en/About/HistoryOfIMO/Pages/Default.aspx (accessed 25 April 2018).

Decisions on the allocation of rescue roles made by the government some-times left the RCAF without a chair when the music stopped because until 1959 other departments often refused to share the workload. This theme of harmonizing resources significantly delayed the development of the Canadian Coast Guard for the maritime component of SAR until deficiencies in the SAR service became glaringly obvious to the public. Cost concerns within the Air Force often fed RCAF reluctance, but conversely, finances drove government decisions to assign SAR to the RCAF. The end result was that the RCAF was forced to pay for aviation and maritime domestic SAR out of its own pockets until the formation of the Canadian Coast Guard.

These three themes are revisited at the end of each chapter to provide continuity of evidence analysis and to highlight key factors that pushed the RCAF towards developing rescue systems well beyond the Air Force's commitment to provide a rescue capability for its own aviators. Although RCAF actions minimized the efforts put towards ASR and SAR in many respects, conclusions made with a broader look at the international and national situation provide the context needed to assess the judgement shown by the RCAF. All three themes demonstrate increasing pressures on the government and the RCAF at different stages to develop a national rescue system, and it is evident that they form a critical framework within which this history unfolded. Despite national, international, and financial pressures working against the Air Force, the following chapters should leave no doubt that the RCAF was solely responsible for successfully developing and delivering SAR services before 1962.

Chapter 2: Combat Requires Rescue

The raging war immediately changed perceptions of rescue. The first nation to change the way it looked at rescue was the UK, during its Battle of Britain conflict with Germany. At the beginning of the 1940 battle, the German Luftwaffe's rescue service, the *Seenotdienst*, dramatically demonstrated the benefits of a search-and-rescue capability for pilots downed at sea during combat. The British development of a similar ASR system in 1941 was a necessary reaction to British aircrew witnessing enemy aircrew being rescued from the sea around the UK. The British response to the German rescue example was a fully integrated organization that immediately saved lives. An ASR system became a new standard for areas where combat operations were expected to take place, and this type of system became the international benchmark that the RCAF had to emulate as the fight came close to Canadian shores.

German U-boat submarine operations threatened Canadian shores by late 1941, and the people of Canada believed that the east and west coasts could be invaded and become operational air combat areas. Following the RAF's proven example for defence, by the end of 1942, the RCAF had developed some rescue procedures in the RCAF's home war establishment— of the Western Air Command (WAC) and the Eastern Air Command (EAC). However, these procedures would not have been sufficient if the fight had transitioned onto Canadian shores. It will become clear that the threat of war near Canadian shores caused the formation of an ASR system in the RCAF, although developments were very slow. The formation of an RCAF ASR system for the expected fight on home territory was the conceptual beginning of an integrated aviation and maritime SAR system in Canada.

THE ASR SYSTEMS OF GERMANY AND THE UK, 1940–1941

When Germany initiated hostilities against the UK to destroy the RAF, it already had an established rescue service operating in the English Channel. The German Luftwaffe had created the *Seenotdienst* for ASR in the spring of 1935 because "the early Luftwaffe could ill afford the unnecessary loss of trained aircrews as it played catch-up with the air forces of its potential enemies."[59] The time-consuming nature of training new aircrew drove the German need to save, and return to flying duties, as many existing aircrew as possible. To save as many aircrew as possible from drowning during upcoming operations against Britain, there were two He-59 seaplanes paired with rescue boats ready for cross-Channel flight operations in each of seven zones, each zone with its own RCC in May 1940. The British became acutely aware of this service during July 1940, when British pilots watched as shot-down German aviators were scooped from the sea after sorties against the RAF to fight again another day.[60]

The RAF, by contrast, only had 13 vessels available for rescue along the UK's entire coast as of June 1940, and at the outbreak of the Battle of Britain in July 1940, it had to resort to impromptu arrangements and borrowed Lysander aircraft to direct surface craft to survivors of downed aircraft.[61] During the battle, the RAF learned quickly that its existing rescue services were insufficient. With only a few aircraft to direct the rescue vessels to crash locations, many downed aircraft went unnoticed, and critically needed pilots drowned at sea as a result. In just two days, 20 and 21 July, 21 aircraft were shot down and crashed into the sea, but only 6 of 40 aircrew were recovered.[62] These losses were unsustainable this early in the battle and at stake was the very survival of the UK.

In August of 1940, the RAF hastily established a sea-rescue service with a mixture of Royal Navy Lifeboat Institution rescue vessels, Royal Navy (RN) ships, and RAF high-speed rescue vessels, all supported by

---

[59] Galdorisi and Phillips, *Leave No Man Behind*, 29.

[60] Jon Sutherland and Diane Canwell, *The RAF Air Sea Rescue Service: 1918–1986* (Great Britain: Pen & Sword Books Ltd., 2005), 31.

[61] Ibid., 9; and Galdorisi and Phillips, *Leave No Man Behind*, 39.

[62] Sutherland and Canwell, *RAF Air Sea Rescue*, 31.

any available aircraft. It was not enough. Continuing losses showed the inadequacy of the service, as 260 more aircrew were lost to the sea in October alone, a result of limited coordination between rescue resources and ground stations.[63] For the rest of the war, it was essential to recover a higher percentage of downed aircrew or risk losing critical battles or even the larger war.[64]

The British could have foreseen a fundamental problem with their rescue capability, and indeed some did worry that they needed better rescue. The RAF had delegated in-flight control of aircraft to stations in the interwar years, and it knew well before the war that the lack of coordination outside a station's radio range was deeply problematic. Stations simply could not communicate or coordinate with aircraft flying even 20 minutes away if they were at low level, let alone attempt to coordinate aircraft missions flying far from their home station. In 1937, the RAF developed a system called Regional Control to solve the problem, but the system would prove ineffective outside of peacetime flying.

By 1939, Regional Control was an organization "responsible for providing assistance to aircrew when lost or in trouble and which, further, could be used by operational staffs for diversions when weather conditions made this necessary."[65] This system allowed for stations in an area to be regionally coordinated by the centre station, but there was no coordination between the UK's eight centres. Regional Control improved upon the previous station-centric command and control of aircraft, but it did not solve problems of increasingly long-range flights or how to coordinate communications with flights between regions of the UK. There were voices of concern within the RAF, arguing in 1939 that the system was still flawed due to the lack of coordination between regions, but those warning voices were not heeded before the Battle of Britain.[66] Air combat in 1940 would prove the critics correct because eight communications and control facili-

---

[63] Ibid., 32.
[64] DHH, AIR 20/4018, 31 October 1945, "RAF Coastal Command Headquarters History of Flying Control." This history was written as an overview of regional control, followed by the Flying Control Organization system.
[65] Ibid.
[66] Ibid.

ties were insufficient for the 132 operational squadrons, 4 balloon groups, and 7 training groups of aircraft operating 2,913 aircraft throughout the UK, often with many of them launching and recovering at the same time.[67] Keeping track of hundreds of flying aircraft from more than 100 stations across the UK with only 8 control centres proved to be impossible.[68]

The problem with the regional-control system was that one central centre served many stations in the vicinity. This meant that a lost pilot could call for assistance from the centre station the pilot was in communication with, but if the battle was raging in one centre's region with many pilots calling for help, then that centre station would be quickly overwhelmed. During the first winter of the war, the large number of aviators who desperately needed assistance inundated the system, and there were more calls for help than ever had been experienced before.[69] Compounding the difficulty of coordination was the large number of aircraft passing through one control area to another, with no handoff of information between the regional centres. In the case of air defence, the lack of a handoff failed Fighter Command's requirement to know the identification of approaching aircraft to determine friend from foe. There were simply too many aircraft flying in too many directions at any one time to deal with effectively and not enough people on the ground to coordinate between organizations. The existing communications-and-control system proved woefully insufficient to meet the wartime need.

Another problem of Regional Control was that the long distances involved in bomber missions meant rescue was impossible. As a prime example, an RAF raid on Heligoland Blight in Germany, 18 December 1939, cost the RAF 13 of 24 launched aircraft, and it had no way to assist those who did not make it back from the raid.[70] The RAF had no resources for

---

[67] Denis Richards, *Royal Air Force 1939–45*, vol. 1, *The Fight at Odds* (London: Her Majesty's Stationery Office, 1974), 406 and 410. The number of squadrons, 132, is based on the RAF organization of September 1939. By the time of the Battle of Britain, there were two RCAF Squadrons in Britain as well as other new squadrons generated by the RAF, compounding the communication problem.

[68] DHH, AIR 20/4018, 31 October 1945, "RAF Coastal Command Headquarters."

[69] Ibid.

[70] Galdorisi and Phillips, *Leave No Man Behind*, 30.

picking up survivors far from home because rescue was the responsibility of the stations from which aircraft had departed, and these stations had zero capability for such long-range rescues and no knowledge of how the mission was proceeding. In the Heligoland Raid, the *Seenotdienst* saved 20 of the British aviators found in the sea from this raid, which in itself was an early indication that ASR would prove necessary in later battles.[71] There were clear signs in 1939 that both Regional Control and the UK's rescue capability had serious flaws, and once the Battle of Britain was over—the RAF fully realized that the sea-rescue service and the Regional Control organizational been very problematic.

The RAF discovered that Regional Control "worked out before the war because the amount of flying over water was comparatively small and not usually at any great distance from the coast."[72] However, distance, massive numbers of aircraft, and a lack of communication between centres made it clear that something better was urgently needed. The answer was a centrally run and interconnected control organization that included personnel at both the main centres and at each flying station to help those aviators who needed guidance or rescue assistance. This system was named Flying Control, and it expanded control personnel from 140 at the beginning of the Battle of Britain to 2,000 control-qualified officers by the end of 1941 to coordinate the control of aircraft and to aid aircrew.[73] The nearly 15-fold increase in flying-control personnel in itself demonstrates the depth of the coordination problem that had to be solved for combat over one's own soil, let alone attacks at a distance.

The RAF established the Flying Control Organization in February 1941, and by November of that year the system was operational and incredibly successful. It supported every station and provided coordination in every part of the UK.[74] Included within the Flying Control Organization was a brand new ASR service. The ASR system was centrally run from the

---

[71] Ibid.

[72] LAC, RG24-D-11, Vol. 11885, CD 18-3-1, West Coast Chart Depot, HMC Dockyard, Esquimalt – Air-Sea Rescue, 18-3-1, 19 September 1942, "RCAF Sea Rescue Bulletin No. 6, Air/Sea Rescue."

[73] DHH, AIR 20/4018, 31 October 1945, "RAF Coastal Command Headquarters."

[74] Ibid.

Air Ministry with an RAF director at the rank of group captain and an RN deputy director of equivalent rank to coordinate efforts between the services.[75] By June 1941, the ASR system of the Flying Control Organization was interconnected by telephone "almost into one 'press-button' chain," and the lines linked RN and RAF coastal units throughout the country.[76] The chance of being rescued from the sea immediately increased from 20 per cent to 35 per cent and would continue to improve over the course of the war. While this increase may not sound like much, it was a 75 per cent improvement and made a significant difference because hundreds of aircrew would ditch into the sea each month. With the improvement, dozens of those aviators, who otherwise would have perished, returned to fly combat missions again.[77] It is possible that the 75 per cent increase of aviators returned to the flight line helped turn the tide of war in Europe.

The ASR organization included the RAF's high-speed rescue vessels and all the RN assets that had previously been in use for aircrew rescue. In a determined effort to stem losses, the number of rescue vessels in 1941 would be expanded to over 300 for the UK coast from just the 13 available during the Battle of Britain.[78] The 1941 Flying Control Organization additions included 36 Lysander aircraft and 8 Walrus flying boats that were assigned exclusively to the ASR mission and held on continuous standby for launch, which greatly increased the speed and reach of rescue.[79] Dedicated ASR resources meant that aircraft and seaplanes could be equipped specifically for the rescue mission and that ASR personnel could become experts in rescue. These experts would soon provide training to Allied aircrew in Britain on ASR best practices, an expertise that would influence RCAF aviators to consider Canada's domestic practices.[80]

The amount of resources assigned to the RAF's ASR in 1941 was significant. Stations with dedicated ASR had a Lysander aircraft and Walrus

---

[75] Sutherland and Canwell, *RAF Air Sea Rescue*, 32.

[76] DHH, AIR 20/4018, 31 October 1945, "RAF Coastal Command Headquarters."

[77] Sutherland and Canwell, *RAF Air Sea Rescue*, 45.

[78] Ibid., 31.

[79] Ibid., 39.

[80] DHH, 181.009 (D4586), RAF File S-7, No. 411 Sqn (RCAF), 11 July 1941 to 31 May 1943, "ASR Procedures and Instructions."

rescue seaplane at immediate availability to launch with another of each aircraft type at 30-minutes notice to launch.[81] The marine vessels assigned had to be at instant readiness to depart, and there was a second vessel on 10-minute notice to move. A duty group controller oversaw the readiness of all assigned resources for effective command and control and was responsive to inputs from the Flying Control Organization on crash locations. By the end of 1942, the British ASR system provided unquestionably robust rescue operations over the English Channel, and a similar system was created in the Mediterranean and in Iceland.[82] Allied aircrew, flying in Britain, immediately benefited from this integrated capability that saved lives daily.

By contrast, the Americans had no rescue system at the start of the war, so US aviators made use of the existing British system, as did RCAF aircrew. Starting in 1943, however, the US would begin creating its own ASR systems in various theatres of operations.[83] The US followed the RAF model of rescue for deployed operations, which was separate from the rescue model used by the well-established United States Coast Guard in North American home waters.

The US had its Coast Guard to operate off the coasts of the continental US and Alaska to continue to provide a domestic life-saving service throughout the war, which was an important difference between the American and Canadian approaches to ASR in North America.[84] This fundamental difference meant that American military services would not be required to build a domestic-rescue service; thus, the US was able to focus on military rescue for deployed combat situations. By contrast, any Canadian rescue system would have to be built from scratch, and it would have to provide the level of service

---

[81] Ibid.

[82] LAC, RG24-D-1-b, Vol. 3896, 1034-3-20, RCAF – Air/Sea Rescue, N.S.S. 1034-3-19, Report to DOD NSHQ from Air Liaison Officer from Atlantic Command HQ to EAC Major R. R. Ings, 25 November 1942, "A.L.O. Visit to the U.K."

[83] L. B. Taylor Jr., *That Others May Live: The Aerospace Rescue and Recovery Service* (New York: E. P. Dutton, 1967), 64.

[84] The United States Coast Guard, "Time Line 1900's to 2000's," *United States Coast Guard Historian's Office*, December 1988, https://www.history.uscg.mil/Complete-Time-Line/Time-Line-1900-2000/ (accessed 25 April 2018).

expected by British and American forces operating in Canadian areas of operation. In particular, British ASR had become a high standard to follow.

The British had followed the operational example of the Luftwaffe's ASR system to create their own successful system, but the British had unknowingly avoided a significant flaw in the Luftwaffe's rescue system. The *Seenotdienst* service had not been kept informed of operational invasion plans, except those against Britain, so the service was not present in the spring of 1940 invasions of Norway, France, Holland, and Belgium.[85] Many lives were lost because this important service was not in place for combat operations in these areas, and post-war documentation confirmed that this had been a significant flaw in operational planning.[86] Having a rescue system in place before combat operations was a lesson immediately understood by the British, followed by the Americans. It would later become apparent to the RCAF, and this important lesson still resonates today.

It can be summarized that by the end of 1941, it was well established among the Allies that any expectation of future combat operations in a given area was going to require a rescue system integrated into operational command and control.[87] Without a rescue system, battles could be lost that otherwise might have been won had aircrew been recovered from the sea. With the UK on the ropes in Europe and operations against North America in the realm of the possible, consideration needed to be given to a combat-rescue capability over Canada's oceans.

RCAF Rescue Developments 1940–1942

Stepping back in time to 1940, the RCAF had yet to become deeply worried about combat operations at home. EAC, based out of Halifax, was concerned about German U-boats and would prosecute sightings, but there

---

[85] Galdorisi and Phillips, *Leave No Man Behind*, 30 and 31.

[86] Ibid., 31.

[87] DHH, 181.009 (D4389), RCAF File S202-85-2, WAC No. 2 Group Standing Orders for ASR June to September 1942, Memorandum from 1 June 1942, "Establishment of Flying Control and Aircraft Safety Services in Canada." There is no name attached to this memorandum, but it is likely that AFHQ staff officer F/L R. J. Lehman produced it, as it was embedded within a package of other letters and memorandums with his signature.

was limited operational activity for RCAF aircraft. WAC, with headquarters in Vancouver, had even less war-related activity.[88] In stark contrast to the hundreds of aviators downed in the sea each month during the Battle of Britain, EAC lost only one RCAF aircraft to a crash near an airport between 1 May and 31 October 1940, and WAC responded to only one RCAF aircraft crash in that time period, which fisherman located immediately.[89] In 1940, all of Canada's Air Force at home responded to only two crashes over a greater time period than the whole of the Battle of Britain. In these circumstances, ASR in Canada was not a significant concern.

Although the RCAF did not have to respond to aircraft crashing in the sea very often, it did have to respond to civilian requests for assistance, as there was no domestic-rescue organization in Canada due to the RCN's lack of funding for the Canadian Lifesaving Service. Throughout 1940, EAC responded to five requests to search for missing civilian vessels.[90] The requests from 1940 were a significant change from 1939, as no mention was found of the RCAF providing assistance to maritime rescues before 1940. By comparison, the RCMP had recorded many maritime rescues prior to the outbreak of war.[91] This demonstrated that the transfer of RCMP vessels to the RCAF for military requirements was having an effect on non-military rescue response. Without the RCMP available to conduct maritime missions for distressed vessels after the war began, the RCAF was morally bound to assist the public, even with combat operations ongoing.

One welcome-but-complicating factor for RCAF rescue was a new American presence in Newfoundland as part of the Leased Bases Agreement

---

[88] RCAF Operations Records Books, C-12160 Western Air Command Headquarters, Daily Diary 6 March 1938 to 31 October 1942, http://heritage.canadiana.ca/view/oocihm.lac_mikan_135766 (accessed 25 April 2018).

[89] RCAF Operations Records Books, Reel ID C-12156 Eastern Air Command Headquarters 1 May 1940 to 30 September 1944, http://heritage.canadiana.ca/view/oocihm.lac_mikan_135766 (accessed 25 April 2018).

[90] Ibid., Images 23, 28, 45, 94, and 109.

[91] LAC, RG12, Vol. 2254, File No. 7800-1, Life-Saving Search and Rescue – General, Miscellaneous Awards Files.

between the US and the UK signed on 27 March 1941.[92] The agreement provided 50 destroyers to the UK in return for 99-year leases of land for bases in Newfoundland and Trinidad, and the destroyers helped keep the UK in the war at a critical time without violating American Congress limits on assistance to the British. Equally important, the leased land in Newfoundland allowed the US to start building a deployed presence to eventually fight the effective and ferocious German naval activity in the Atlantic. The US built air and naval bases in Newfoundland as a way to defend itself from the furthest point away possible, and this was welcome by both the Government of Canada and the RCAF to provide additional protection to Canadians from a possible German invasion.[93] The first American troops arrived in St. John's in January 1941, and by 1945, more than 100,000 American military troops had been stationed in Newfoundland and Labrador.[94] The increasing American presence meant more possible rescue requirements in an area controlled by the RCAF; although, it also meant that American resources could assist in rescue situations when the need arose.

To limit the number of Canadian military aircraft used for searches, more emphasis was put on high-speed vessels to rescue RCAF aircraft operating over the sea on missions. The RCAF had wanted to expand its numbers of aircrew and aircraft defending Canada, but there was intense pressure from the UK to provide maximum capability where the need for resources was clearly the greatest, in the European theatre. As part of the compromise solution, aircraft were limited for Canadian operations, and rescue services were not given priority. In August 1940, the Chief of the Air Staff issued standing orders for rescue vessels "to carry out patrols at sea for the purpose of aiding aircraft in need of assistance or any other necessary patrol or duty they may be required to perform by the Officer in Command."[95] Using vessels was a convenient way to avoid the optics

---

[92] Jenny Higgins, "The American Presence in Newfoundland and Labrador," *Heritage Newfoundland & Labrador*, 2006, http://www.heritage.nf.ca/articles/politics/american-presence-newfoundland-labrador.php (accessed 25 April 2018).

[93] Strauss, "Diplomatic Negotiations Leading," 22.

[94] Higgins, "American Presence in Newfoundland."

[95] DHH, 89/625, August 1940, "Standing and Maintenance Orders for High Speed Rescue Vessels."

of combat aircraft used for non-combat roles and still provide a limited service. The rescue vessels were very useful and not just for the RCAF, as patrols often assisted with local civilian emergencies.[96] With the RCMP very limited in its wartime maritime capability and the RCN operating further out to sea, the RCAF had become acutely aware that it would have to be involved in civilian rescue activities as well as meet its own rescue requirements.

For RCAF domestic operations, the RAF's long-abandoned station command and control of aircraft was still used by the RCAF. Surprisingly, station control was quite workable in 1941 due to the limited numbers of aircraft operating in EAC, which meant that the problems were nowhere near as glaring. As an example, on 3 June 1941, a Bolingbroke aircraft clipped an RCN vessel while out at sea on a mission and eventually crashed in the ocean, which initiated an immediate station rescue response.[97] In this case, the station launched aircraft to search and reported to EAC; EAC arranged for additional search aircraft and, in turn, reported to Air Force Headquarters (AFHQ) in Ottawa, Ontario. There was genuine interest at all levels of command in the fate of the crew of three, and AFHQ was kept well informed of progress. The two headquarters involved had the time and capacity to keep each other well informed while maintaining oversight on all operations. However, this was still 1941 with a lot less aircraft activity in contrast to 1943 when the Battle of the Atlantic was at high pitch and the operational tempo was far quicker. AFHQ involvement in individual missions would not survive the massive 1943 increase in air activity, despite the precious lives involved in the crashes, especially with the limited effectiveness of station flying control in the RCAF prior to the fall of 1942.

The loss of life resulting from these aircraft crashes were heart wrenching and demanded attention. On 10 November 1941, an RCAF DH 82C Tiger Moth crashed near Calgary, Alberta. Leading Aircraftman Karl Mander Gravell, 19 years old, was one of two people onboard. He died while attempting to pull his pilot out of the burning wreckage, despite the

[96] DHH, 96/24 Air Force Headquarters fonds, Box 7, File 2, "Air Council Minutes from 3 November 1942."
[97] DHH, 181.003 (D7) Summary of RCAF Activities 1941, Bolingbroke message traffic, 2–3 June 1941.

fact that he had lost an eye in the crash and his own clothes were on fire.[98] His sacrifice was awarded posthumously with the first George Cross of the Second World War for the RCAF, the highest gallantry award given to military personnel not in the face of the enemy. Although bravery and courage were clearly a part of the RCAF culture, as crashes became more frequent, the need to rescue those who did make it out of the wreckage was certain to become more of a priority for RCAF leadership. Crashes that occurred close to stations would receive station help, as Gravell's crash suggests, but crashes outside of communication range of the station needed procedures to be developed and resources to be assigned for an avoidable loss of life.

By early 1942, RCAF leadership was indeed quite concerned about rescue, specifically the number and type of vessels it needed for sea-rescue operations, given that U-boat operations had increased along the Atlantic coast.[99] The RCAF had replaced older seaplanes in the bomber-reconnaissance role with Canso seaplanes, and these new seaplanes extended the radius of operations from 300 miles from the coast to an improved maximum of 600 miles.[100] The rescue vessels had a 200-mile radius, and it was normal for the vessels to patrol halfway between the station and the seaplane patrol area, but the range of the new Cansos considerably exceeded the range of the rescue vessels.[101] Even the newest vessels would not have the range required to provide an effective rescue capability for the new seaplanes. Coupled with the threatening presence of U-boats in the operational flight areas, AFHQ needed assistance to be able to rescue aircrew operating far out to sea.

AFHQ's Air Council—consisting of the Minister of National Defence for Air, Charles Gavan Power, and the most senior officers of the RCAF—discussed vessels for rescue work at length the year prior.[102] They had concluded that deep-sea rescue work was not appropriate for the RCAF to attempt, so

---

[98] The Para Rescue Association, *That Others May Live*, 9. The information provided was supplemented by information from a story in the *London Gazette*, 5 June 1942.

[99] Douglas, *Official History of the Royal Canadian Air Force*, 473.

[100] LAC, RG24-D-11, Vol. 11885, CD 18-3-1, West Coast Chart Depot, HMC Dockyard, Esquimalt – Air-Sea Rescue, 18-3-1, Letter to CNS from AOC EAC, 24 August 1942, "Rescue Boats."

[101] Ibid.

[102] DHH, 181.003 (D7) "Summary of RCAF Activities 1941."

they had made a formal request to the RCN to take on oceanic rescue work further than 200 miles from shore.[103] The RCN agreed that rescue vessels operating that far from shore should indeed become a naval commitment, but agreement was not achieved on what vessels to purchase or how to coordinate efforts.[104] The lack of effective range for available rescue craft was not resolved.

In the interim, the rescue resources that were available by 1942 were well-regarded vessels. Canada had six Scott-Paine 70-foot high-speed rescue vessels, built in Montreal in 1941 specifically for RCAF rescue work, complete with weapons and a rugged but attractive appearance.[105] The names of the six vessels were the Abnaki, Huron, Malecite, Montagnais, Nootka, and Takuli.[106] These vessels were the best known of the RCAF marine craft, and initially, they remained at the command of the station commanding officer (CO) where the vessel was based. This meant that COs of stations without such vessels would have to ask the CO of the station with a vessel for authority to use the rescue resource, knowing the request would strip the owning station of its primary rescue resource. EAC would quickly get involved if there were competing demands for resources, but the procedure wasted critical time during emergencies for stations without immediate access to the vessels.[107]

EAC had an important operational responsibility in the Atlantic theatre, but the amount and complexity of flying operations was vastly simpler than RAF activity in the UK, and that slowed flying-control development in Canada. Without the large number of operational missions and combat losses, it was difficult to justify the increase of capability in Canada while the overseas situation remained dire. Even at the height of EAC operations, there were never more than 200 aircraft operating out of 18 squadrons from 19 different stations throughout the Atlantic

---

[103] LAC, RG24-D-11, Vol. 11885, CD 18-3-1, West Coast Chart Depot, HMC Dockyard, Esquimalt – Air-Sea Rescue, 18-3-1, Memorandum to CNS from CAS, 28 December 42, "Rescue Boats for RCAF."

[104] Ibid.

[105] Vernon, "RCAF Marine Craft," 100.

[106] Halliday, "Role of the Boats."

[107] Vernon, "RCAF Marine Craft," 105.

provinces.[108] In 1940, there were fewer than 80 aircraft flying out of EAC stations.[109] That was in stark contrast (see Figure 2) to the RAF's 2,913 aircraft operating on high-risk missions at day and night over a much smaller area.

Figure 2. EAC Operating Area Comparison[110]

As there was such a low number of RCAF aircraft flying over a large area, the station control of aircraft did not have the obvious deficiencies of the UK's defunct Regional Control system. As depicted in Figure 2, a total of no more than 200 aircraft operated in an area at least twice the size of

---

[108] Douglas, *Official History of the Royal Canadian Air Force*, 349, 352, and 357.

[109] Ibid., 352.

[110] This map was drawn by Dawn J. Hill.

the UK; that is, fewer than 10 per cent of the aircraft flying over Britain operated in twice the area, and that greatly lessened the requirement for detailed control of aircraft. Aircraft and seaplanes in Canada could depart their station, communicate one-on-one with other stations they might pass near, and switch to operational frequencies without worrying about other aircraft from other stations flying in the vicinity. This meant that there was little incentive for the RCAF to follow the RAF example of a flying-control organization throughout Canada until combat forced the issue.

Although the RAF Flying Control Organization was well established by September 1941, the RCAF had not taken any similar action in late 1941 because of the expected expense of setting up flying-control facilities in Canada and because the British Air Ministry "had not defined any long-term policy regarding training of flying control officers."[111] However, the war appeared to be approaching Canadian shores at the end of 1941, and RCAF views on flying control would change as a result. A professionalization of flying control was inevitable.

In October 1941, German U-boats were creating havoc off Newfoundland in daring raids against Allied shipping close to RCAF air stations, and they significantly raised the threat against Canada and Newfoundland.[112] The disaster at Pearl Harbor in December 1941, along with the Atlantic U-boat threat, greatly increased Canadian government concern for military flying, as there was a perceived threat on both coasts. In fact, the number of squadrons to defend Canada was increased dramatically in response "to an atmosphere of near panic in British Columbia."[113] The dangers posed by enemy forces on the East Coast were significant, as outlined in Figure 3, and the increase of threat raised awareness of the inadequacies of both station flying control and the RCAF's lack of an ASR organization.

---

[111] DHH, 181.009 (D4389) 1 June 1942, "Establishment of Flying Control."

[112] Douglas, *Official History of the Royal Canadian Air Force*, 484.

[113] Ibid., 341.

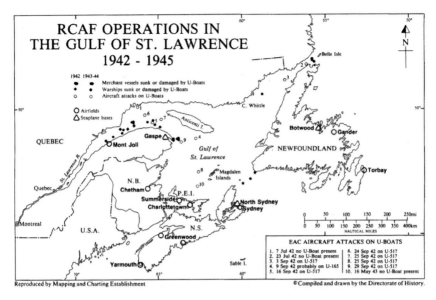

Figure 3. East Coast RCAF Operations 1942–1945[114]

Subsequently, in March 1942, AFHQ concluded that there was an urgent need for flying control so that the RCAF system, so similar to the flawed RAF system of 1936, could be corrected before it proved disastrous in combat.[115] There is no coincidence that the RCAF saw an urgent need to revisit a flying-control organization in Canada after the public and government became concerned about invasion. The Battle of Britain in 1940 had firmly established that combat operations over water needed a well-organized flying-control system with an embedded ASR capability. Canada needed to act before an invasion to have a better chance at repelling the enemy by developing an ability to rescue as many aircrew as possible from combat missions close to Canadian shores. The impetus to create a flying-control organization became even more urgent after the Japanese

---

[114] DHH, 181.009 (D4389) 1 June 1942, "Establishment of Flying Control,"499. © All rights reserved. RCAF Operations in the Gulf of St. Lawrence 1942–1945 reproduced with the permission of DND/CAF in 2018.

[115] DHH, 181.009 (D4389), "Establishment of Flying Control."

invaded Alaska's Aleutian Islands in June 1942, making a Canadian invasion seem quite possible.[116]

To create a flying-control organization, the RCAF sought recommendations from two officers with RAF flying-control experience. RCAF Wing Commander (W/C) Andrews and Squadron Leader (S/L) Mouatt were tasked to investigate the issue.[117] They produced a detailed report in August 1942 recommending "the provision of a Flying Control, Aircraft Safety and Sea Rescue organization" that would work in tandem with the civilian air-traffic-control system.[118] This report was accepted, and orders were given immediately to develop a flying-control organization in Canada to include procedures for ASR.[119] The Air Ministry in the UK provided "one of its ablest Flying Control Officers as advisor, and the nucleus of the Canadian organization was made up of ten RCAF officers who each had a year's experience in flying control in the United Kingdom."[120]

A new Deputy Directorate of Flying Control, within AFHQ's Air Member of Air Staff, was made responsible for the Flying Control Organization, with staff assigned to Flying Control, Flying Control Air Safety, and Sea Rescue Services.[121] A W/C headed the Flying Control Organization and 490 personnel were needed to set up the services at all levels.[122] Not all of the recommended positions were established. For example, although it was recommended that an S/L should head the Sea Rescue Services, the rank was downgraded to a flight lieutenant (F/L) because the

---

[116] The Para Rescue Association, *That Others May Live*, 13.

[117] DHH, 181.009 (D4389), "Establishment of Flying Control."

[118] DHH, 181.002 (164), RCAF File S.204-2-1 Part 1, by W/C Andrews, 8 August 1942, "Operations – Operational Procedure and Control – WAC." No other details were provided on the document.

[119] DHH, 181.002 (164), RCAF File S.204-2-1 Part 1, Operations – Operational Procedure and Control – WAC, 12 August 1942, "Organization Order No. 93, Formation of No. 1 School of Flying Control."

[120] DHH, 181.003 (D984), Monthly Review of RCAF Ops in North America 43–44, "July 1943 Edition."

[121] DHH, 181.009 (D4389), RCAF File S202-85-2, WAC No. 2 Group Standing Orders for ASR Jun to Sep 42, 14 September 1942, "Standing Orders and Instructions for Flying Control Officers."

[122] DHH, 181.002 (164) 8 August 1942, "Procedure and Control – WAC."

plan did not include dedicated ASR officers at EAC or WAC to supervise and direct, and that made the higher rank unnecessary at AFHQ.[123] Thus, by the end of summer 1942, a plan to build a Flying Control Organization with ASR potential was well underway, even if it was planned to have a less-than-ideal number of personnel.

The creation of formal RCAF ASR procedures as part of the creation of Flying Control solved some other problems, such as communications between RCN vessels and RCAF aircraft, best demonstrated by the *Empire Seal* rescue of 17 June 1942. An RCAF aircraft located the *Empire Seal*, with people on board clearly needing assistance, and the aircraft tried to contact the nearest RCN vessel, but the aircrew could not acquire radio communications with the RCN vessel, so they had to use a signaling device known as an Aldis lamp to flash lights using Morse code and get a nearby merchant vessel to affect the rescue instead.[124] RCN and RCAF communications at all levels could fail at times without coordinated procedures, and ASR procedures were issued in September 1942.

Although communications problems would be partly resolved by new orders, one problem that was not solved was aircrew procedures for rescue missions. EAC and WAC had different procedures, and they were very vague with how to conduct the actual missions. As well, specific equipment to support SAR activities had not yet been tested or ordered. At first blush, the changes had the appearance of a duplication of the RAF's rescue system, but there was little real depth to the number and type of changes affecting Canadian ASR.

The standing orders for ASR in the RCAF included several significant differences from the organization developed in the UK. Rather than assigning air sea rescue officers (ASROs) with specialty training at each station, group, and higher headquarters (HQ), the RCAF included ASR training at the Flying Control School and ordered the senior flying-control

---

[123] F/L R. J. Lehman was the signing authority for Sea Rescue Services in 1943.

[124] DHH, 181.002 AFHQ file 9325-11 Vol. 2 Operations – RCAF Cover for Convoys, Air Sea Rescue File folder four, *Sea Rescue Operations in EAC*, 17 June 1942.

officer at each station to be responsible for initial ASR response.[125] As well, the senior flying-control officer was responsible for equipment, close-in searches, and the training of aircrew to include search procedures and dinghy drills. If flight operations at the station were slow, then the workload could be manageable. If the station entered a busy period, this was a massive amount of work for a small organization at any station. Consider that a station responsible for an ongoing search could have found itself communicating with many aircraft operating in the local area to assist with a search, while still being responsible for other duties such as hunting submarines. As combat flying operations increased, this over-tasking of flying-control personnel would become a serious concern.

The senior flying-control officer was also the assigned position responsible for ASR at group HQs. One immediate change initiated by the new standard procedures was that the senior flying-control officer at group HQ was now responsible for overall coordination of ASR operations throughout the area instead of the closest station, as had previously been the case.[126] This change was very significant because it took away rescue responsibility from individual stations and moved it to the higher level of authority of the group where coordination could occur with all the group's stations. The new direction to provide ASR from the group level increased safety and established sensible ASR procedures, but the RCAF Flying Control Organization still did not have the dedicated ASR experts of the RAF example.

There were still major differences between the RAF and RCAF systems in 1942, but the RCAF Flying Control Organization was an effective response that, in hindsight, was completed in a timely fashion. Similar to the UK system, the flying-control officers had little-to-no flying experience, but were trained "to assist pilots with the safe landing of aircraft," "keeping an accurate record of aircraft movements," and "assisting aircraft

---

[125] DHH, 181.009 (D4389), RCAF File S202-85-2, WAC No. 2 Group Standing Orders for ASR Jun to Sep 42, *Draft Standing Orders for Air/Sea Rescue Services in the RCAF*, September 1942. An attached minute sheet states that the orders were accepted with minor grammatical changes.

[126] LAC, RG24-D-1-b, Vol. 3896, 1034-3-20, RCAF – Air/Sea Rescue, N.S.S. 1034-3-19, *RCAF Sea Rescue Bulletin #A1*, 28 November 1942.

lost over sea or land by direction finding services."[127] Many existing deficiencies had been rectified as stations, groups, and commands would now have flying-control officers to coordinate aircraft whereabouts and safety needs. It would have been far better had ASROs been added to stations and groups, but the initial RCAF flying control organization was a step in the right direction.

From an ASR perspective, however, the deficiencies were still considerable, even after the policy changes of 1942.[128] There were still only six high-speed rescue vessels to provide rescue coverage on both coasts. Aircraft could be sent out for rescues from any RCAF station, but the crews had no survival gear to drop to aviators in the sea. They had no training for that type of mission, and the aircraft could be taken from a high priority combat mission without clear authority from higher HQs. The coordination of rescue missions fell upon the senior flying-control officer of the group missing the aircraft, who already had a very busy job keeping track of all flying operations. Additionally, if a rescue situation would greatly benefit from Navy resources, there was no ability to coordinate directly. Any assistance required by the Navy had to be requested by the commands, so there was a potential failure point for communications between the Flying Control Organization running the search and the higher HQ authorizing and coordinating the request for urgently needed Navy resources. These were failings that would need to be resolved while there was still a threat that large air combat operations could take place over Canada.

The development in Canada of the Flying Control Organization, and its embedded ASR, was taking place at the same time as Allied pressure had started to mount on Canada to build these organizations and prepare for combat in Canadian areas. In July 1942, an American major from the ASR Directorate in the UK wrote a report detailing the differences

[127] LAC, RG24-E-1-b, Vol. 5421, 67-16-2, Sea Rescue Services – Liaison with Royal Canadian Navy, Memorandum to AMO from AMAS A/V/M N. R. Anderson, 3 August 1942, "Flying Control, Aircraft Safety and Sea Rescue Services."
[128] DHH, 181.009 (D4389), RCAF File S202-85-2, WAC No. 2 Group Standing Orders for ASR Jun to Sep 42, September 1942, "Draft Standing Orders for Air/Sea Rescue Services in the RCAF." There is a minute on these draft orders that they were accepted. All information for this paragraph is taken from this source.

between the RAF and RCAF organizations and concluded; "if some such [ASR] organization were established on the Atlantic Cost, many valuable lives could be saved."[129] The report highlighted a linkage between the number of lives saved in UK waters and the increasing wartime casualties in Canadian waters.[130] The RAF ASR system was held up as an example for the RCAF to follow.

Separately, a Major R. R. Ings, the Air Liaison Officer from Atlantic Command HQ of the United States Army Air Corps, wrote a similar report in November 1942 that stated his team "felt that an [ASR Directorate] might be started on the East Coast of Canada and Newfoundland, where not only the valuable lives of aircrew might be saved, but that some worthwhile attempt could be made to rescue survivors from torpedoed ships."[131] These criticisms likely reinforced the formation of the Flying Control Organization in Canada, as the RCAF was more than a year behind the changes the RAF was making in response to wartime lessons. With the Battle of the Atlantic approaching its height, the expected combat losses would require an RCAF rescue system capable of providing a service to Allied aviators similar to that of Britain's.

Canadian ASR Development at the End of 1942

In summary, the transfer of RCMP and volunteer resources to the RCAF and RCN meant that what little domestic rescue there had been in Canada before the war was abandoned. As RCN activities moved further from shore on convoy duties in the first two years of war, a gap of potential rescue resources was created within 200 miles of shore, and demands on the RCAF were inevitable. The RCAF had six high-speed rescue vessels to fill the gap, but these few vessels would be insufficient for large combat

---

[129] LAC, RG24-E-1-b, Vol. 3410, 466-1-3, Air/Sea Rescue Services – Minutes of RAF Monthly Air/Sea Rescue Meeting – Policy, File 464-3-3 Vol. 2, July 1942, "Air Sea Rescue." The major's signature is illegible and a day of the month was not provided.

[130] Ibid.

[131] LAC, RG24-D-1-b, Vol. 3896, 1034-3-20, RCAF – Air/Sea Rescue, N.S.S. 1034-3-19, Report to DOD NSHQ from Air Liaison Officer from Atlantic Command HQ to EAC Major R. R. Ings, 25 November 1942, "A.L.O. Visit to the U.K."

operations as well as civilian-rescue activity. The gap of rescue left by the RCMP had fallen to the RCAF, and few, if any, resources were added to acknowledge the civilian aspect of the ASR requirements. National sovereignty was weakened by the lack of a Canadian ability to rescue aircrew or civilians without help from the US.

With U-boat operations on the East Coast and a Japanese threat on the West Coast in 1942, there was undeniable international pressure to create a flying-control organization and ASR system in Canada. The Luftwaffe and the RAF had fully demonstrated the benefits for an ASR system to support combat operations, and the RCAF now needed to establish flying-control and ASR operations to prepare for combat operations within Canada. The lesson in flying control was partly learned, as the Flying Control Organization was created in 1942, but ASR in Canada was not as well developed as it had been in the RAF before the changes of 1941. Further progress was urgently required for the expected air combat near Canada's shores in 1943 to avoid learning British lessons the hard way.

For military flight operations, AFHQ acknowledged that cost was initially a factor in delaying the development of the Flying Control Organization. The threat of war approaching Canada's shores eliminated cost as a concern during 1942.[132] The focus of operational capability had remained on the overseas situation, and that necessarily slowed the growth of ASR in Canada. However, the limited number of RCAF vessels and aircraft in the rescue role meant that there were known deficiencies in the ASR system immediately upon its formation, and funding was not obtained for additional rescue vessels or aircraft. Overall, cost was a significant factor in RCAF reluctance to develop a flying-control organization and ASR prior to spring 1942.

With the war closing in on Canadian shores, the RCAF had responded with the creation of the Flying Control Organization system with ASR potential in 1942. In the progress towards today's SAR system, this chapter has shown that little was achieved. As illustrated in Table 3, a rudimentary national system had been formed in 1942, but it was developed only to meet the needs of aircrew downed at sea. Resources assigned to rescue

---

[132] DHH, 181.009 (D4389), "Establishment of Flying Control."

activities were limited to a few high-speed rescue vessels. For civilians, rescue at sea was less likely than before the war, as the few dedicated pre-war rescue resources had been transferred from the RCMP and the Canadian Lifesaving Service to the military. The following chapter demonstrates how the RCAF developed a system for its own needs and that the improved system started to fill in rescue gaps for civilian domestic emergencies.

Characteristic	Aviation	Maritime
National Standards	**Aviation rescues.** The RCAF had a rescue policy, but it had inadequate plans for crashes over land	**Maritime rescues.** None
Available Resources	**Aircraft.** RCAF aircraft could be tasked, but they had no training or procedures	**Vessels.** Six RCAF vessels and assistance available from the RCN provided coastal coverage only
Formalized Policy	**Military rescues.** Commands and groups were mandated to respond, but searches overloaded the senior flying-control officer	**Civilian rescues.** The RCAF started to respond to civilian rescues, but there was no requirement to do so

Table 3. Canadian ASR in 1942

Chapter 3: A Domestication of Air Sea Rescue

The initial Canadian ASR system of August 1942 was developed to prepare for combat operations over Canada's land and oceans. As will become evident, rising Allied expectations and internal pressures caused the RCAF to fully develop ASR into a robust national capability by the end of the war. The practical reality of the RCAF's ASR system, however, was that it developed less for combat rescues and more to assist any aviator or mariner in distress, military or civilian. The lack of any other national rescue system compelled the RCAF to provide resources to missing civilian aviators and mariners due to the Air Force's existing procedures and available resources. Without a doubt, the lack of a combat focus for the new rescue organization would have long-term repercussions on rescue developments in Canada.

EAC and WAC had been involved in military rescues in Canada since the outbreak of war. While the initial focus of ASR operations had been on military aircraft ditching into the sea, more concerning were American military aircraft crashes along the Northwest Staging Route (NWSR), a route from Edmonton and through Alaska to Russia. This route was used by the Americans to transport new American aircraft to Russia for use on the Eastern Front against Germany. The importance of this route to ASR development is that any response to crashes over land along the NWSR did not need to take into account an enemy presence. A civilian manager of 2 Air Observer School in Edmonton, former Captain Wilfrid Reid "Wop" May, developed a parachute-rescue capability that would extend the ASR concept over land, specifically along the NWSR, where most of the overland crashes were taking place. The parachute-rescue capability continued the RCAF's inadvertent creation of a domestic rescue expectation.

THE DEVELOPMENT OF FLYING CONTROL AND ASR PROCEDURES

The 1942 initial ASR capability was part of the Flying Control Organization that provided little actual rescue potential because it had few resources assigned. The RCAF high-speed rescue vessels were the main resources for the new procedures, but they could not reach even half of the patrol areas of the new aircraft and seaplanes.[133] Meanwhile, RCAF squadron personnel in Britain were being rescued by the effective RAF ASR system, and knowledge of the British rescue capabilities contributed to internal RCAF pressure for better Canadian ASR even as the combat component of RCAF operations moved further offshore.[134] Whether the threat to Canada remained or not, there was a clear desire for a better rescue system in Canada to match the expectations of aviators returning from European combat operations.

To improve rescue policy and overall flying operations in Canadian airspace, Canadian Air Publication (CAP) 342 was issued in May 1943.[135] CAP 342 outlined flying-control procedures in the RCAF and included much better guidance and resources for ASR. Changes from the 1942 version of ASR were the requirement for commands to provide aircraft for rescue purposes, direction for the groups to assume responsibility for searches within 200 miles of shore with marine craft, procedures for aircrew prosecuting rescue missions, and for the RCN to provide "maximum effort" for searches further out to sea.[136] Changes did not include additional personnel, but there were much improved regulations and guidance for equipment management. There were even regular ASR articles in the *Monthly Review of RCAF Ops* [Operations] *in North America* that was first published in June of 1943. The CAP and the monthly publication greatly increased ASR communication to all RCAF members.

Concurrently with the CAP 342, WAC developed its own procedures, which included providing rescue for "civil planes passing through command areas" and "ships in distress," demonstrating RCAF awareness of the need

[133] LAC, RG24-D-11, Vol. 11885, 24 August 1942, "Rescue Boats."
[134] DHH, 181.003 (D893), 434 Squadron File "Air Sea Rescue," July 1943 to May 1945.
[135] DHH, 81/301, RCAF, CAP 342, *Orders and Instructions for RCAF Flying Control and Air Sea Rescue Service*, May 1943.
[136] Ibid., 33.

for it to assist in providing domestic rescue to the Canadian public.[137] It is not clear what official EAC procedures on ASR were in 1943, but it is known that EAC responded to civilian marine emergencies on a regular basis.[138] Basically, both EAC and WAC were not busy enough to ignore pleas for help from the public, and they ensured that help was made available through procedures and practice. Fundamentally, mid-war Canadian steps in the development of ASR included procedures for domestic maritime rescue, and this began a trend that the RCAF could not escape.

One example of RCAF assistance in domestic maritime rescue took place on 16 January 1943. An RCAF detachment at Cape Scott, Vancouver Island, British Columbia, witnessed a vessel listing badly to starboard, and it appeared to sink during a gale.[139] The vessel was identified as the Union Steamship Co. of BC's *S.S. Northolm,* and it had 15 persons on board. An RCAF aircraft, notably already flying on a search mission for a missing civilian aircraft, was redirected to locate survivors from the sinking vessel.[140] Two other aircraft were tasked to assist as well as the *BC Star,* an RCAF-operated converted fishing boat chartered to transport supplies. Unfortunately, after two days of searching, the search was called off, and all 15 crew were assumed lost at sea. Similar examples are available for civilian maritime rescues within EAC's area of operations, making it clear that domestic rescues for distressed mariners were quite common on both sides of the country.[141]

Six months after the *Northolm* sinking, the *BC Star* came to grief while transporting gravel to the southern tip of Haida Gwaii from Bella Bella,

---

[137] LAC, RG24-E-1-c, Vol. 17870, Orders, Instructions, Directives – SAR, Letter to CAS, attention DDFC, from AOC WAC, signed by F/L J. M. H. Langford, 3 May 1943, "WAC ASR Services."

[138] RCAF Operations Records Books, Reel ID C-12156 Eastern Air Command Headquarters 1 May 1940 to 30 September 1944, http://heritage.canadiana.ca/view/oocihm.lac_mikan_135766 (accessed 25 April 2018).

[139] DHH, 181.003 (D3569), RCAF File S-202-21-1, January 1943, "Report of RCAF Participation in Search for Survivors of *S.S. Northolm.*" All information for this paragraph is taken from this source.

[140] Details of the air search were not available.

[141] DHH, 181.002 AFHQ file 9325-11 Vol. 2 Operations – RCAF, Cover for Convoys, ASR File folder four, 17 June 1942, "Sea Rescue Operations in EAC." The *Empire Seal* rescue of 17 June 1942 is an example.

both locations in British Columbia. On 23 July 1943, she failed to arrive but was not reported missing until 3 August, due to notification problems between the RCAF and the charter organization.[142] It was subsequently determined that all ten crew had perished at sea without an air search ever having been conducted. The *BC Star* sinking is important for two reasons. First, the Air Officer Commanding (AOC) WAC ordered an inquiry into the sinking to identify lessons that could be learned, accepting a rescue responsibility for even civilian charter vessels. Apparent RCAF ownership of fault in this case blurred the line between military- and civilian-rescue efforts and highlighted Canada's lack of any other domestic-rescue system. Second, this incident was of enough political importance that it was included in the briefing package for the Minister of National Defence and raised awareness at the highest levels in Canada that the RCAF was involved in maritime-rescue situations, as there was no other organization that could effectively respond to emergencies close to shore. Expectations of RCAF assistance in domestic rescue were rising.

The two incidents identified above took place within 200 miles of shore, which had become the RCAF operating area for marine-rescue vessels. The Air Council was still trying to coordinate a marine-rescue capability with the RCN that was effective farther out to sea than 200 miles. One possibility that was explored was the purchase of a few specific vessels by the RCAF for the RCN to man and operate. Arrangements had been made with the US for the RCAF to purchase American 104-foot vessels that were suitable for long-range rescue work, but the deal was subject to RCN agreement.[143] As the talks progressed, however, there was less need for larger rescue vessels because the U-boats had changed their operational areas to mid-Atlantic in July 1942, due to the increased effectiveness of RCAF antisubmarine operations.[144] The aircraft had the range to patrol far

---

[142] DHH, 181.003 (D3543) RCAF Binder – *Minister's Information Book: Regulations and Policies Relating to RCAF, January to March 1944*. All information for this paragraph is taken from this source.

[143] LAC, RG24-D-1-b, Vol. 3896, 1034-3-20, RCAF – Air/Sea Rescue, File C.1034-3-20, Minutes produced by AMAS (DOR) G/C W. I. Clements, 22 June 1943, "Minutes of Meeting Held 22nd June at AFHQ on ASR Organization."

[144] Douglas, *Official History of the Royal Canadian Air Force*, 519.

out to sea and hunt German U-boats, which put RCAF operations firmly outside a reasonable range for one or two rescue vessels operating far out to sea. Vessels operating in rapidly changing mission areas would be too far apart from each other to make effective use of limited large rescue vessels to support flight operations. On 28 June 1943, the RCN announced that the American rescue vessels were not suitable for the proposed tasks, and this decision scuttled Air Council efforts to purchase a better maritime vessel for rescue work as the need was less and the combat activity kept moving farther offshore.[145]

The Air Council concluded that there would be no advantage to handing over the control of the existing rescue boats to the RCN, as had been discussed at length in 1942.[146] EAC and WAC would have to make do with the maritime resources already in their possession and that another meeting would be called to discuss rescue vessels only if the "Commands indicated that further action was required to improve the ASR service."[147] Unlike the British ASR example from 1941, the RCAF and RCN did not pool resources together for ASR within 200 nautical miles, largely due to the lack of enough resources for the large area that had to be covered. One implication of the Air Council decision was that the number of rescue vessels in Canada remained very limited.

Due to the failure to purchase more vessels for rescue, the Air Council made the best of existing resources. Maximization of resources was partly accomplished by grouping all the marine resources on each coast into a squadron in June 1943, to provide higher-level oversight into vessel assignments, and assigning full authority for vessel missions to the group responsible for that area.[148] The amalgamation took away station-commander involvement in high-speed rescue mission authority so that the group

[145] LAC, RG24-D-1-b, Vol. 3896, 1034-3-20, RCAF – Air/Sea Rescue File C.1034-3-20, Memorandum with enclosed minutes to the Naval Service from the Deputy Secretary (staff), Minutes signed by AMAS DOR G/C W. I. Clements, 28 June 1943, "Coordination of RCN-RCAF Facilities for Joint Air/Sea Rescue Service."
[146] Ibid.
[147] Ibid.
[148] DHH, 73/1177 Vol. 2, RCAF Organization and Establishments, 1942–1951, "A.M.O. Progress Report for Period June 12 to June 18, 1943."

could move rescue vessels within the area of responsibility as operational demands warranted. The change of authority saved time by eliminating discussions that needed to occur before the vessel departed the dock, thus improving the limited maritime-rescue capability provided by the RCAF.

In EAC, where there were two air groups needing access to these maritime resources, the new maritime squadron was renamed the EAC Marine Squadron and reported to No. 3 Group that was collocated with EAC HQ in Halifax, Nova Scotia.[149] The Marine Squadron established detachments of vessels to RCAF stations in Quebec and Newfoundland so that rescue resources were made available throughout EAC's area.[150] It is interesting, however, that despite all the effort to maximize the rescue potential of the Marine Squadrons, the marine vessels only conducted six aircrew rescues over the remaining two years of the war.[151] As combat operations largely occurred outside the vessel rescue range of 200 nautical miles, the RCAF's vessels were not used anywhere close to full capacity. Marine-rescue requirements were further deflated by the defeat of German wolf packs of submarines in late 1943, decreasing the number of RCAF combat sorties and, by extension, the usage of the RCAF's vessels.[152]

It did not go unnoticed that the Marine Squadron was not busy conducting rescues for RCAF aircrew. The DoT had not been able to offer sufficient assistance to civilian mariners on either coast with resources left over from the ongoing war effort, so it sent a letter to the Deputy Minister of National Defence for Air to request possible standing ASR assistance from the RCAF in the Bay of Fundy area and along the west coast of Vancouver Island.[153] The Department of National Defence (DND) Air responded that they would assist as much as possible.[154] Without a mandate for civilian res-

[149] Vernon, "RCAF Marine Craft," 106. EAC and No. 3 Group were collocated and used the same personnel.
[150] Vernon, "RCAF Marine Craft," 106.
[151] Pilborough, *Royal Canadian Air Force Marine Squadrons*, 33.
[152] Douglas, *Official History of the Royal Canadian Air Force*, 568.
[153] LAC, RG24-E-1-c, Vol. 18113, Search and Rescue – Policy, File 976-1, 10 November 1943, Letter without title from DM DoT to DMND (Air).
[154] LAC, RG24-E-1-c, Vol. 18113, Search and Rescue – Policy, File 976-1, Enclosure to Letter to AOC WAC from CAS, 26 December 1943, "Air Sea Rescue Services."

cue, but with compassion for those in distress, expectations of the RCAF in domestic maritime rescue were ever increasing. Interestingly, the increased numbers of civilian rescues also increased the operational experience of aircrews, so there was an upside to rescue requests from the public.

The aircraft and seaplanes used for rescue were still provided on an as-available basis when the May 1943 ASR regulations provided by AFHQ made commands responsible for the "provision of RCAF aircraft for air/ sea rescue searches when required, having regard to the operational commitments at the time."[155] AFHQ was well aware of the benefits provided by dedicated ASR aircraft in the UK, and in October 1943, staff sent a letter to the commands requesting their input on a plan to either form dedicated ASR squadrons in Canada or to allocate specific station aircraft or seaplanes solely for ASR purposes.

The WAC response to the concept of assigning specific standby aircraft was that "morale building benefits would be lost if the Air Sea Rescue was confined to a single squadron."[156] EAC agreed that an ASR squadron was not required, as they preferred to have each station identify "a standby aircraft at immediate readiness at all times, subject, of course, to operational commitments and serviceability."[157] With this input from both commands, AFHQ shelved the idea of dedicated ASR squadrons. However, the exchange of letters led to an agreement that any airframe identified as "on standby" had to be equipped with supplies specific to ASR. Airframes placed on standby were an important step forward from relying on empty seaplanes or armed aircraft and was considered an effective compromise to ensure that air-droppable survival equipment was

[155] DHH, 81/301, CAP 342, *Orders and Instructions for RCAF Flying Control and Air Sea Rescue Service*, 32.

[156] LAC, RG24-E-1-b, Vol. 3199, Equipment and Supplies – Aircraft – RCAF Requirements and Supply of Search and Rescue Aircraft, letter from AOC WAC to DDFC, 24 January 1944, "Air Sea Rescue Aircraft."

[157] DHH, 181.009 (D2283), RCAF File S-2164, No. 36 Operational Training Unit Greenwood, ASR Procedure and Policy, October 1943 to May 1945, a group of letters attached together, 1–22 October 1943, "Standby Aircraft for Air Sea Rescue."

available for stranded aircrew lost at sea.[158] Airframes and crews were still not specified for the ASR role, but the new standby requirement showed incremental progression.

At the end of 1943, the RCAF had an ASR system very comparable to the ad hoc arrangements the RAF had made in August 1940 during the Battle of Britain. There was a long way yet to go to match Allied rescue operations elsewhere in 1943, both in knowledge and ASR personnel. Only at the end of 1943 did the Flying Control Organization School in Patricia Bay, British Columbia, start to produce ASRO graduates with a comprehensive understanding of ASR operations to close the knowledge gap.[159] Again at the end of 1943, an ASRO-qualified position at the rank of F/L was created in both commands to take the pressure off the senior flying-control officer positions and to provide greater rescue expertise. The Flying Control Organization was further expanded to provide "a uniform system of control over the movements of aircraft" in Canada and Newfoundland.[160] To provide ASR direction from AFHQ to subordinate positions in the commands, the Sea Rescue Service staff position in AFHQ was upgraded in rank from F/L to S/L.[161] Although these personnel added significant value to the system, it was only two additional personnel and one promotion to improve ASR throughout the entire country.

In a clear sign that personnel with ASR expertise were few and far between, F/L R. J. Lehman was promoted to S/L in mid-1944 and remained in the same AFHQ ASRO position until the summer of 1946.[162] He had been working the same ASR issues in the Sea Rescue Service position as

---

[158] Ibid.

[159] DHH, 181.003 (D984), *Monthly Review of RCAF Ops in North America 43–44,* "November 1943 Edition," 3.

[160] LAC, RG24-E-1-b, Vol. 5421, 67-16-2, Sea Rescue Services – Liaison with RCN, Letter to the Department of National Defence for Air from AOC EAC, 24 September 1943, "Flying Control Establishment in EAC."

[161] LAC, RG24-E-1-b, Vol. 5421, 67-16-2, Sea Rescue Services – Liaison with RCN, Memo to distribution list from AMAS A/V/M N. R. Anderson, 14 October 1943, "Flying Control Establishments."

[162] This was determined by examining the signature blocks on the letters from AMAS DDFC.

part of the Directorate of Flying Control since its inception in 1942, but after the promotion, the Chief of the Air Staff (CAS) often authorized his work. The change in authorization was a subtle but important difference to the status of ASR in Canada in 1944. It was no longer just staff positions sending out ASR information and orders; these were now specific directives with the full authority of the CAS. AFHQ was leading change in the rapidly developing area of rescue operations.

Part of the reasoning behind further expansion in the ASR service was that "it had been apparent for some time that RCAF aircrew proceeding overseas [were] greatly handicapped through lack of sufficient knowledge of the RAF ditching procedures, emergency equipment, distress procedures, etc."[163] The RAF offered to send British ASRO experts to Canada and to train a Canadian ASRO in Britain to resolve this problem.[164] The offer was intended to help the RCAF develop a rescue system that met Canadian requirements but to also provide the ASR expertise expected for operations overseas where knowledge of ASR was critical to survival. The offer was declined, likely because the RCAF priority for ASR was not driven by military requirements.

Regardless of missed opportunities, the increase of ASR activity at higher headquarters reflected the greater importance that rescue was developing, right down to the marine-station level. In early 1943, two aircraft had to let down on ice flows in the Gulf of St. Lawrence to avoid crashing.[165] Rescuing the crews was very problematic, and it demonstrated that the RCAF had no ice rescue capability. A marine-rescue capability was desired that could withstand the pressures of ice flows in the winter months. EAC's marine section vowed to fix the problem for the following

[163] LAC, RG24-E-1-c, Vol. 18113, Search and Rescue – Policy, File 976-1, Memorandum to D/A.M.A.S./Ops from DDFC, signed by F/L R. J. Lehman, 27 December 1943, no title given.
[164] LAC, RG24-E-1-b, Vol. 3411, Letter to CAS A/M R. Leckie from RCAF Liaison with HQ No. 45 Group RAF, W/C L. de S. Duke, 30 May 1944, "Air/Sea Rescue."
[165] LAC, RG24-E-1-b, Vol. 5421, 67-16-2, Sea Rescue Services – Liaison with RCN, H.Q.S. 67-16-6, letter with enclosure to the Secretary Department of National Defence for Air from AOC EAC, signed by S/L C. F. W. Burns, 25 January 1944, "Amphibious Sea Rescue Equipment."

winter and created the Gulf Winter Rescue Flight. Men in small special dories trained in January 1944 to have a rescue capability in the event another aircraft had to land on an ice flow. This capability demonstrated a grassroots effort to resolve rescue deficiencies at all levels. RCAF personnel were not waiting for guidance or regulations to improve sea rescue; they were proactively solving problems to save lives.

RESCUE BY PARACHUTE-EQUIPPED SPECIALISTS

As important as sea rescues were to RCAF aircrew, the NWSR from Edmonton to Alaska and then Russia was a vast area where many aircraft crashed. Land-rescue parties simply took too long in this area because there were so few roads to use. Once search aircraft did find survivors from crashes along the NWSR, help would be sent, but there were many deaths during the long wait for rescue.[166] To better assist downed aircrew in Canada's Northwest, the civilian manager of 2 Air Observer School in Edmonton, "Wop" May, supplied aircrews from his school for searches from the air. He came to believe that parachute-equipped rescuers could jump out of aircraft at the crash site, stabilize crash survivors, and clear an area near the site of the crash from which the survivors could be safely extracted by aircraft.[167] This parachute-rescue capability was developed entirely for domestic rescues of military aircrew, and it proved to be an important area of ASR growth.

May came to the parachute-rescue idea during a search mounted from Edmonton in February 1943 for two missing transport aircraft. The search lasted 19 days, and although there had been survivors, the two pilots did not survive long enough after the crash to be rescued.[168] May was aware that smokejumpers in the US had started using parachutes in 1939 to deploy into an area to fight forest fires, and he knew this could be an answer for future crashes along the NWSR.[169] In June 1943, May wrote a proposal for an RCAF parachute-rescue team and sent it to the

---

[166] Denny May, "RCAF Rescue Service," *The Adventures of W. R. (Wop) May*, http://www.wopmay.com/current/adventures/rcafRescue.htm (accessed 25 April 2018).

[167] The Para Rescue Association, *That Others May Live*, 14.

[168] Ibid.

[169] May, "RCAF Rescue Service," *The Adventures of W. R. (Wop) May*.

Air Council in Ottawa, requesting RCAF permission to train a number of civilian personnel in parachute jumping "who could be dropped at the scene of aircraft crashed in isolated localities to give assistance."[170] Without any explanation, the Air Council rejected the proposal.[171] Apparently, AFHQ could not yet see beyond the limited view of sea rescue in 1943.

May remained undeterred. The Civilian Public Service Program in the US, which trained smokejumpers, offered a brand new parachute-training course in late 1943 to military personnel for the American ASR system that was in development.[172] May sent two volunteer civilian mechanics from his school, Owen Hargreaves and Scotty Thompson, to begin training in the fall of 1943, and they conducted regular training afterwards to maintain their readiness for future rescues.[173] They trained two additional mechanics, Larry Poulsom and Wilf Rivet, so there were four parachute-rescue specialists in Edmonton by the spring of 1944. These personnel were available for rescue work, as were aircraft for searches, through coordination with May. Even though the jumpers did not deploy from aircraft in any actual searches during the war, the Americans were very grateful for this standing rescue capability and the unfettered access to Canadian search aircraft for missing American aircrew. The Americans were so pleased by the Canadian service that, after the war, Brigadier General Dale Gaffney of the United States Army Air Corps presented Wilfrid May with the American Medal of

---

[170] DHH, 96/24 Air Force Headquarters fonds, Box 7, File 2, "Air Council Minutes from 7 June 1943."

[171] Ibid.

[172] Forest History Society, *History of Smokejumping*, updated 12 September 2011. However, the website was changed circa 2017 to a pay-for-use model and the article is no longer available for free.

[173] Forest History Society, *History of Smokejumping*. This source states that the courses for rescue personnel started after the fire season ended in September 1943 due to the high demand for firefighting training that summer. There is a discrepancy between The Para Rescue Association, *That Others May Live* and other available sources on the timing of the course these mechanics took in Missoula. They started the course either May or October, and this author has assumed October is the correct date because W. R. May is assumed to have waited for a response from AFHQ, after his request for authorization in June, before obtaining company permission and making course arrangements for the mechanics after the summer firefighting season.

Freedom for providing "a rescue service indiscriminately to Americans and Canadians thus saving many of our fliers."[174] It is notable that the praise May received was for a purely domestic-rescue service that operated under no enemy threat. The US appreciated not having to provide this service itself, and this praise almost certainly encouraged RCAF improvements to ASR late in the war.

In March 1944, the highly experienced Group Captain (G/C) Z. L. Leigh of AFHQ, previously discussed as a commercial aviator in the 1930s, conducted a routine inspection of facilities in Western Canada as part of his duties. Hargreaves and Thompson provided him with a demonstration of May's parachute-rescue capability.[175] Leigh had left TCA and joined the RCAF shortly after the onset of war, and he had risen through the ranks very quickly. Leigh was very impressed by parachute rescue, possibly assisted by the fact that May was an old friend, and Leigh recommended that the RCAF absorb this capability.[176] His recommendation was immediately acted upon, and it turned out that including parachute rescue into the RCAF marked a significant turning point in Canadian rescue, as the parachute-rescue capability was a highly capable addition to the otherwise lackluster ASR service.[177] The transfer of the capability was partly initiated by the fact that May's school was about to close, and if arrangements were not made, the RCAF would lose access to the four trained parachute-rescue mechanics and that would decrease the deeply appreciated rescue services available to American aircraft transiting through the area.[178] From an RCAF perspective, the parachute-rescue capability was a cost-effective method of increasing a capability highly valued by the Americans.

Prioritizing a parachute-rescue capability that asserted Canadian

---

[174] May, "RCAF Rescue Service," *The Adventures of W.R. (Wop) May.* The award was presented to May in 1947.

[175] LAC, RG24-E-1-c, Vol. 18113, Search and Rescue – Policy, File 976-1, Letter to DDFC from AMAS/D of ATC, G/C Leigh, 4 April 1944, "Air Rescue Development."

[176] Leigh, *And I Shall Fly*, 179.

[177] LAC, RG24-E-1-b, Vol. 3411, File Part 1-3, 466-1-5, Air/Sea Rescue Services – Parachute Rescue Personnel and Equipment Policy, Vol. 1, 20 July 1944, Letter to AOC EAC from CAS, "Parachute Rescue Personnel."

[178] LAC, RG24-E-1-c, Vol. 18113, 4 April 1944, "Air Rescue Development."

authority over Canadian territory for rescue purposes meant that Canada was meeting basic needs that the Americans did not have to provide. The parachute-rescue service helped limit the American presence on Canadian soil and later affected Canada's decision making in the post-war environment.[179] A clear example of American involvement in Canadian sovereign issues was when the US Army authorized a pipeline with Imperial Oil from Norman Wells to Whitehorse, entirely within Canadian territory, "more than a fortnight before the Canadian government signified its approval!"[180] Undoubtedly, Canada needed to prioritize efforts such as parachute rescue in its northern terrain to protect its own aviators and to prevent the Americans from asserting itself on Canadian soil even further.

Parachute rescue became a very high-demand capability because the RCAF acquired a new responsibility in the north part of Canada. Due to RCAF concern at American dominance of Canadian airfields from Edmonton to Whitehorse, the RCAF created the NWSR in October 1942, but DoT had retained communications and construction functions of NWSR airfields in Canada. Management of the NWSR ceased to be a DoT responsibility in March 1944 when the responsibility was assigned to WAC.[181] Owning up to this responsibility, the CAS, Air Marshal Robert Leckie, fully supported integrating May's civilian parachute-rescue capability into the RCAF for the recovery of crashed military and civilian aircrew operating along the NWSR.[182] On 22 April 1944, he requested that staff investigate the feasibility of urgently enlisting the four civilian parachute-rescue mechanics into the RCAF.[183] As the NWSR was increasingly important, he also created the North West Air

179 Barry and Bratt, "Defence Against Help," 63.

180 Donald Creighton, *The Forked Road: Canada 1939–1957* (Toronto: McClelland and Stewart Limited, 1976), 73.

181 LAC, RG24-E-1-b, Vol. 5421, 67-16-2, Sea Rescue Services – Liaison with RCN, H.Q.S. 67-8-2, Vol. 1, letter to the Secretary DND for Air from AOC WAC, A/V/M L. F. Stevenson, 15 March 1944, "Establishment – WAC Headquarters, Flying Control Section."

182 LAC, RG24-E-1-c, Vol. 18113, Search and Rescue Policy, SAR – Organization and Administration, Letter to AMP from AMAS A/V/M W. A. Curtis, 22 April 1944, "Enlistment RCAF – Procedure re."

183 Ibid.

Command (NWAC) to relieve the NWSR commitment from WAC.[184] A great deal of effort was expended to ensure that a rescue effort could be made available for any Allied aircrew lost on that route, and it is clear that these rescue improvements were greatly appreciated by the Americans.[185]

The process to enlist the four mechanics happened very quickly, and by 1 June 1944, the four civilian parachute-rescue mechanics had become sergeants in the RCAF, specifically assigned to provide a rescue service on the NWSR.[186] Not only was the enlisting complete, but plans were in place by 1 June for the four new sergeants to begin a training syllabus to produce 20 more parachute specialists for NWAC, EAC, and WAC.[187] Part of the impetus to increase the parachute-rescue activity was that the Americans had made it known that they were interested in setting up rescue units along the northern staging routes, which included Canadian territory between Alaska and Edmonton.[188] The fact that they did not do so is testament to the seriousness with which the RCAF owned up to NWSR responsibilities and the rapid increase of rescue capability. It is no coincidence that the Americans showed decreased interest in setting up ASR units in Canada after parachute rescue was established.

The development of this land-based rescue service was logical based on the context of mid-1944. One can assume that RCAF personnel were readily available by this stage of the war, with 20,000 applicants for the 20 new parachute-rescue specialist positions, and the British Commonwealth Air Training Plan was producing enough pilots that the RAF was no longer accepting fighter pilots from Canada in August 1944.[189] By using some of

[184] Douglas, *Official History of the Royal Canadian Air Force*, 491.

[185] May, "RCAF Rescue Service," *The Adventures of W.R. (Wop) May.*

[186] LAC, RG24-E-1-b, Vol. 3411, File Part 1-3, 466-1-5, Air/Sea Rescue Services – Parachute Rescue Personnel and Equipment Policy, Vol. 1, Memo to AMAS from DAC W/C H. B. Norris, 1 June 1944, "Parachute Rescue Personnel and Equipment."

[187] Ibid.

[188] DHH, 181.009 (D6412), RCAF File 64-1-3, AFHQ General Air Research Oct 42 to Aug 44, Memorandum to CAS from and AMAS from DGR A/V/M E. W. Stedman, 14 Feb 1943, "Helicopters."

[189] The Para Rescue Association, *That Others May Live*, 18; and Douglas, *Official History of the Royal Canadian Air Force*, 291.

the personnel coming out of the training pipeline to provide greater rescue effectiveness in existing aircraft, the RCAF maximized the capabilities of the few aircraft assigned to ASR. This use of personnel was a cost-effective way to increase the rescue capacity without allocating greater numbers of expensive aircraft to commands in Canada. Additionally, the development of land- and sea-rescue roles increased the professionalization of the rescue service to military and civilians.

Further incremental advances were taking place to outfit aircraft with specialized gear to enable more effective rescues, such as complex air-droppable survival equipment, thus using easily available resources to improve rescue efforts.[190] Personnel and equipment improvements were not the only ones needed, as the search procedures for aircraft looking for survivors over land were nowhere near as well developed as search procedures over water. Search patterns for missing aircraft over oceanic areas were built upon procedures developed to hunt U-boats, and the searches were overseen by RCN experts collocated with RCAF search planners.[191] These patterns took into account wind, sea drift, tides, and all available radio-direction-finding data. Plus, the RCAF had developed effective procedures for communications between RCAF vessels and aircraft and had improved both coordination and request-for-assistance procedures with the RCN.[192] Rescue at sea was efficient, despite the lack of dedicated aircraft to the role.

By contrast, the search pattern for land-based searches was arbitrarily assigned as 50 nautical miles on either side of the aircraft's planned track for the initial search, followed by an expansion to 100 nautical miles on either side of track if the aircraft was not found in the initial search area.[193]

---

[190] DHH, 181.003 (D984), *Monthly Review of RCAF Ops in North America 43–44*, "April 1944 Edition," 24.

[191] DHH, 181.003 (D984), *Monthly Review of RCAF Ops in North America 43–44*, "March 1944 Edition," 35–37.

[192] DHH, 181.003 (3439), EAC – Searches for Missing Aircraft – 20 Dec 1943 to 10 May 1944. A review of operations reports show fewer coordination problems with the RCN than searches in 1942 and earlier.

[193] LAC, RG24-E-1-c, Vol. 18113, Search and Rescue Policy, SAR – Organization and Administration, 7 June 1944, "Suggested Search Procedure for the NWSR." A hand-written minute states this procedure was accepted.

Given that one assigned search area could encompass thousands of square nautical miles to search if the departure and arrival points of the missing aircraft were far apart, it could take a search aircraft over 100 hours to search that one area out of many that might be assigned. The search procedure is depicted in Figure 4, and it is worth noting that a search aircraft would take over two hours just to search from one side of the search area to the other, and the crew was only searching half a mile out on either side of the aircraft.[194] The massive search areas made it clear that the RCAF had the time and resources in 1944 to commit to long and costly searches in Canada. However, the RCAF did not research or think through the procedures that were used to identify search areas.

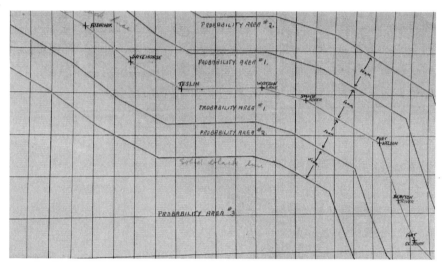

Figure 4. NWSR Search Procedure in June 1944[195]

By the end of 1944, 20 additional personnel were selected for parachute training in Edmonton for employment in EAC, WAC, and NWAC,

---

[194] LAC, RG24-E-1-c, Vol. 18113, Search and Rescue Policy, SAR – Organization and Administration, 976-1, Letter to Air Member CJS from CAS, signed by F/L R. J. Lehman, 24 April 1944, "ASR – Policy and Procedure in the RCAF."

[195] LAC, RG24-E-1-c, Vol. 18113, Search and Rescue – Policy, File 976-1, 7 June 1944, "NWAC Suggested Search Procedure for the NWSR."

and another 20 trainees were planned.[196] An interesting twist to this second parachute-rescue course was that it was offered to the Air Sea Rescue Agency of the United States Coast Guard, making the Americans well aware of rescue developments in Canada and establishing close relationships across the border.[197] During the development of the parachute-rescue capability, there was no discussion in any document of utilizing this capability in a combat environment. The additional parachute-rescue personnel allowed for rescues anywhere over Canadian territory and advanced the theme of the RCAF ASR system as a domestic capability. The lack of combat focus for this capability was perhaps not intentional, but ASR was clearly designed only for use in Canada.

THE PUSH AND PULL FOR A FULL ASR SYSTEM

The introduction of parachute-rescue specialists was but one development in a string of changes starting in 1944 that was rapidly enhancing ASR in the RCAF. These developments included the expansion of specially trained ASROs right down to the station level, standby crews for the ASR service, and an increasing interest in ASR operations by commands. The driving force was a mixture of pushing from Allied nations and pulling from operationally experienced personnel internal to the RCAF with a deep interest in saving lives. Despite some remaining rescue concerns in the Atlantic area, in 1944, Canada had a fully developed ASR system that proved effective for aviation and maritime rescue throughout the country.

The RCAF's increasing rescue effectiveness was perhaps surprising, as the demand for ASR services in Canada simply was not at the same level as that of operational theatres elsewhere. ASR in Canada responded to very few missions in comparison to many other operational areas, so one might

[196] LAC, RG24-E-1-c, Vol. 18113, Search and Rescue Policy, SAR – Organization and Administration, Letter from No. 3 Training Command to No. 10 AOS in Chatham, 2 November 1944, "Emergency Equipment Room."
[197] LAC, RG24-E-1-b, Vol. 3411, File Part 1-3, 466-1-5, Air/Sea Rescue Services – Parachute Rescue Personnel and Equipment Policy, Vol. 1, letter to the Secretary Department of National Defence for Air from Air Member, Canadian Joint Staff, signed by W/C E. E. Smith, 25 July 1945, "Detail Relative to RCAF Parachute Rescue Personnel."

have expected much reduced pressure to increase capabilities and services. As an example of the lower number of rescues, in September 1944, EAC reported no searches while WAC reported one search for an aircraft that crashed near Vancouver. Yet, in the UK, a typical month around the same time would have 360 aircrew rescued, let alone the number who perished in the sea.[198] Therefore, it is somewhat surprising that ASR in Canada received the level of interest that it did.

It is probable that part of the explanation for the RCAF drive for ASR was based on increased numbers of RCAF personnel returning from operational theatres where ASR was a critical component of operations. These personnel had come to expect a certain level of effort to rescue them if they crashed, and that expectation is likely the cause of the ever-increasing resources and expertise in the ASR service in Canada. Once the capability was grown and fostered, it would have been primed for rescues, military or civilian. One can reasonably surmise that the drive to increase the ASR capabilities without the combat requirement resulted in a natural domestication of the ASR service in Canada by aircrew looking for rescue work.

Despite the domestic nature of rescue activity in wartime Canada, those involved took their role very seriously. Just after midnight on 16 June 1944, Warrant Officer Simpson was flying an Anson aircraft in poor weather over Lake Manitoba, and he watched an aircraft in front of him ditch into the lake.[199] After communicating the distress to flying control so the appropriate station could arrange a vessel rescue, he flew to Portage La Prairie to get fuel and equipment to support the rescue and then flew back out. In the pitch dark and with clouds at 50 feet above the lake, Simpson flew multiple passes to allow his crew to drop emergency equipment to support the five people clinging to the wing of the downed aircraft. The Anson he was flying was 56 feet across, so turns over water and in the dark

---

[198] DHH, 181.009 (D95), Air Sea Rescue No. 423 Sqn, Dec 42 – May 45, Summer 1944, "Maps of RAF Rescues"; and DHH 181.003 (D5186), Summary of RCAF Activities, Progress Reports September 1944 to February 1945, "AMAS Division Report for September 1944."

[199] LAC, RG24-E-1-b, Vol. 5421, 67-16-2, Sea Rescue Services – Liaison with Royal Canadian Navy, letter to AOC No. 2 TC in Winnipeg from CO No. 1 CNS, G/C W. A. Murray, 20 October 1944, "Crash of Anson Aircraft #12395 in Lake Manitoba."

with such low ceilings were a very high-risk endeavour. As he needed to keep the aircraft over water and out of the clouds, his wingtips would have been barely 20 feet over the water during turns while maintaining speeds above 150 kilometres per hour, but Simpson ensured all crew members freezing in the lake were saved, despite the extreme danger to himself and his crew.[200]

At some point, the level of risk that was taken during flights like Simpson's would have to be managed by AFHQ to achieve some form of risk-versus-reward balance. During the war, casualties and crashes were routine due to the risk inherent in combat. However, after the war, the dynamics would have to change to preserve personnel and equipment in a restrained financial environment. The reason this point is made is because it is important to note that wartime experiences forced the RCAF and all other militaries to accept high risk, but then manage those risks during times when resources were scarce. High risk was certainly evident in Simpson's flight, but his clear skill saved lives and left an amazing story in its wake.

Equally important to daring flying was the work to provide the equipment and procedures that pilots like Simpson needed at the ready when the call for help was received. Improvements in ASR needed individuals within the RCAF to drive policy forward, and in all the documentation found, there were very few specific rescue personnel mentioned, as committees were a popular way to resolve ASR issues below the command level. In EAC, these committees were established at all stations in May 1944 as a way to increase the effectiveness of procedures.[201]

However, one individual who really stood out was the EAC ASRO in 1944, F/L Alguire, who wrote a detailed report in April 1944 that drove EAC ASR policy until the end of the war. This report recommended the addition of ASRO positions at each station and provided solid evidence

---

[200] Current SAR regulations require fixed-wing aircraft to maintain 500 feet above ground level during turns.

[201] DHH, 181.009 (D2283), RCAF File S-2164, No. 36 Operational Training Unit Greenwood, ASR Procedure and Policy October 1943 to May 1945, letter to CO of 36 Operational Training Unit from AOC EAC A/V/M G. O. Johnson, 16 May 1944, "Air-Sea Rescue Committee."

that the Flying Control Organization and the people within it were occasionally overwhelmed with ASR duties.[202] Subsequently, the AOC EAC started sending letters to AFHQ requesting the creation of an ASRO position for each of the 18 stations across the command. In December 1944, AFHQ agreed, but to only 16 ASRO positions due to lower flying levels at two stations.[203] The new positions were an effective compromise that not only acknowledged the effective argument made by Alguire and his chain of command but also positively affected the ASR service across the country.

All of the people needed to fill the new positions required a significant increase in training, but the system proved well prepared for the expansion. The Flying Control School in Patricia Bay, British Columbia, arranged for specialty courses to produce ASROs within a few months in the quantity required by both EAC and WAC.[204] AFHQ took matters even further and ordered all Air Force operational training units to create an Air Sea Rescue room to standardize specialist equipment for ASR across the RCAF and indoctrinate personnel to ASR early in their training.[205] F/L Alguire's persistence had paid off, and the additional ASRO positions created at the station level made the RCAF's ASR congruous with the RAF system, from a rescue-coordination personnel perspective. Interestingly, the RCAF was instituting a broad-based military-rescue culture long after combat operations ceased near Canada.

Unlike the satisfactory ASRO increases, assigning dedicated aircrew and aircraft to the ASR mission was still a hurdle. EAC continued to resist dedicating aircrew to ASR, although that resistance was challenged by a

---

[202] LAC, RG24-E-1-c, Vol. 18113, Search and Rescue Policy, SAR – Organization and Administration, Report by F/L Alguire, 24 April 1944, "Report on Air/Sea Rescue in EAC."

[203] LAC, RG24-E-1-b, Vol. 3210, Letter to AOC EAC from CAS, 9 November 1944, "Establishments Air/Sea Rescue Officers."

[204] LAC, RG24-E-1-b, Vol. 3210, 185-A-6, Requirements and Establishments, Letter to AMSO from AMAS A/V/M W. A. Curtis, 9 December 1944, "Requirements and Establishments Air/Sea Rescue Officers."

[205] DHH, 181.009 (D2283), RCAF File S-2164, No. 36 Operational Training Unit Greenwood, ASR procedure and Policy October 1943 to May 1945, letter to all Operational Training Unit COs from AOC 12 OTG, signed by W/C J. R. Davenport, 10 July 1944, "Training at OTUs – Air Sea Rescue."

new AFHQ requirement to have at least some aircrew trained in specialty rescue equipment, which eliminated the ad hoc nature of assigning aircrew to rescue missions.[206] Two differing approaches to producing the trained aircrew were considered: to train specific ASR aircrew dedicated to the rescue role and to train all aircrew on the new procedures. The first approach limited the usefulness of those crews when not employed on ASR duties, while the second approach was very expensive.[207] The compromise solution employed was to limit the types of aircraft and seaplanes that could hold ASR duties and to train three crews per airframe type at select stations on how to use the specialty equipment.[208] The idea was that the trained aircrew would be used for other types of flying duties when not holding ASR standby, but not all aircrew received the specialty rescue training.

The driving factor for increased training was the introduction of airborne lifeboats as necessary equipment for rescue aircraft. The airborne lifeboats were major additions to the equipment that was to be carried by aircraft identified for rescue work, as the lifeboats could be dropped to aircrew or mariners stranded at sea.[209] The boats had emergency equipment, food, and water to allow the occupants to survive for days while a rescue was conducted, if the ditching had happened far out to sea. If the ditching had occurred close to shore, the occupants could use the outboard motor included in the lifeboat to reach the safety of the nearest shore. Dropping equipment like this, close to people in the water who could be injured or killed if struck by the falling items, was the driving factor for specialist training. Improvements such as airborne lifeboats were a direct result from close attention to reports such as one from September 1943 that described

---

[206] LAC, RG24-E-1-b, Vol. 3210, 185-A-6, Requirements and Establishments, Letter to AMSO from AMAS A/V/M W. A. Curtis, 16 November 1944, "Establishments Air/Sea Rescue Officers."

[207] LAC, RG24-E-1-b, Vol. 3199, Equipment and Supplies – Aircraft – RCAF Requirements and Supply of Search and Rescue Aircraft, Letter to DND for Air from AOC WAC, signed by W/C E. W. Beardmore, 16 September 1944, "Airborne Lifeboats – Operating Crews."

[208] Ibid.

[209] DHH, 181.003 (D984), *Monthly Review of RCAF Ops in North America 43–44*, "March 1944 Edition."

treatment of 150 survivors from the Atlantic theatre who spent between 30 hours and 22 days adrift on the high seas.[210] The RCAF learned from the September 1943 report, and others, about how to treat aircrew after rescue in order to return them to the cockpit as soon as possible. The lessons resulted in new and specialized equipment.

EAC's approach to training for the special equipment was to train more crews than needed just for the ASR role, but the aircrew flew multiple mission types, unlike RAF and American aircrew who were assigned only to the ASR mission.[211] At roughly the same time, this multipurpose aircrew approach was extended to WAC, keeping the system similar across the country.[212] The squadrons where these multirole-qualified personnel were stationed were renamed "composite" squadrons, and this multipurpose approach to holding rescue duties, and yet flying other mission types, is still in use today.[213] Multirole qualifications were, and still are, a cost-effective approach to rescue standby in Canada. The main benefit was to maximize the operational use of all trained aircrew on a limited number of available airframes.

A potentially unintended consequence of the increasing number of resources available for rescue was that sufficient numbers of aircrew were trained that could respond to large rescue missions, making the RCAF an obvious choice for conducting large searches for missing civilians. It is clear from documentation that the RCAF actively assisted in any distress case brought to its attention, and the likely reason for this was to practise their specific rescue skills in any rescue mission available. Those who were

---

[210] Milberry, *Canada's Air Force*, 149.

[211] Galdorisi and Phillips, *Leave No Man Behind*, 39–47.

[212] LAC, RG24-E-1-b, Vol. 3199, Equipment and Supplies – Aircraft – RCAF Requirements and Supply of Search and Rescue Aircraft, Letter to Dept of National Defence for Air from AOC WAC L. F. Stevenson, 21 April 1944, "Air/Sea Rescue Aircraft."

[213] LAC, RG24-E-1-b, Vol. 3199, Equipment and Supplies – Aircraft – RCAF Requirements and Supply of Search and Rescue Aircraft, letter to DDFC from AOC WAC, 24 January 1944, "Air Sea Rescue Aircraft." This author was posted to a SAR squadron until September 2014, and transport missions were still conducted by SAR squadrons. However, very recent decreases in funding mean that, at present, SAR squadrons are largely limited to SAR only.

provided the specialty training developed standards over time that had to be maintained to remain proficient at the specific operational skills needed to conduct rescues. One interpretation of the dynamic achieved was that the military needed the civilian-rescue missions nearly as much as the public needed these brave aviators.

Late in the war, AFHQ planned to establish one ASR flight in each command as the primary unit responsible for rescue. Moreover, the flight would coordinate the training of other units in the vicinity that were also providing rescue assistance. The Army and the Navy were involved in these discussions, as available resources were identified to assist with various components of rescue.[214] For the RCN, involvement meant more integration of the procedures to ensure that rescues conducted with the RCAF would benefit from shared communications procedures. For the Canadian Army, this meant assistance with ground searches for aircraft crashed on land. ASR had become a concern for all the services even though it mostly benefited the Air Force. The RCAF's leadership of the rescue role had become well established.

One of the major changes initiated by AFHQ in 1944 was the requirement for stations to have pre-identified ground search teams, which often incorporated Army personnel in the vicinity. However, the station could not just send out Army personnel and expect them to know where to search; the RCAF required expertise in aviation search procedures.[215] Trained aviators from the station provided this expertise, as they could lead the teams of volunteers and Army personnel into the most likely search areas based on the last information received from the missing aircraft. Late in the war, parachute-rescue personnel often provided this leadership due to their specific training experiences.

All of the changes initiated by AFHQ appeared to be driven by ASR experiences of RCAF personnel in combat missions overseas and were

---

[214] LAC, RG24-E-1-c, Vol. 18113, Search and Rescue Policy, SAR – Organization and Administration, 976-1, Minutes prepared by W/C H. S. Gawler of RAF TC, "Minutes of Air/Sea Rescue Conference 7th September 1944, Dorval."

[215] LAC, RG24-E-1-c, Vol. 18113, Search and Rescue Policy, SAR – Organization and Administration, 976-1, Letter to AOC RCAF Overseas, from CAS, signed by F/L R. J. Lehman, 21 March 1944, "Mountains, Jungle, and Desert Rescue Service."

to ensure that RCAF operations in Canada were kept similar to RAF operations. Apart from the standby crews, the rest of the ASR system had been ordered integrated from the station level all the way to AFHQ.[216] The composite squadrons became the central point of trained personnel for all rescue activity, and it was believed that training and identifying some aircrew as experts for search flying would increase the safety margins of searches and solve the identified problems.[217] Despite the fact that dedicated ASR squadrons were not formed, that single difference from the RAF example was not enough to devalue the rescue organizations that had formed on both coasts.

Within WAC, a single-rescue-flight concept introduced in September 1944 integrated the existing land- and sea-rescue organizations that had been developed in 1942, as per AFHQ direction. The command viewed the new direction very favourably and stated, unequivocally, that the integration of the organizations and the addition of parachute-rescue specialists would greatly improve the rescue capabilities on the West Coast.[218] Some of the problems had been the difficulty in obtaining Canadian Army support for ground searches and the lack of personnel familiar with aircraft operations leading searches on the ground. The concept planned on trained individuals responsible for all rescue activity within the commands, and this was a major step forward from the communications challenges that had previously existed between the air and land organizations.

Despite all the advances in ASR for over-land areas and close to shore, the North Atlantic remained a troublesome sector for rescue until the end of the war, and not just for Canada. Flying over the Atlantic was largely coordinated by Ferry Command, an RAF organization whose function was to deliver aircraft built in North America to the RAF, and it operated out of Dorval, Quebec. Ferry Command was a very successful organization, but it still lost a great many personnel to transoceanic flying. The

---

[216] Ibid.

[217] LAC, RG24-E-1-c, Vol. 18113, untitled letter to DDFC from AOC WAC, 29 June 1944.

[218] LAC, RG24-E-1-c, Vol. 18113, Search and Rescue Policy, SAR – Organization and Administration, 976-1, untitled letter to DDFC from AOC WAC, signed by W/C D. Galloway, 29 June 1944.

command reported 560 personnel lost in 151 crashes over five years of operation.[219] Flying over the Atlantic was anything but routine, and the resulting loss of aircrew to bad weather and mechanical breakdowns was nearly double all the losses of EAC and WAC over the same time period.[220]

There were similar aircraft losses in the American ferry organization flying over the Atlantic. Surprisingly little was done about this problem, even though the Americans felt that the presence of just one surface ship might be enough to noticeably reduce loss of life.[221] A meeting was held in March 1944 with RCAF, RAF, and US Army Air Forces personnel to resolve some of the concerns, but the most they could agree to was to pool all rescue equipment of the three services at stations used by two or more of the air forces.[222] The meeting was not enough to convince their respective commanders to take action and reduce the loss of aircrew over the Atlantic. Transoceanic rescue was beyond the will and resources of all involved.

In all fairness, the large distances involved in Atlantic rescues could create unusual problems. Take the case of Warrant Officer R. Lenton.[223] He was an RCAF aircrew member flying a combat mission against the enemy in the mid-Atlantic on 16 October 1943. He had flown out of Ballykelly, Northern Island, and was shot down that day. A Canadian

---

[219] Carl Christie, *Ocean Bridge: The History of RAF Ferry Command* (Toronto: University of Toronto Press, 1995), 305.

[220] The numbers of lost and rescued aircraft are not all compiled in one, or even several, location. From 1 January 1944 to 1 June 1945, EAC reported 29 lost or crashed aircraft, and it is clear that the losses were significantly lower in WAC. Other evidence shows there were only 3 RCAF crashes in Canada in 1940 and 51 crew were saved from 18 crashes in the eighteen months prior to the EAC report. Therefore, a reasonable estimate over the five years of war is 60–80 crashed aircraft.

[221] LAC, RG24-E-1-b, Vol. 3410, 466-1-3, Air/Sea Rescue Services – Minutes of RAF Monthly Air/Sea Rescue Meeting – Policy, 7 April 1945, "Minutes of Monthly RAF ASR Meeting."

[222] LAC, RG24-E-1-c, Vol. 18115, Search and Rescue – Operations, Letter to AOC No. 3 TC from AOC EAC, signed by G/C W. A. Orr, 18 March 1944, "Search for Lost Aircraft."

[223] LAC, RG24, Vol. 20614, No. 1 Group, RCAF HQ file C.22-8 – Personnel – Survivors, letter to W/C Parkinson from Civil Officer (finance and accounts) F. J. Lowes, 12 May 1944, "1108755 W/O R. Lenton."

corvette of the convoy he had been protecting picked him up out of the water, badly injured, and cared for him during the convoy's transit to Canada. Lenton was hospitalized in Newfoundland on 23 October and, after several transfers, he was able to leave a hospital in Toronto to return to duty on 12 May 1944. However, he had no clothes and no identification, so no one knew what to do with him or where to send him. Finally, it was suggested that he be posted to Moncton, New Brunswick, to earn pay so the RCAF could recover the $120 given to him to obtain new clothes. The lack of administration coordination between agencies for the rescues that were successful over the North Atlantic was a pretty surprising state of affairs.

Later in 1944, an ASRO specialist from the RAF, Flying Officer (F/O) Alexander, toured Atlantic rescue stations to determine the effectiveness of rescue over the Atlantic. He concluded that procedures were faulty in all the services and that more should be done. Examples of his recommendations to improve the chances of rescue were to modify the routes for transiting aircraft to have more possible diversion airports, to place weather ships along known transatlantic routes, and to monitor emergency frequencies.[224] However, it appears the report was never acted upon by any of the services involved.[225] Alexander did not single out the RCAF in his report, so by and large, it appeared that the RCAF ASR service in 1945 was aligned with expectations and resource levels compared to other Allied nations operating in the same area, even if the RCAF was the only service without dedicated rescue squadrons.

The end of the war in Europe, May 1945, meant a realignment of resources for the continued war against Japan, and ASR was included as a required Canadian capability for the new force to be deployed to the Pacific theatre. In Canada, this meant bringing some squadrons home and disbanding many others, but it also meant sending some squadrons into the Pacific theatre.[226] As one of the eldest squadrons still in service, 404 Squadron was selected for conversion to Canada's first dedicated

[224] Christie, *Ocean Bridge*, 260–64.

[225] Ibid., 264.

[226] Brereton Greenhous et al., *The Official History of the Royal Canadian Air Force, Vol. 3, The Crucible of War, 1939–1945* (Toronto: University of Toronto Press, 1994), 117.

ASR squadron to support Allied forces in the Pacific.[227] However, Japan surrendered before the deployment happened, so the ASR squadron was never formed. Canada never did take that final step to a dedicated ASR squadron oriented to combat rescue, and it missed an opportunity to follow the established ASR footsteps of the UK and the US.

However, the overall capability that was created in Canada was surprisingly advanced. The final configuration of ASR was effective, especially for the limited amount of rescue activity experienced. There was only one squadron dedicated to ASR on each coast, 122 Squadron at Patricia Bay, British Columbia, and 167 Squadron in Dartmouth, Nova Scotia, but trained crews at various stations supplemented them with additional search-capable aircraft and crews.[228] The squadrons had parachute-rescue specialists that could be deployed to land crashes to save survivors, and there were ground search teams available at each station.

In addition, responses could take advantage of other Allied resources in the area. On 20 April 1945, a crashed Canso between Moncton, New Brunswick, and Goose Bay, Labrador, was in a really difficult spot to reach by ground.[229] EAC responded by borrowing a helicopter and pilot from the Americans to extract all survivors, as the area around the crash was unsuitable for any other aircraft to access. The helicopter was a new resource at the time, and only one or two survivors could be airlifted at a time. However, it demonstrated that for some missions helicopters were the only effective rescue resource.

As the war wound down, a rescue flight was added in Trenton, Ontario, to provide an additional rescue capability for RCAF activities over the

[227] Ibid.
[228] LAC, RG24-E-1-b, Vol. 3199, Equipment and Supplies – Aircraft – RCAF Requirements and Supply of Search and Rescue Aircraft, letter from AOC WAC to DDFC, 24 January 1944, "Air Sea Rescue Aircraft"; and letter from AOC EAC to DDFC, 16 September 1944, "Airborne Life Boats – Operating Crews."
[229] DHH, 181.009 (D4436), RCAF File 2-36-1, WAC ASR, Searches General September 1944 to October 1945, Report written by ORS/EAC/WHC, 24 July 1945, "A Review of Searches for Missing Aircraft, EAC, 1 January 1944 to 1 June 1945."

Great Lakes.[230] This new flight went a long way towards closing the gap in rescue that existed between the two coasts. Overall, RCAF resources for these missions were few, but as a system to save lives, it was quite effective for the limited scope of rescue at that time.

The coordination of all of these resources for missing aircraft was conducted by ASROs within the flying-control organization. The search centres were in Goose Bay, Halifax, St. John's, Edmonton, and Vancouver.[231] Reports of distressed civilians in aircraft crashes or vessels at sea would receive initial RCAF response from the flying-control personnel, and if searches were required, the full-time ASRO would report to duty and coordinate the station response. The ASRO was responsible for training and maintaining the equipment room at each station, so there was considerable efficiency achieved within the ASR coordination set-up.[232] Canada finally had a well-developed rescue organization, comparable with Allied capabilities.

The final statistics of the war would later indicate that ASR worldwide had saved 13,269 lives, of which 8,604 were British and Allied aircrew.[233] By contrast with the number of American and British lives saved through ASR, Canadian ASR was much less utilized. Two reports would provide limited clarity on ASR achievements in Canada during the war. One report from AFHQ covered the period of August 1942 to April 1944, the initial period of the ASR capability, and "18 successful rescues have

---

[230] DHH, 181.005 (D1761), RCAF File – RCAF Regular and Auxiliary (Interim Forces) – Preliminary Estimates 1946–47 – Report dated 18 December 1945, "Working Establishments 1946–1947."

[231] LAC, RG24-E-1-c, Vol. 17870, Orders, Instructions, Directives – SAR, Letter to AOC No. 9 Group in Rockcliffe, from CAS, signed by S/L R. J. Lehman, 20 August 1945, "ASR Instruction, etc."

[232] LAC, RG24-E-1-b, Vol. 3210, 185-A-6, Requirements and Establishments – Air Sea Rescue Officers, letter to AOC WAC from CAS, signed by A/C J. L. Plant, 30 May 1945, "Air Sea Rescue Officers."

[233] Peter Whittle and Michael Borissow, *Angels Without Wings: The Dramatic Inside Stories of the RAF's Search and Rescue Squadrons* (Great Britain: The Angley Book Company Ltd., 1966), 36.

been effected, involving some 55 persons."[234] The second report was from EAC and reviewed searches from 1 January 1944 to 1 June 1945, and it identified that 29 aircraft were lost in that period, with 25 of them located within five days.[235]

This data is hardly exhaustive because it is not known how many aircraft were lost in the first period or how many of these incidents were included in both reports. However, it does suggest that a reasonable estimate of overall rescue activity, extrapolated to cover the entire duration of the war, was fewer than three military aircraft crashes per month in Canada during the war. That was miniscule loss of aircrew in comparison to the hundreds downed at sea off the UK each month as well as the substantial losses in other operational theatres. With such little rescue work required for military operations, it is easy to see how the system would have embraced domestic-rescue missions as a way to gain rescue experience for ASR aircrews in the limited combat environment that was wartime Canada.

By the end of the war, the ASR service in Canada included ASROs at all the busy stations. There was command and staff involvement, a reasonable policy framework, and specialty aircrew flying aircraft with dedicated equipment for civilian and military rescues. All of this was overseen by AFHQ for national ASR standards. Allied interoperability had been a factor in developing Canadian ASR, as was the need to provide a rescue service to prevent the Americans from providing ASR on Canadian soil. The transition to an effective system took far longer than it took the UK or US, but at the end of the war, RCAF ASR was a very effective system used for military and domestic rescues.[236]

---

[234] LAC, RG24-E-1-c, Vol. 18113, 24 April 1944, "ASR – Policy and Procedure in the RCAF."

[235] DHH, 181.009 (D4436), RCAF File 2-36-1, WAC ASR, Searches General September 1944 to October 1945, Report written by ORS/EAC/WHC, 24 July 1945, "A Review of Searches for Missing Aircraft, EAC, 1 January 1944 to 1 June 1945."

[236] LAC, RG24-E-1-c, Vol. 18113, Search and Rescue Policy, SAR – Organization and Administration, 976-1, Letter to Air Member CJS from CAS, signed by F/L R. J. Lehman, 24 April 1944, "ASR – Policy and Procedure in the RCAF."

Summary of Canadian ASR

The RCAF had initiated an ASR service in August of 1942, but the limited size and sophistication of both the Flying Control Organization and the ASR organizations had been based on the unfettered use of personnel already busy with other duties. Changes were made in 1943, and shortly afterwards, it was evident by the number and type of changes that ASR had become a high priority service for the RCAF to provide due to the bolstered national sovereignty that a rescue system provided. The RCAF ASR organization was further developed after 1943, despite a reduced enemy threat to Canadian shores, and it became remarkably useful for domestic rescue. The threat of combat along Canadian shores had been key to the RCAF decision to follow RAF ASR development, but when that threat moved offshore, the Canadian system continued its progression to protect Canada's sovereignty from American expansion in Canada.

By mid-1944, the increases had produced a system comparable to that of the RAF in organization, if not in size. Allied pressure and internal willingness to expand ASR meant that the capability became comparable to other Allied services by the end of the war; although, the RCAF had created a system far more suited to domestic rescue than the combat rescue for which it was originally intended. The domestication of ASR, and the experience the Air Force obtained in rescue organization, would provide obstacles to the RCAF to potentially handoff rescue services to another organization after the war.

International pressures were important to the growth and development of the RCAF's ASR system. The RAF applied pressure on the RCAF to produce trained aircrew who had a solid understanding of ASR procedures, which Canadian-produced aircrew did not have in 1943. The RCAF needed to reduce the operational training requirements in the UK so the aircrew could join the fight more quickly. An increase in ASRO personnel and dual-qualified aircrew within Canada resolved the majority of these concerns. Additionally, the US was expanding its ASR requirements over the globe, and if Canada wished to avoid an American ASR presence on its territory, it had to provide a rescue capability along the NWSR. The RCAF development of Wilfrid May's fledgling parachute-rescue capability resolved this concern in 1944, but the parachute-rescue capability furthered the domestication of the RCAF rescue system. One can reasonably conclude that international pressure furthered ASR improvements in Canada, but the lack of operational rescue missions meant that the system developed became far more domestic than combat capable.

Cost was always a factor in the allocation of squadrons and capabilities. Cost may have prevented the RCAF from purchasing large American rescue vessels that would have been operated by the RCN, and it was certainly a factor that limited the number of airframes in Canada. Because airframes for EAC and WAC were limited, the commands resisted using aircraft solely for the ASR role. Maritime vessels were amalgamated into one squadron on each coast to maximize efficiency, and multirole-qualified aircrew manned aircraft or seaplanes that did not have to remain completely dedicated to ASR. Compared to airframes, personnel were not expensive. Personnel increases in the Flying Control Organization and ASR were viable solutions to the rescue-system problems and increased the overall rescue capability while minimizing equipment requirements. Aircraft were desperately needed overseas, which was a constant limitation to the growth of ASR. Overall, cost can be considered an important factor that limited the growth of ASR to just the Canadian area of operations, thus limiting the RCAF from providing a combat-rescue squadron in operations overseas.

All of the rescue developments that occurred in Canada over the course of the war led to one clear conclusion: ASR was deemed to be an essential requirement for the military mission in a large-scale conflict. Whether one considers the British and American developments, the Canadian developments, or even just the attitude of returning aviators in expanding the rescue capability despite the lack of a military-rescue requirement domestically, an ASR system was developed from scratch in five years while the nation waged a war. Those facts speak volumes about the requirement of a military to have a rescue system in place when combat operations may take place, even at home in Canada.

From today's perspective, some rescue progress was made between 1943 and 1945. A national rescue system was available for military-aviation rescue, as depicted in Table 4, and the system was incidentally used to support civilian aircraft crashes as well as mariners in distress. Aircraft and seaplanes, increasingly specialized for rescue throughout the war, were added as rescue resources. The system was developed for military needs, but it had proved capable for civilian rescue. This chapter has shown the evolution of combat rescue in Canada and how civilian-rescue requirements became integrated within the rescue efforts provided by the Air Force. The following interlude will describe the international civilian-aviation planning for post-war rescue that was discussed near the end of the Second World War.

Characteristic	Aviation	Maritime
National Standards	**Aviation rescues.** The RCAF had a rescue policy, but it had inadequate plans for land rescues	**Maritime rescues.** None
Available Resources	**Aircraft.** RCAF aircrew had training and procedures, but there were no ASR aircraft for Prairies rescues	**Vessels.** Six RCAF vessels and assistance available from the RCN provided coastal coverage only
Formalized Policy	**Military rescues.** AFHQ had well-developed policy and trained personnel to handle investigation and coordination	**Civilian rescues.** The RCAF still responded to civilian rescues, but there was no requirement to do so

Table 4. Canadian ASR in August 1945

Chapter 4: An Interlude for Planning

As time would very soon show, the increasing weakness of the Commonwealth in world politics made its revival forever impossible. The return which Canada was most likely to experience was a return to an older and more primitive status—colonialism, with a new imperial suzerainty, the United States.[237]

Donald Creighton

In the waning days of the Second World War, the question within the Air Force was no longer whether an ASR system in Canada was needed, but who would take the lead role in domestic-rescue operations after the war. The RCAF's views on peacetime ASR as a military role will become quite clear, and this short chapter describes the efforts that the Air Force took to prepare the rescue service for a transfer to any other organization after the war. The changing international climate for rescue is also described here, as the international community, and the US in particular, played a critical role in post-war rescue developments worldwide.

In Canada, the RCAF took the lead on initiating post-war rescue discussion and called a meeting in November 1944 to discuss the "amalgamation of the marine services of the various departments into one government

---

[237] Creighton, *Forked Road*, 14.

marine service."[238] The Departments of Transport, Mines and Resources, and Fisheries, as well as the RCAF, RCN, and RCMP attended the meeting. The Minister of National Defence for Air had approved in principle an amalgamated rescue service that "could look after marine-rescue work and provide patrol and preventative services."[239] The RCAF had suggested that maritime-rescue resources from all departments with a sea-going role could be placed within the authority of one organization that would retain the responsibility for aviation and maritime rescue.[240] The proposed service was a coast guard, so that experts in coastal-water responsibilities would take over the rescue role from the military. A Canadian coast guard was the desired end result for the RCAF and, ideally, would have provided aviation- and maritime-rescue services.

The DoT challenged the need for a new organization, as it "doubted if air-sea rescue work could be classed as a national responsibility."[241] The RCMP, RCAF, and RCN disagreed and were convinced that one amalgamated rescue organization was necessary. If support for a new organization was not possible from all organizations involved, then the military and police organizations agreed that the RCMP "would take over air-sea rescue if necessary."[242] In the aftermath of the meeting, the Canadian Cabinet did consider a coast-guard service, as recommended by the military and the RCMP, but concluded "the establishment of a Coast Guard to provide new services offers no apparent advantage."[243]

For reasons that are unclear but likely have a lot to do with money, there was little government interest in a post-war rescue organization, so interest in amalgamation or a coast guard was still a long way off. The

---

[238] LAC, RG24, Vol. 8164, File Part 1-2, 1700-27 SUB 1, Memorandum to D. of P. from A/Dir of Plans Commander F. A. Price, 23 November 1944, "2nd Meeting of the Inter-Departmental Committee on Water Services."

[239] Ibid.

[240] Ibid.

[241] Ibid.

[242] Ibid.

[243] LAC, RG-2, Vol. 124, Cabinet Documents, 9 February 1949, "Document No. 890." This document refers to, and details, a 17 July 1945 report on the suggested formation and subsequent rejection of a Canadian coast guard.

lack of government interest in rescue could have had a lot to do with the development of ASR during the war as a grassroots capability that was completely embedded within the RCAF. Because ASR was such a small organization and six vessels had seemed sufficient for maritime rescue during the war, it is quite possible that the true amount of rescue activity and the public's legitimate requirements for a coast guard were simply unknown to the Canadian Cabinet.

Rescue was largely associated with the sea at this time, where there appeared to be little public or community interest outside of those involved in ASR; however, there was considerable focus on aviation matters. In fact, interest in civil aviation was expected to reach new heights after the war, and that would affect Canadian developments in due course. It was widely anticipated that international aviation would become a massive area of growth, and most nations wanted to be in on that action.

Discussion among the Allies on post-war international civil aviation started as far back as October 1943, with the UK deeply concerned about potential post-war economic dominance by the Americans, specifically regarding international air travel.[244] Canada was deeply interested as well and remained close to all discussions on post-war aviation. Prime Minister Mackenzie King had made it very clear that aviation was critically important to Canada's post-war future when he stated in April 1943 that Canada was prepared to support "whatever international air-transport policy can be demonstrated as being best calculated to serve not only the immediate national interests of Canada but also our overriding interest in the establishment of an international order which will prevent the outbreak of another war."[245] The idea was that an interdependent and international aviation organization would integrate nations enough that it might limit future wars, or at least keep future wars regional. Combined with the economic expectations of Canada's position along major new international flight paths, the rescue and other regulatory expectations of a future international aviation organization had the highest support possible in Canada.[246]

---

[244] David MacKenzie, *Canada and International Civil Aviation 1932–1948* (Toronto: University of Toronto Press, 1989), 142.

[245] Ibid., 125–26.

[246] Ibid., 124. However, support did not include funding.

Initial international post-war planning for civil aviation took place at the Chicago Convention in December 1944 and became "the single largest gathering of air-minded nations during the Second World War."[247] The development of international aviation was considered a critical component of any nation's post-war economic well-being, which is why so many nations attended the convention. This storied meeting created the Provisional ICAO, which laid the groundwork for the final organization, ICAO, which was to become very important to later Canadian rescue developments. The mindset of Canadian officials entering into these negotiations likely reflected that of Prime Minister King: a co-operative Commonwealth policy in foreign affairs, mostly in matters of defence but certainly contained within post-war air-transport arrangements, might involve Canada "in undesirable external communications which could prove fatal to Canadian unity."[248] Canada entered these discussions wary of British influence.

During the initial Provisional ICAO discussions, Canada found itself in the enviable position of mediator between the big powers of the US and the UK.[249] The role of mediator was initially considered a large success; however, it came at the cost of increased tension with the UK, as Canada was clearly favouring the US position.[250] At the heart of the talks were executive powers for ICAO, which would have wide-ranging authority over international aviation standards to interconnect air-minded nations. The UK, however, desired a less prescriptive approach to an aviation governing body to allow more freedom. Therefore, the British saw Canada's stance as a serious drift away from Commonwealth authority. These talks laid the foundation of a Canadian metaphorical transfer from a British orbit to an American one, and the British were unhappy with the change.[251]

Tension was most evident in the vote over the proposals for the location of ICAO HQ. Canada proposed Montreal as the permanent home of ICAO; the location was strongly supported by the Americans due to the close proximity and their influence over the Canadian government.

---

[247] Ibid., 172.

[248] Creighton, *Forked Road*, 3.

[249] MacKenzie, *Canada and International Civil Aviation*, 170 and 190.

[250] Ibid., 199.

[251] Ibid., 192.

The British voted against this proposal for precisely the same reasons and, instead, supported a bid for Paris to permanently host ICAO.[252] After considerable debate, the end result of the Provisional ICAO meetings was international agreement on an aviation organization with executive powers that was based in Montreal. Strong support of executive powers for ICAO and sponsoring the HQ meant that ICAO would have considerable influence over Canadian aviation policy but that was a worthy price for the influence Canada would maintain on the international stage.

The decision to place ICAO HQ in Montreal was a win for Canada, and the clear Canadian ties to the US publicly demonstrated a change in allegiance from the UK to the US. Even though Prime Minister King publicly stated that the war had made Canada a sovereign nation and that remaining emblems of colonialism must be removed, in private, he and others "suspected that Canada had simply exchanged the free and equal association of the Commonwealth for an increasing economic and military dependence on the United States."[253] Regardless of the political machinations behind the scenes, developing clear international aviation standards, in Montreal with Canadian influence, was of benefit to Canada.

It became obvious right after the Chicago convention that the ASR capability in Canada needed to be maintained because a rescue service was deemed essential to developing ICAO safety standards, and Canada was deeply invested in ICAO because there were massive post-war benefits expected from the growth of aviation.[254] The RCAF supported ICAO involvement because it believed that Canada could not obtain strategic security in isolation and that support for international organizations would assist in the RCAF's desired "distant defence" strategy, as a clear set of international regulations were thought to result in a regional approach of conflict resolution as opposed to another worldwide conflagration.[255] The

[252] Ibid., 193.
[253] Creighton, *Forked Road*, 127.
[254] MacKenzie, *Canada and International Civil Aviation*, 119.
[255] DHH, Raymont fonds, box 125C, letter with attached resport from the joint secretary of the Canadian Joint Staff Mission to Lieutenant General Montague, Chief of Staff of Canada House, London, 27 March 1945, "Military Aspects of Canadian Participation in Mutual Defence Organizations."

RCAF was amenable to support any tasks that the government requested of the Air Force in order to leverage ICAO's authority in the international arena because most ICAO developments had so far favoured Canada.

Included in the agreements from the convention were statements that rescue services were considered essential to the growth of international civil aviation, based on the wartime experiences. American and British forces had ASR squadrons all over the globe, and the addition of this type of service to post-war aviation was simply not questioned. When the Provisional ICAO delegates discussed the requirements of post-war aviation, even the first draft of the text contained the statement: "each contracting State undertakes to provide such measures of assistance to aircraft in distress in its territory as it may find practicable."[256] ICAO's insistence on a rescue service for civil aviation, at least a nominal one, was a direct result of the Allied ASR experiences around the world during the war.

Back in Canada, the post-war rescue discussions resumed in June 1945, after the RCMP had concluded a detailed study of the ASR system and the DoT finally conceded that a national rescue system for aircraft was indeed required. The RCMP's study noted in part that "the position of the RCAF is now such that they cannot support an air/sea rescue force on a scale adequate to meet service and commercial needs on their projected annual appropriations"; it also noted that the RCAF "proposed that the liability for the future provision of an air/sea rescue service should be assumed by the RCMP."[257] The RCN was in full agreement that the ASR functions should transfer to the RCMP and proposed to return resources back to the RCMP, as it had taken control of many RCMP vessels when war broke out.[258] Post-war rescue planning in Canada was well underway to meet the new ICAO requirements.

The RCAF supported the proposed transfer of rescue activities to the RCMP with its stated intent "to provide search and rescue assistance for both military and civil aircraft during the transition period with such

[256] ICAO, Convention on International Civil Aviation (Chicago: 7 December 1944), 11.
[257] LAC, RG24-D-1-c, Vol. 33825, File Part 7, 1700-27, Organization and Administration – ASR Services, Memorandum to the MND Naval Services from CNS, 19 June 1945, "Air/Sea Rescue."
[258] Ibid.

facilities as is practicable to retain."[259] It really was not clear what was practical to retain. After the transition, the rescue process for military aircrew was even further unclear, as post-war planning by the Air Force would eliminate the rescue component from all three of the post-war RCAF establishment and organization plans proposed to the government.[260]

Post-war planning proposed five composite flights located in Dartmouth, Trenton, Winnipeg, Edmonton, and Vancouver, but rescue was not included in the list of tasks. The five multirole units would conduct "communication flying, target towing for the Navy, Army and Air Force, practice flying for General List Officers not posted to flying units, and air salvage operations."[261] It can only be assumed that the RCAF expected the RCMP to conduct all domestic-rescue missions and to potentially provide support for military aircraft search missions. The RCAF appeared intent on providing only functions it considered military in nature, and ASR had not met that definition based on the RCAF wartime experience within Canadian territorial lands and waters. The hard-fought-for ASR capability embedded in the RCAF from stations to AFHQ would not survive the transition to peace.

The apparent ease with which the ASR service disappeared from the RCAF needs a little scrutiny. There was no evidence found to explain the decisions that were made to so rapidly reduce ASR, but some deductions can be made. First, the mindset that had developed around ASR was that any operational area needed an ASR capability to support combat flight operations. This had been true overseas, and it was true when the threat had developed in Canadian waters. Without a threat over Canadian waters, however, the RCAF apparently accepted that an ASR system was not required because Canada was no longer a theatre of combat operations. Second, ASR had been so integrated in the Flying Control Organization

[259] LAC, RG24, Vol. 8164, File Part 1-2, 1700-27 SUB 1, minutes by Chairman F/L G. L. Alguire, 3 December 1945, "EAC Post-war Rescue – RCAF – RCN Conference December 3rd."
[260] DHH, 96/24 Air Force HQ fonds, Box 9, File 4, 23 August to 2 May 1946, 29 January 1946, "Air Council Minutes" and RCAF Plan B in the same file.
[261] DHH, 96/24 Air Force Headquarters fonds, Box 9, File 4, "Report of the Post-war Planning Committee, 31st October, 1945." Air salvage operations were not defined.

that it might easily have been assumed that the processes for responding to rescues would still exist even if specifically trained aircrew and rescue-equipped aircraft were no longer maintained. Third, risk was viewed as simply inherent in flying operations for military crews, so a specific rescue capability could come from any organization and the RCAF could accept a little extra risk. Regardless of the accuracy of all or none of the reasons above, the RCAF demonstrated no desire to retain the ASR service it had laboured so hard to create.

When the war ended, there was still no agreement from the DoT on amalgamation of all rescue services, despite the Provisional ICAO developments. However, the RCN, RCMP, and RCAF were aligned in their understanding of a civil organization's role in peacetime domestic rescue; they had ministerial agreement that civilian rescue was required in the post-war world. Therefore, they planned to proceed with a limited amalgamation of rescue services under the lead of the RCMP.[262] Next up is a description of what happened in the post-war environment when the best-laid plans of the military and the police met the Canadian Cabinet. The Air Force could not escape its own creation.

[262] LAC, RG24-D-1-c, Vol. 33825, File Part 7, 1700-27, Organization and Administration – ASR Services, Letter from MND Air to MND Naval Services, 12 June 1945, untitled.

Chapter 5: Voluntold in 1947 and Beyond

The Canadian Cabinet formed an Interdepartmental Committee in mid-1945 to make recommendations for post-war ASR in Canada, and it would unanimously conclude that the RCAF's ASR organization would best be transitioned to the RCMP. Cabinet discussed methods to meet ICAO's requirement for a rescue organization, and all eyes were on the ASR organization that the RCAF had so successfully developed in the latter part of the war. ASR was viewed by the RCAF as a transferrable organization that could support the RCMP's proposal to lead Canada's rescue service as mandated by ICAO. The planned transfer of ASR to the RCMP would allow the RCAF to focus on what it felt was military matters, and as a bonus, the RCMP plan included a robust maritime-rescue component that would improve the overall service.

The requirement for a post-war rescue organization was a serious matter. The Second World War had proved that aviation was a critical component of international travel and transport, and if Canada wanted to be part of the massively expanding post-war international trade using aviation, it would have to be an integral partner in developing international aviation regulations and rescue services. Despite a clear interest in post-war civil aviation, the Canadian government had no appetite for expensive new organizations that aimed to provide capability outside the core ICAO demand of aviation rescue resources. Equally, the government wanted no part of an RCAF with interest in only roles the Air Force deemed to be military, which was one of several factors that led to Cabinet's decision making in 1946 and 1947. The decisions on SAR organization made in 1946 and 1947 formalized a civilian role for the RCAF that the Air Force would struggle to accept for a long time.

THE RCMP BID FOR SAR

The ASR organization developed by the RCAF during the war had become a source of pride in 1945, and the rescue missions had included searches for missing mariners and civilian aircrew.[263] In the last year of the war, the system had saved 52 RCAF personnel, and it had conducted 18 humanitarian flights.[264] Although ASR had been tied to defensive operations in Canada, with the end of the war, the RCAF no longer viewed the system as critical to ongoing operations. Despite the RCAF's lack of interest in its ASR, it was well aware that civilian rescue desperately required an ASR organization.

The ASR organization needed a lead agency, and quickly, as the RCAF was "rapidly curtailing its Air Sea Rescue facilities in line with the general policy of contraction of that service."[265] Because the DoT had refused to participate in an amalgamated marine-rescue service in 1944, the RCN, RCAF, and RCMP had worked together and concluded that the RCMP was the best organization to take on ASR in the post-war period. The transfer of ASR to the RCMP would relieve the RCAF "of an obligation which has developed since the outbreak of war and will continue to exist in the post-war period."[266]

The wartime RCAF's only dedicated ASR capability was 122 Composite Squadron in Patricia Bay, British Columbia, 121 Composite Squadron in Dartmouth, Nova Scotia, and the command composite flight in Trenton, Ontario. The RCAF committed to retaining these rescue facilities after the war "on a reduced basis" until a transfer to another agency could take

---

[263] LAC, RG24-E-1-c, Vol. 18113 Search and Rescue Policy, SAR – Organization and Administration, Letter to Dept of National Defence from AOC No. 2 AC, A/V/M K. M. Guthrie, 25 April 1946, "Air Land Sea Rescue Facilities for No. 2 Air Command."
[264] DHH 181.009 (D5200), Department of National Defence for Air 1945–1946, AMA Directorate, "Annual Report."
[265] LAC, RG24, Vol. 8164, File Part 1-2, 1700-27 SUB 1, Prepared by Chairman S/L R. J. Lehman, 30 November 1945, "Minutes of Meeting 4 of the Interdepartmental Committee on Post-war Air Sea Rescue."
[266] LAC, RG24-E-1-c, Vol. 18112 Search and Rescue – Organization and Administration 1945–1954, Letter to Hon. D. Abbott from Hon. C. Gibson, 8 June 1945, untitled.

place.[267] ICAO was the driving force for a continued rescue service, but "no explicit agreement was reached as to the minimum air search rescue facilities which would be supplied by the contracting countries within their territorial limits."[268] The lack of minimum limits was wise as the standards developed in war were strictly concerned with aircrew involved in combat operations, so there had not been enough information available with which to develop civil rescue standards. ICAO deliberately left it to each nation's discretion on how many resources would be required for the SAR service they felt was necessary; although, it was understood that standards would come later.[269] In 1945, a national rescue system could be as small as the existing RCAF version or as big as Canada could afford.

One of the changes that occurred during this time was the name of this type of service due to the inclusion of land-rescue capabilities for aviation. "Following the lead of [Provisional ICAO], it is proposed that hereafter the [air sea] rescue organization be referred to as the Search and Rescue Service."[270] The non-military nature of the proposed new service, captured in the duties and new name of the service, factored considerably into the interdepartmental recommendation to transfer the SAR service to the RCMP. Another factor was the domestication of the ASR service throughout the war, even though the service had been prepared to rescue aircrew from combat situations close to shore. However, AFHQ did not appear to value the service as an ongoing capability for military aircrew, so it felt no post-war attachment to the term "air sea rescue."

The RCAF was reducing rapidly in the post-war environment, and it was

---

[267] LAC, RG24-E-1-b, Vol. 3199, Equipment and Supplies – Aircraft – RCAF Requirements and Supply of Search and Rescue Aircraft, Letter to Air Member Canadian Joint Staff, Washington, from CAS, signed by S/L R. J. Lehman, circa July 1945, "Air Sea Rescue Aircraft."

[268] LAC, RG24, Vol. 8164, File Part 1-2, 1700-27 SUB 1, Minutes produced by W/C A. M. Cameron, Secretary of ICSAR, 25 January 1946, "First Meeting of the Revised ICSAR at 1000 hours on 24 January 1946."

[269] DHH, 112.3M2 (D340), May 1947, "Report of Interdepartmental Committee on Search/Rescue."

[270] LAC, RG24, Vol. 8164, File Part 1-2, 1700-27 SUB 1, circa January 1946, "Proposed Plan – National and International Commitments for Search and Rescue Throughout Canada."

trying to remain focused on the possibility of further war in an uncertain world. Air Force priorities were summed up as follows: "due to the radical change in warfare brought about by the introduction of the atomic bomb, and homing and guided missiles as offensive weapons of tremendous destructive power, it is not possible to state specifically the role of an Air Force of the future."[271] What was clear was that the RCAF had larger military concerns than domestic rescue immediately after the war ended, which is the most likely explanation for its willingness to abandon the rescue role it had created.

Between June and November of 1945, an Interdepartmental Committee on Post-war Rescue met four times to make detailed recommendations on SAR for Canada.[272] This committee was formed of RCMP, RCAF, RCN, and DoT personnel. The fourth meeting included a detailed proposal for the RCMP to assume responsibility for SAR, and this proposal was unanimously accepted by the agencies involved.[273] The agreement can be summarized as follows: a rescue service was needed to meet ICAO requirements, the RCAF had built a satisfactory ASR system that could form the basis of a post-war SAR system, and the RCMP was a civil organization with experienced aviation and marine organizations that could easily be expanded to lead the SAR function. The main recommendation of this committee was that the RCMP should become the lead agency for post-war SAR in Canada, and this recommendation went to Cabinet for consideration in December 1945. No other option had been documented as a possible alternative to the RCMP proposal.

The recommendation from the post-war rescue committee was a very robust proposal for post-war rescue. The plan included an increase of 1,066 personnel for the RCMP, of which 366 would have provided the air-rescue component and 700 personnel would have provided the marine-rescue

---

[271] DHH, 96/24 Air Force Headquarters fonds, Box 9, File 4, 23 August 1944 to 2 May 1946, "Report of the Post-war Planning Committee," 31 October 1945.

[272] LAC, RG2-B-2, Vol. 103, File T-30-1, Territorial Waters and Districts – Official – Air Search Rescue, Canadian Coast Guard, Prepared by Chairman S/L R. J. Lehman, 30 November 1945, "Meeting Four of the Interdepartmental Committee on Post-war Air Sea Rescue."

[273] Ibid.

component.[274] Of the marine component, approximately 420 of those personnel would have been dedicated mariners and the other 280 of those personnel would have been RCMP officers conducting duties in the protection of revenue service as well as providing oversight for the rescue service. The RCAF and RCN agreed to provide 38 aircraft and 44 vessels from left-over wartime resources to be based at police locations across the country in order to respond to aviation and maritime emergencies. The large number of vessels was surprising, as the RCAF had relied on only six high-speed launches for its coastal rescue service on both coasts that had been used for domestic rescues during the war, but this plan wisely expected that the maritime-rescue requirement would expand over time.[275] The RCMP proposal was based on the assumption that the RCMP and the military would achieve support from the Cabinet level that the marine portion of rescue was of enough importance, in addition to the ICAO requirements, to justify the $5,859,370 expense of the RCMP proposal for SAR.

One aspect of the proposal that was not addressed in the documentation of the SAR discussions was the potential inclusion of Newfoundland and Labrador into Canada as an additional province. The RCMP proposal did not include any resources or bases in Newfoundland or Labrador, and any resources added to these areas would have increased the cost of the proposal. This potential problem was magnified by the fact that the US had a SAR capability at Goose Bay and at Argentia, which was an ICAO-demanded capability that would eventually have to be replaced with Canadian resources.[276] Interestingly, the RCAF already had limited SAR resources established in Goose Bay, Labrador, for its own military requirements, which perhaps might have been expected to remain as an RCAF contribution to the overall plan.[277]

---

[274] LAC, RG2-B-2, Vol. 103, File T-30-1, 30 November 1945, "Meeting Four, Rescue." All of the information in this paragraph is obtained from this document.

[275] Halliday, "Role of the Boats."

[276] LAC, RG24-E-1-c, Vol. 18112, SAR – Organization and Administration 1945–1954, 976-0 Vol. 6, Letter to CAS from AOC TC, signed by A/C W. W. Brown, to CAS, 19 May 1949, "SAR – Commitments, Newfoundland."

[277] LAC, RG24-E-1-c, Vol. 17554, Co-operation and Liaison with ICAO – SAR, 1945–1953, File 004-4 SAR Vol. 1, Letter from Acting SSEA to High Commissioner for Canada in Newfoundland, 16 August 1946, untitled.

The RCMP bid for SAR was very generous. Figure 5 shows only the air bases, but the vessel locations were largely collocated with the air bases to ensure interoperability between the differing capabilities.[278] The relatively short distance between various rescue locations ensured that Canadians could have received assistance within a few hours. The inclusion of a marine-rescue component was one potential difficulty in obtaining Cabinet approval for this plan, as there was no international requirement yet for the maritime aspect of a SAR service.[279] As well, there were two other problem areas that would need to be resolved.

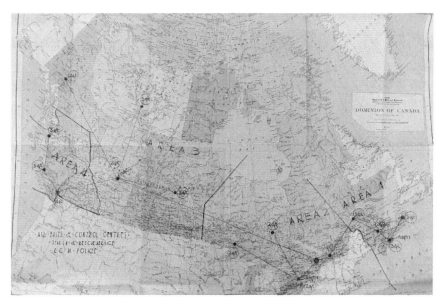

**Figure 5. Aviation Portion of Proposed
RCMP SAR Bid, November 1945**

The first problem was poor communications over the oceanic areas. The RCAF and RCN knew that any vessels and aircraft operating at

---

[278] LAC, RG24, Vol. 8164, File Part 1-2, 1700-27 SUB 1, Draft document to His Excellency the Governor General in Council, to be signed by Ministers of Justice, Naval Services, National Defence for Air, Transportation, and Reconstruction, 10 December 1945, "Recommendation for Search and Rescue."

[279] Ibid. The minutes clarify that the committee was fully expecting Cabinet support.

distances of several hundred miles out to sea at that time would not have communications with shore-based services.[280] A high frequency direction finding (HF/DF) system that covered all of the Canadian area would be required to provide basic communications with transoceanic flights and bearing information on aircraft declaring a distress situation. The HF/DF system that had been used in wartime had been specific to military needs and was insufficient for the large area of coverage needed for ICAO purposes due to the rapid expansion of transatlantic flight routes for civilian aircraft. The only organization with detailed expertise in this area was the RCN; therefore, the RCN would have to provide personnel and equipment for the new service to communicate over long distances.

The second potential problem was the integration of flying-control personnel from the RCAF into the RCMP. It may be recalled that the RCAF had developed the Flying Control Organization that was integrated with the civilian air-traffic-control system in Canada. The purpose of the integration was to ensure that all aircraft movements were communicated properly between the various agencies involved to prevent accidents and to respond quickly to changing weather situations. The proposed RCMP bid would add a layer of complexity to the air-traffic-control system by introducing a third organization into the system.[281] This complication was not discussed at all in the available documentation, but it should have been apparent to knowledgeable observers that the RCMP SAR plan would require additional personnel for coordination and control of aircraft in Canada, beyond what was already in place for civil- and military-aviation needs. It had been established in 1941 that any rescue service required complete integration into the air-traffic organization, and this would not

---

[280] LAC, RG24, Vol. 8164, File Part 1-2, 1700-27 SUB 1, Minutes Prepared by EAC ASRO F/L G. L. Alguire, 3 December 1945, "EAC Air Sea Rescue RCAF–RCN Conference." This source provides all the facts for this paragraph.

[281] LAC, RG24-E-1-c, Vol. 17870, Orders, Instructions, Directives – SAR, Letter to AOC No. 9 Group in Rockcliffe, from CAS, signed by S/L R. J. Lehman, 20 August 1945, "ASR Instruction, etc."

change in the post-war environment.[282] It is reasonable to assume that the RCMP proposal had duplication included.

Based on the two problems outlined above, one can conclude that any move out of ASR by the RCAF would result in duplication of functionality or some level of reliance on military organizations for specific rescue requirements. However, the RCMP proposal did have planned solutions to the problems. The solutions required personnel and equipment from the RCAF and RCN, but that was readily coordinated, and by the end of 1945, solutions were well underway.

The RCAF had identified key ASRO personnel, including the previously discussed persuasive EAC ASRO F/L Alguire, who were screened and kept in service beyond the end of 1945 specifically for a transfer to the RCMP as soon as approval was obtained for the new service.[283] It was important that these experts were retained in the SAR system because they understood the integration required into the Flying Control Organization and civilian air-traffic-control systems, they had operational rescue experience, and they had been involved in the ICAO SAR discussions.[284] The CAS demonstrated very high-level RCAF support for the RCMP proposal to lead the SAR organization by ordering the screening and retention of ASRO personnel specifically for transfer to the RCMP.[285]

What is not clear is how the RCAF planned to provide expertise for its own post-war rescue requirements or if it would maintain any expertise for military rescue. The approved plan for the RCAF did not contain an ASR capability in the fall of 1945, but it did in January 1946.[286] Obviously,

---

[282] DHH, AIR 20/4018, 31 October 1945, "RAF Costal Command Headquarters History of Flying Control."

[283] LAC, RG24-E-1-b, Vol. 3210, 185-A-6, Requirements and Establishments – Air Sea Rescue Officers, Memorandum to D/AMP from DPC G/C W. I. Clements, 19 December 1945, "Air Sea Rescue Officers."

[284] Ibid.

[285] LAC, RG24-E-1-b, Vol. 3210, 185-A-6, Requirements and Establishments – Air Sea Rescue Officers, by DPC G/C W. I. Clements, 17 December 1945, "Message from AFHQ to EAC."

[286] DHH, 96/24 Air Force Headquarters fonds, Box 9, File 4, 23 August 1944 to 2 May 1946, "Report of the Post-war Planning Committee," 31 October 1945; and "Air Council Minutes," 29 January 1946.

plans were very much in flux. The Air Force had to juggle massive downsizing all the while figuring out what roles it would need to perform and what aircraft it needed. Aircraft that were identified as surplus could then be handed over to other organizations.

No transfer of aircraft had been processed before Cabinet viewed the proposal for the SAR service, but the War Assets Corporation had already transferred over 25 marine craft to the RCMP from the RCAF and the RCN, primarily for the protection of revenue, but also in anticipation that the RCMP bid for SAR would be accepted.[287] In the rapidly changing post-war environment, it was assumed that the unanimously agreed-upon proposal from the SAR experts would be accepted. In order to minimize the disruption to SAR operations while decisions were formalized, personnel and equipment were pre-identified for transfer as concurrent activity.[288]

It can be summarized that the RCMP bid was a robust and well thought-out SAR proposal that envisaged rapid growth of SAR requirements in Canada. Multiple departments would be directly involved in providing capabilities for SAR because the proposal relied on assets and personnel from the RCN and RCAF, so the final proposal was not the amalgamation that had initially been anticipated. An underlying issue was that military organizations not only had created initial rescue systems in Canada but also had to expect that they would continue to be involved in rescue to some extent. This continued involvement could be viewed as inefficient if the RCMP was responsible for the SAR service, and that put the cost of the RCMP proposal in a critical light. The price tag associated with the RCMP bid was considered a necessary expense by the organizations directly involved in SAR, but this price had yet to be scrutinized by the Canadian Cabinet against other post-war requirements.

THE SAR MANDATE DECIDED

The Cabinet members directly involved with the RCMP proposal for SAR were the Ministers of National Defence for Air and Naval Services as well as the Minister of Justice, who was responsible for the RCMP. All

---

[287] LAC, RG2-B-2, Vol. 103, File T-30-1, 30 November 1945, "Meeting Four, Rescue."
[288] LAC, RG24, Vol. 8164, 3 December 1945, "EAC, RCAF–RCN Conference."

three ministers had supported the idea, but the planning had been conducted in isolation from the Cabinet. When the proposal went to Cabinet, the full scrutiny of ministers was brought to bear on the plan to analyse costs versus benefits. The war had been expensive, and new costs had to be weighed against all budgetary priorities.

Canada's finances were a mess after the war, like many other nations, and there were many new pressures on the government. Minister of Finance James Lorimer Ilsley was particularly concerned due to "defence expenditures several times larger than before the war; increases in the normal overhead costs of government; and 'vastly increased' expenditures on social security and social welfare activities."[289] These concerns made Cabinet look deeper into the RCMP's proposal for cost effectiveness.

The new Minister of National Defence in 1945, Douglas Abbott, gave several speeches after the decision on SAR was made that are useful to shed light onto the cost concerns that were considered by Cabinet during SAR decision making. Cabinet was deeply concerned about defence expenditures of the late 1940s, as they were significantly higher than the 1930s and other departments—such as External Affairs and the Department of Finance—required millions more than pre-war budgets due to the need for complex post-war international engagement and financial complications arising from the war.[290] In addition, costly DoT expenditures were a priority because infrastructure maintenance in Canada had been deferred during the war, and bridges and ferry replacements required millions more in new investment. All of these pressures were combined with annual interest costs of up to $200 million on $13 billion of debt, which was debt pressure nearly five times higher than 10 years earlier in the aftermath of the Great Depression.[291] Ministers were feeling pressure from constituents to decrease taxation and yet to provide new services that a war-weary nation believed it deserved.

---

[289] Colin Campbell, "J. L. Ilsley and the Transition to the Post-war Tax System: 1943–1946," *Canadian Tax Journal* (2015), 13.

[290] LAC, MG32 B6, Vol. 15 Speeches, 11 July 1946, "Memorandum to Mr. Abbott re: Government Expenditures."

[291] LAC, MG32 B6, Vol. 15 Speeches, 18 November 1946, "Speech to Eastern Townships Associated Board of Trade."

The financial pressures on the federal government were critically relevant when the $5.8 million RCMP proposal for a new SAR service in Canada came before Cabinet, and questions were asked. Although it is not clear how long the meeting lasted, the decision did not match the expectation of the ministers involved in the preceding discussion. Minister of Justice Louis St. Laurent, who had been an advocate for his RCMP's plan, was the first to bow to the pressure from other ministers, rather than pursuing agreement on the proposal. He asked his fellow Cabinet members during the meeting on 28 December 1945 if the SAR service required for ICAO requirements "might be carried on adequately and with less expense under the auspices of the Navy and/or the Air Force," and support for the proposal collapsed.[292] The RCMP's proposal for SAR remained on the table as a possibility for the month it required the Cabinet Defence Committee to consider the military options, but effectively, the RCMP proposal was finished by just one Cabinet meeting.

High cost was an understandable explanation for the failed RCMP bid, but cost was supplemented by another significant concern. The Cabinet applied surprising pressure on the military, through the Minister of National Defence, to reintegrate the military services into civilian society. The RCAF had proved its mettle in combat, and there could not have been an expectation that it would return to its "bush pilots in uniform" reputation from the 1930s. However, members of the government clearly wanted a military that supported the civilian populace, even in times of peace.[293] Undersecretary of State A. D. P. Heaney clarified the Cabinet's position that although DND was "known to be reluctant to undertake such additional responsibilities [such as SAR] of a non-military nature ... there is considerable goodwill to be maintained by co-operating closely with civil departments in such matters."[294] Heaney was one of the Prime Minister's most important private advisors, so his guidance to the military

[292] CJOC Historical Files, "Cabinet Defence Committee Minutes for 10 January 1946," 2.
[293] Douglas, *Official History of the Royal Canadian Air Force*, 117.
[294] LAC, RG2-B-2, Vol. 103, File T-30-1, Territorial Waters and Districts – Official – Air Search Rescue, Canadian Coast Guard, Privy Council Office – Air Search Rescue, 8 January 1946, "Cabinet Document D-30."

on its integration with other departments was fundamentally indicative of the Canadian government's overall outlook on the post-war roles the military would be expected to perform.[295] The military would not be allowed to avoid all "non-military" tasks.

It can be surmised that the government wanted to retain the rescue experience of the military and ensure that the RCAF took on a civil peacetime role. It must be remembered that the military requirement to search for and rescue its own aircrew was not going away, so the Air Force argument that it was not an appropriate organization to lead the rescue mandate was considerably weakened by the recent wartime experience. The new civilian requirements of SAR made sense to be within the existing military SAR service in order to reduce overall costs and utilize existing experience, resources, and processes. These factors were clearly understood by Cabinet, as they mused over the civilian roles the military would have to acquire in the post-war period.[296]

In addition to experience and the RCAF's own requirement to provide rescue for aircrew, the pre-war experience and post-war expectations are important factors. Since the origins of Canada's air force in 1920, only 5 of 26 years had been spent at war. Fighting wars was an essential component of any military, but Canada had a somewhat unique expectation of its military: that it would perform services for Canadians even when not at war, which was most of the time. In that light, using military forces for SAR purposes made good sense because of the unlimited liability of serving Canadian military members. Using military forces meant using personnel who were prepared to give their lives, that others may live, which was not an expectation that could be expected from civilian resources. RCAF aviators risked their lives in non-military missions before the war, so there was a natural fit between conducting post-war SAR missions in terrible weather and the pre-war well-established civil-aviation duties. This liability has since been codified in the Canadian military's 2003 *Duty with Honour*: a clear internally generated outline of the values and expectations

---

[295] Creighton, *Forked Road*, 93.
[296] Ibid.

of military personnel.[297] The post-war expectation that a return to long-term peace, especially given the military prowess of the American military protecting much of North America, can be interpreted as a rational reason for the RCAF to return to civil-aviation activities, as a way of integrating the military back into Canadian society.

The idea of integrating the military into civilian affairs was not a passing phase. Brooke Claxton, an experienced soldier from the Great War, became the Minister of National Defence in December 1946, and the following summer, he produced formal defence-objective guidance that "the Armed Forces form an integral part of the life of the community."[298] The RCAF had been assigned responsibility for the NWSR, also a role the RCAF considered to be a civilian airline activity, and tension began between the Liberal Government's desire to integrate the RCAF into civilian aspects of aviation and the RCAF's noted desire to avoid tasks it considered "non-military."[299] The RCAF was not going to be allowed to focus only on wartime tasks even though it was clearly against providing any civil domestic role.

At the beginning of January 1946, once the Cabinet decided to look into cost options for the RCAF or RCN to assume responsibility for SAR, the way forward was decided very quickly. The RCN had neither the manpower nor the aviation experience over land that the ICAO SAR service would require.[300] The RCAF, however, had both the experience and sufficient aircrew to include SAR missions. The Cabinet Defence Committee discussed alternatives to the RCMP SAR proposal and, on 10 January 1946, decided "that an adequate rescue organization for aircraft in distress could be provided by existing services in co-operation and that the

[297] Chief of the Defence Staff, *Duty with Honour: The Profession of Arms in Canada* (Kingston: Canadian Defence Academy, 2003), 14.
[298] LAC, RG24, Vol. 18826, Box 159, July 1947, "Canada's Defence: Information on Canada's Defence Achievements and Organization."
[299] DHH, 96/24, Air Force Headquarters fonds, Box 9, RCAF Plan G, 1 September 1950 Revision.
[300] LAC, RG24, Vol. 8164, File Part 1-2, 1700-27 SUB 1, Report by RCN Director of Plans, Captain H. N. Lay, 7 February 1946, "RCN Facilities Available for ASR."

DND for Air should undertake responsibility for necessary coordination to this end."[301]

Over the following year, details were produced to finalize the RCAF SAR organization. The RCAF had initially offered to maintain the wartime ASR structure of three rescue locations, but three locations were assessed as insufficient to ICAO's developing standards.[302] While it is not written anywhere, it is highly likely that the UK and US examples were used as a baseline for ICAOs developing standards. The rescue services in both of those countries had many rescue locations on both coasts of their respective territory, so by comparison, only three squadrons for the vastly larger expanse of Canada was not justifiable.

The RCAF then proposed to add rescue resources to the five composite squadrons that were already in the process of becoming operational, but this plan too was deemed insufficient for total coverage of Canada.[303] Again, the most likely rationale for the decision is the comparison that was certainly made with other Western nations. The agreed-upon solution was five composite flights as well as an additional four air stations with a SAR capability, and three of these additional locations were approved in the northern areas of Canada: Whitehorse, Yukon; Churchill, Manitoba; and Goose Bay, Labrador. The final addition to the SAR system was a temporary and small aircraft detachment in St. John's, Newfoundland, dispatched from the rescue unit in Greenwood, Nova Scotia.[304] The number of marine vessels on each coast and at Trenton was considered adequate and the aircraft were leftover from the war, keeping expenses at a minimum.

During 1946, the RCAF had restarted training of parachute-rescue personnel and ASROs. As the expansion was taking place, the first

---

[301] CJOC Historical Files, "Cabinet Defence Committee Minutes for 10 January 1946," 2.

[302] DHH, 112.3M2 (D340), May 1947, "Report of Interdepartmental Committee on Search/Rescue." This source supports all the information in this paragraph.

[303] DHH, 96/24 Air Force Headquarters fonds, Box 9, File 4, 23 August 1944 to 2 May 1946, "Report of the Post-war Planning Committee," 31 October 1945; and "Air Council Minutes," 29 January 1946.

[304] Smith, *Seek and Save*, 25.

operational jump of the parachute-rescue specialists took place on 7 July 1946.[305] In a classic example of a SAR mission, the search aircraft spotted the aircraft wreckage they were looking for and dropped Corporal George Bartlett and Sergeant Larry Poulson by parachute down to the crash site to locate and stabilize the hoped-for survivor. In this case, the pilot had survived the crash but walked away from the site and was never heard from again. Pilots are now taught to stay at the crash site, highlighting that SAR policy and procedures, as well as the regulations governing civilian pilots, were developed as a result of real-world experience in this era.

As the organization developed and learned other lessons, the RCAF formalized its first RCC in Halifax on 1 January 1947.[306] Each RCC would require 25 personnel, but the number of Flying Control Organization personnel already conducting rescue duties across the nation meant that only 11 additional positions would be required to transition the military ASR command and control to the domestic service that would provide both military- and civilian-aviation rescue coordination.[307] This demonstrates some of the efficiencies that were achieved by using RCAF resources to meet ICAO requirements and internal flying-control responsibilities. Some lessons, such as the numbers of personnel needed to coordinate rescue missions, had already been learned.

ICAO's importance to the development of international SAR was clearly growing. F/L Strouts, an RCAF Liaison to ICAO, reported in January 1947 that the SAR Division of ICAO "recommended that search and rescue should be integrated with the *International Convention for Safety of Life at Sea.*"[308] The personnel within ICAO's SAR Division clearly understood that, in addition to aviation rescue, maritime SAR would eventually

---

[305] The Para Rescue Association, *That Others May Live*, 29.

[306] LAC, RG24-E-1-c, Vol. 18113, Search and Rescue – Policy, File 976-1, Letter to CAS from AOC #10 Group, A/C F. G. Wait, 26 June 1947, "SAR Coordination Centre."

[307] DHH, 112.3M2 (D340), May 1947, "Report of Interdepartmental Committee on Search/Rescue."

[308] LAC, RG24-D-1-c, Vol. 33825 File Part 1, 1700-27, Organization and Administration – Air Sea Rescue Services, untitled memorandum to DSD from Director of Naval Plans and Intelligence, Captain H. N. Lay, 13 January 1947, on the second meeting of Provisional ICAO.

have to be mandated. Apparently, if the maritime community was not going to fight for increased services on their own behalf, ICAO was willing to do it for them. The potential growth of the SAR role meant that the additional Air Force rescue resources that Interdepartmental Committee of Search and Rescue (ICSAR) had demanded were likely going to be necessary. The RCAF was likely concerned about this expansion into the maritime domain, much as had happened during the war, but it faithfully expanded as requested.

Composite flights were the rescue units in most parts of the country, but on the East Coast the RCAF established 103 Search and Rescue Flight on 1 April 1947 to respond to the highest number of rescue missions in the country.[309] It was established initially in Dartmouth, but then moved when facilities were ready in Greenwood, Nova Scotia. It was the only specific rescue flight created as part of the SAR organization, and on 11 October 1947, it received its first helicopter, an S-51, to ensure the flight had a rescue component as well as search capabilities.[310] This unique squadron remains the only dedicated air-rescue unit in Canada.

On 2 June 1947, the Cabinet was made aware that the initial SAR organization developed by the RCAF had cost $1,066,000, but another $696,000 was needed to upgrade the system to the nine air stations needed to meet new ICAO standards.[311] It had been found that the RCAF needed an additional 142 personnel to its establishment to complete the SAR organization, and the RCN required an additional 10 personnel to establish and maintain the HF/DF system over oceanic areas.[312] As a bonus for the government, the RCAF committed to absorbing costs for SAR operations in the 1947–48 main estimates because rescue costs at the time were still

---

[309] Smith, *Seek and Save*, 17.

[310] Larry Milberry, *Air Transport in Canada, Volume 1* (Toronto: CANAV Books, 1997), 420.

[311] LAC, Canada, Cabinet Documents, RG-2, Vol. 66, 2 June 1947, "Document No. 468."

[312] DHH, 112.3M2 (D340), May 1947, "Report of Interdepartmental Committee on Search/Rescue."

minimal.[313] SAR operations were a very small role for the Air Force to provide, and it was conducted by the RCAF throughout this period as the system expanded.

The additional personnel for the military, 152 total, was a lot less than the RCMP proposal for 1,066 personnel. The financial cost savings of $4 million was equally attractive, so on 9 April 1947, the Cabinet Defence Committee ordered the RCAF to take immediate responsibility for SAR in Canada, in anticipation that Cabinet would agree.[314] Cabinet formally approved the new RCAF SAR organization on 18 June 1947, as SAR became functional on the coasts and was expanding rapidly throughout the country.[315]

The approval of the RCAF SAR organization saved the government over $4 million when compared to the RCMP proposal, but the RCAF organization operated in only nine locations across the country, compared to the RCMP plan for 15 locations.[316] Five RCCs were organized around the country, still embedded into flying control, and five personnel manned each RCC.[317] The personnel in each RCC were available for other air-station duties, meaning that the RCC personnel were cost-effective for both rescue and RCAF purposes.[318] Therefore, duplication between

---

[313] LAC, RG24-E-1-c, Vol. 18113, Search and Rescue Policy, File 976-1, Letter to AOC NWAC from CAS, signed by A/C J. M. Murray, 24 June 1947, "Financial Recoveries Arising Out of SAR Operations."

[314] DHH, R. L. Raymont fonds 73/1223, Memorandum to Distribution List from CAS, signed by S/L R. B. Inglis, 9 April 1947, "Air Force: SAR Arrangements." This document summarizes Cabinet Defence Committee guidance from 31 March 1947.

[315] LAC, Cabinet Conclusions, RG-2, Privy Council Office, Series A-5-a, Vol. 2640, No. 5435, 18 June 1947, "National Defence – Air Search and Rescue Service."

[316] DHH, 112.3M2 (D340), May 1947, "Report of Interdepartmental Committee on Search/Rescue."

[317] DHH, 181.009 (D3311), RCAF Aircraft Control, SAR Generally, 15 January 1945 to 9 May 1948, Letter from AOC NWAC to S/L Greenwood, 1 December 1947, untitled.

[318] There is no list available of work duties for RCC personnel in 1947, but documentation from both 1943 and 1948 make it clear that maintaining rescue equipment and training of aircrew were key duties performed by ASROs and, later, RCC controller personnel.

RCMP and the RCAF was avoided by the RCAF SAR organization, existing ties between the RCN and RCAF were augmented through the HF/DF system, and the RCAF was already integrated into ICAO SAR standards and the Canadian systems of air traffic control. Given the pressures from the public for the government to utilize existing resources to the fullest, the decision to assign SAR to the RCAF was logical and cost-effective.

IMPLEMENTATION OF THE RCAF's SAR ORGANIZATION

The cost of SAR increased after 1947 with more and more missions, so the RCAF lobbied the new ICSAR for costs to be shared. The annual recurring SAR costs for the RCAF after the first year of operations were estimated at $1,544,362, and it was proposed that a cost-sharing arrangement should be coordinated due to DoT's responsibility for civilian air traffic.[319] Surprisingly, the proposal was refused without an explanation. Another attempt at obtaining funding support from DoT was made on 28 May 1947; this time for a lowly $8,100 that had been spent by the RCAF searching for a Transport Canada aircraft.[320] The $8,100 bill was given to Claxton for transfer to the DoT, but Cabinet refused that as well.[321] With no financial support from the Minister of Transport, or anyone else, the RCAF had to foot the bill for civilian SAR operations, aviation and marine.

Another potential avenue for cost recovery was ICAO, but with many nations involved in this sensitive area of discussions, ICAO had yet to make any decisions on what costs, if any, commercial airlines would have to pay for search or rescue efforts.[322] ICAO would discuss the potential of cost recovery well into the 1950s, which was not a surprise to the Air Force based on its experience with previous long decision-making processes, meaning

---

[319] LAC, RG24, Vol. 8164, File Part 1-2, 1700-27 SUB 1, Vol. 1, Memorandum to the Cabinet from Minister DND (Air), 9 December 1946, "Report of the ICSAR."
[320] CJOC Historical Files, "Cabinet Defence Committee Minutes for 28 May 1947," 4.
[321] Ibid.
[322] LAC, RG24-E-1-c, Vol. 18113, Search and Rescue Policy, File 976-1, Letter to AOC NWAC from CAS, signed by A/C J. M. Murray, 24 June 1947, "Financial Recoveries Arising Out of SAR Operations."

that the RCAF needed interim options. After financial arrangements were reviewed and it was determined that any cost recovery was going to prove extraordinarily challenging, the RCAF decided to simply absorb all the costs for domestic SAR, at least temporarily.[323]

Wrangling over money aside, the Canadian decision to assign SAR to the Air Force was not unique, as both the UK and the US came to similar conclusions: that military organizations were best suited for domestic-rescue work. The RAF had kept marine-rescue vessels and aircraft assigned to domestic SAR and were actively looking at helicopters to supplement SAR resources to reduce the requirement for RAF marine vessels.[324] However, the RN Lifeboat Institution supplemented domestic SAR requirements with a network of non-RAF rescue resources. In the US, the Aerospace Rescue and Recovery Service was formed in 1946 as a global rescue service to American military personnel and a service to provide domestic-rescue resources for military and civilian aircraft crashes within all states.[325] One significant difference, however, was that the US had a coast guard with an assigned responsibility for all SAR matters over coastal waters.[326] One can conclude that it was common practice in the post-war Western environment to use military resources for rescue services. Given the actions of Canada's major allies and the fact that the RCAF would have to continue to provide rescue services for its own aircraft, it could not have been much of a surprise to the RCAF that Canada had chosen a similar SAR-mandate path as its closest allies and had assigned rescue to its Air Force.

As the SAR system became fully manned in 1948, the SAR mandate was not initially a large requirement. In the first year of operations, there were only 50 SAR missions performed by the nine rescue units at stations across the nation, which meant that each SAR flight within the composite squadron was averaging a mere five or six missions that year.[327] There was plenty of time for

[323] Ibid. Little did it know, temporary turned into permanent, as the RCAF still pays for its entire portion of SAR operations.

[324] Sutherland and Canwell, *The RAF Air Sea*, 135–37.

[325] Taylor, *That Others May Live*, 73 and 77.

[326] Galdorisi and Phillips, *Leave No Man Behind*, 109.

[327] DHH, 79/631, RCAF SAR Operations 1947–1970, DIS Files 1–14, SAR Ops 1947, File 1, "RCAF SAR Operations 31 March 47 to 31 March 48."

the RCAF to use those crews and aircraft for other flying operations; although, aircrews had to conduct SAR training as well as operations.[328] Figure 6 shows the locations of RCAF aircraft stations and the medical personnel attached for rescue purposes, although the SAR facilities in Newfoundland were not made permanent until 1954.[329] The locations were Torbay, Newfoundland, Goose Bay, Labrador; Greenwood and Halifax, Nova Scotia; Trenton, Ontario; Churchill, Manitoba; Edmonton, Alberta; Vancouver, British Columbia; and Whitehorse, Yukon. Although this was not as robust as the RCMP plan, it was still a reasonable number of resources spread across the nation.

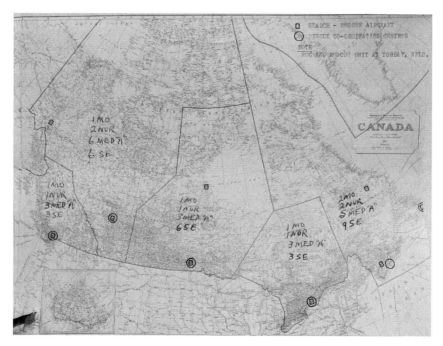

Figure 6. RCAF SAR Resources in 1947[330]

---

[328] Smith, *Seek and Save*, 22.

[329] LAC, RG24-D-1-c, Vol. 33825, 6 August 1947, "Interim SAR Organization"; and Smith, *Seek and Save*, 48.

[330] LAC, RG24-D-1-c, Vol. 33825, File Part 7, 1700-27, Organization and Administration – ASR Services, Letter to Distribution List from A. T. Cowley, Director of Air Services, 6 August 1947, "Interim SAR Organization."

Each boxed-in area of Figure 6 represents a region served by an RCC, with six total to support coordination of rescue activity and a reasonable number of resources assigned. Figure 6 includes handwritten notes on the placement of medical officers, nurses, medical assistants, and parachute-rescue technicians, called safety equipment workers in those days. The entire SAR personnel component of the RCAF in 1948 consisted of the previously identified 142 new positions, which was only half of one per cent of the planned military strength of the RCAF and easily viewed as a very small commitment.[331] Even the aircraft and vessels were inexpensive to provide. The aircraft the SAR system used were left over from the Second World War, like the C-47 Dakota, Canso seaplane, and Lancaster bomber.[332] The high-speed rescue vessels were split evenly with two each at Dartmouth, Trenton, and Vancouver.[333] Therefore, SAR was a very small portion of the post-war RCAF with no new expensive requirements, when the organization was first operational.

Despite the small size of the SAR organization, it was embedded into all aspects of the RCAF with changing organizational linkages. As a result, the command and control of the new SAR organization became quite different from the wartime ASR organization. During the war, EAC and WAC had been responsible for command and control and were overseen by AFHQ. The two commands had a fair amount of autonomy, but keeping rescue standards similar was relatively easy, as there were only two organizations involved and they communicated regularly with each other. After the war, new commands were organized on a regional basis, and then further changes were made circa 1951 to split command and control into capability-based commands, such as Training Command, Transport

---

[331] DHH, 96/24 Air Force Headquarters fonds, Box 9, RCAF Plan F 1949. The RCAF was planning to expand to 25,135 service personnel and 5,341 civilians in 1949, which were the figures used to obtain the percentage.
[332] DHH79/631, RCAF SAR Operations 1947–1970, DIS Files 1–14, SAR Ops 1949, File 3, 1950 (exact date not provided), "RCAF Press Release No. 7615."
[333] DHH79/631, RCAF SAR Operations 1947–1970, DIS Files 1–14, SAR Ops 1949, File 3, late 1947 (exact date not provided), "RCAF Press Release No. 7350."

Command, Maritime Air Command, and others.[334] The point here is not to outline all of the numerous changes, but to point out that SAR flights reported to the command that ran the station where they were located, and this meant standardization efforts were made more challenging. Many new organizations had a stake in rescue efforts, and that likely prevented the SAR organization from speaking with one voice as the number of missions increased and the mandate became more complex. The convoluted chain of command would have repercussions later due to the inherent lack of coherency in identifying systemic problems.

The majority of SAR cases in 1948 were marine and humanitarian missions, as only 12 of the 50 missions in the first year were directly related to ICAO-required aircraft searches.[335] The low number of military aircraft crashes in the immediate post-war period appears to have been a factor that significantly limited the RCAF's view of the importance of this post-war capability. No matter the reasons, RCAF planning documents from 1948 until 1959 do not outline any expectation from SAR resources during war scenarios, domestic or deployed.[336] Given the wartime pressures that created the rescue system in the first place and the military response that was proven to be necessary during those years, the lack of war planning for SAR is disappointing.

One post-war military application of SAR was the response to foreign military aircraft downed inside Canada, and there were two large foreign military searches after 1947 that demonstrated the RCAF's thorough response to American military aircraft crashes. The SAR organization's response to military aircraft crashes in Canada would arguably have been the type of mission that the RCAF would have had to respond to no matter which department ran the SAR service, as military professionals could not

---

[334] LAC, RG24-E-1-c, Vol. 17870, Orders, Instructions, Directives – SAR, Command Instruction SOAT/10 signed by AOC Training Command, A/V/M C. R. Slemon, 15 May 1951, "TC Search and Rescue Organization."

[335] DHH, 79/631, RCAF SAR Operations, "RCAF SAR Operations 31 March 47 to 31 March 48."

[336] DHH, 96/24 Air Force Headquarters fonds, Box 9, RCAF Plan E 1948, to Plan H 1951; and LAC, RG24-E-1-c, Vol. 18117, SAR – Operations, File 976-100, Memo to CAS from CNS Vice-Admiral H. G. DeWolf, 15 July 1960, "Responsibility for SAR."

just stand by while fellow military members prosecuted a search for their own aviators in the RCAF's home turf. The friendly and professional relationship between American and Canadian air forces demanded that special attention was provided to searches for their missing aircrew. Of the two searches that the RCAF conducted for the Americans that are important here, the first very significant foreign aircraft search mission for the RCAF was Operation (Op) Attaché in September 1948.

A United States Navy aircraft vanished between Churchill and The Pas, Manitoba, on 12 September 1948.[337] Onboard the aircraft was the United States Navy Attaché to the American Embassy in Canada, Captain Ouster, with three other American servicemen and a senior British Navy liaison officer. The United States Air Force (USAF) immediately provided a B-17 Flying Fortress aircraft with parachute-equipped doctors among a total of 40 aircraft provided by Canada and the US. The Americans had regulations that stated they were to command searches in foreign territory for their own aircraft.[338] However, the US worked within the Canadian SAR structure because the RCAF responded immediately and robustly with Air Commodore (A/C) Martin Costello of Winnipeg, who commanded the overall effort with over 300 RCAF personnel involved.

Coordinating the search effort was G/C Leigh, the officer who had initially recommended a parachute-rescue capability within the RCAF.[339] He was a good choice because he had deep experience in complex air-transport operations that allowed him to effectively control a massive number of aircraft in a small area. His enthusiasm for SAR was alive and well, and he expanded the search well beyond the initial search areas in an acknowledgement that pilots did not always stick to the plans they submitted before departure. At the time and because of poor adherence to routes provided in

---

[337] DHH 79/631, RCAF SAR Operations 1947–1970, DIS Files 1–14, SAR Ops 1948, File 2, *Operation Attaché*, 12 September 1948. All the information for this paragraph has been taken from this official report.
[338] LAC, RG25-A-3-b, Vol. 8012, File Part 1, ICAO – Standards and Recommended Practices for SAR, 72-ADU-39-40 Pt 1, Memorandum for Mr. Wershof from R. A. J. Phillips, 28 May 1952, "Costs of SAR Operations by Air."
[339] Leigh, *And I Shall Fly*, 184.

flight plans, search-area definition appeared more art than science. Leigh described the process of search-area allocation like this:

> The operation lasted 12 days, with the search areas now expanded to what was considered the maximum fuel range, under any condition, of the missing plane. I was beginning to fear that it was at the bottom of a lake. Rather than cancel the search, however, I decided to expand further and continue for one more day.[340]

Due to Costello and Leigh's leadership, the Americans did not need to take command of the search and were able to limit the number of aircraft provided. The mission ended successfully, due to the large Canadian expert response that located all five personnel alive and well after 13 days of searching, in the area added on by Leigh. It is only supposition that USAF would have responded differently if another Canadian organization had been responsible for SAR at the time, but it is important to note that the relationship between Canadian and American militaries was very strong in the post-war environment.[341] In fact, both Costello and Leigh received the US Legion of Merit for their role in saving the five lives, most of them American.[342] It is quite possible that if the RCAF did not respond to American military crashes in Canada, the Americans would have intervened with more resources and perhaps would have taken a more commanding role of search operations over Canadian soil.

Op Brix in 1950 was another mission where RCAF leadership and military involvement was essential. A USAF B-36 Peacemaker bomber declared an emergency on 13 February 1950, north of Vancouver Island,

---

[340] Ibid., 185. Normally, one is not so confident that the search object is not in the area already searched, due to thick trees and the like. In this part of Manitoba, however, the trees are short and less dense, so aircrew would have had high certainty that the search object was not actually in an area that was thoroughly searched.

[341] DHH, R. L. Raymont Collection (73/1223) Series VII, Box 124, File 3122, Post Hostilities Planning – Joint Draft Group of Working Committee on Canada – United States Post War Defence Relationship, circa September 1945.

[342] Leigh, *And I Shall Fly*, 186.

during a flight between Eilson Field, Alaska, and Fort Worth, Texas.[343] This type of aircraft was known to carry nuclear weapons for flight testing, and when the distress call was received, there was a possibility of nuclear weapons on board.[344] The initial response to the developing emergency revealed a crucial cryptographic communications problem between the RCN and the RCAF, slowing both organizations' response to the potential nuclear crisis, as they were unable to communicate the secret information they had on the situation.[345] As in many SAR incidents, the situation was complicated by terrible weather: low ceilings, poor visibility, and winds nearing 100 kilometres per hour in mountainous terrain.[346]

RCC Vancouver, a military entity, then contacted American military authorities with a synopsis of the problem and made an urgent request for help after the cryptographic failure. Immediately, the Americans dispatched 28 military aircraft and 4 United States Coast Guard cutters to assist with the search, supplementing the large Canadian response that included the RCN destroyer, Her Majesty's Canadian Ship *Cayuga*.[347] The SAR response in this instance was wholly military with two of the RCAF high-speed launches and over 40 aircraft total airborne within a few hours to respond to the distress and, with a nuclear weapon potentially involved, necessarily so.[348] In this instance, the RCC was able to initiate action with the American military organizations while HQ sorted out the cryptographic problem.

Five USAF personnel died in the B-36 tragedy, but 12 personnel bailed out before the crash over very remote islands between Prince Rupert and

[343] LAC, RG24-D-11, Vol. 11807, COPC 115-45 (B36), Flag Officer Pacific Coast File, ASR B36 File, report drafted by F/L D. G. Bell-Irving, 8 July 1950, "Operation Brix 1950."

[344] LAC, RG24-D-11, Vol. 11807, COPC 115-45 (B36), Flag Officer Pacific Coast File, ASR B36 File, Letter to Naval Secretary from H. G. Dewolf, Flag Officer Pacific Coast, 8 July 1950, "Operation 'BRIX.'"

[345] Ibid.

[346] Flying Officer P. R. Gilliam, "Rescue Co-ordination Centre, Vancouver," *The Roundel* 3, no. 8 (July–August 1951): 20.

[347] LAC, RG24-D-11, Vol. 11807, ASR B36 File, Report to Flag Officer Pacific Coast from Captain (N) Medland, 21 June 1950, "Operation 'BRIX' – Conference 27th February 1950."

[348] Gilliam, "Rescue Co-ordination Centre, Vancouver," 20.

Vancouver, British Columbia.[349] However, the fact that there were survivors was not known at the time, and an intense search was initiated. After a week of searching, an oil slick on the water provided a solid clue as to the crash location of the aircraft. Vancouver RCC personnel, with knowledge of military bailout procedures that non-military personnel could not have known, worked out a new search area for subsequent searches. Based on the revised search area, two survivors were found on Princess Royal Island. The following day, search efforts were further refocused and concentrated based on input from the two located airmen, and another 10 survivors were found. The 12 lives were saved through heroic efforts of all the personnel involved in the rescue but also because RCAF personnel knew how to translate information from military authorities into available rescue assets and effective search areas.[350] The expertise of the Air Force RCC proved critical to saving lives from this tragedy.

The lesson, however, was that the RCAF, and indeed even the RCN, needed to be immediately involved in SAR communications efforts to be able to respond quickly to emergencies that could so clearly impact the safety of Canadians. Despite the majority of SAR missions involving civilian aircraft or vessels, military aircraft flying over Canada with nuclear munitions meant that air defence authorities needed to be immediately aware of military aircraft emergencies. As RCAF officers were the coordinators in RCCs, coordination could occur quickly with Canadian or American military agencies in response to any military aircraft emergency.[351] RCAF SAR personnel performed an essential role in rescue communications in this instance that stressed the importance of military integration between air-traffic-control and rescue services.

Given the RCAF effort in SAR missions for Canadian and American military aircraft, the apparent lack of RCAF SAR planning for deployed

---

[349] LAC, RG24-D-11, Vol. 11807, 8 July 1950, "Operation Brix 1950."

[350] Ibid.

[351] LAC, RG24-E-1-c, Vol. 18112 Search and Rescue – Organization and Administration 1945–1954, Letter to CAS from AOC NWAC, 20 May 1950, "RCC Officer Establishments." Trenton, Winnipeg, and Edmonton RCCs had one officer answering the RCC phone system during normal working hours; after hours, an NCO was on call from home.

Air Force rescue resources was surprising due to USAF's successful use of helicopters for combat SAR in Korea, 1950. USAF used helicopters on the battlefield to save 996 men from enemy territory over the course of the Korean War, which demonstrated the continued importance of SAR forces in a combat environment.[352] The RAF ASR service had already proved the importance of rescue after the Battle of Britain, making the military provision of SAR services a fairly obvious linkage. The RCAF, however, relied on Allied capabilities for the combat applications of SAR and failed to include the capability in any war planning until 1960.[353] Within the RCAF, the military applications of SAR operations were either misunderstood or ignored.

Arguably, a military use of Air Force resources for civilian-aviation rescue was a new post-war reality. Another mission type that the RCAF could not escape, no matter who led the SAR mandate, was the humanitarian mission. Although humanitarian missions were a provincial or RCMP responsibility, the RCAF was the only national post-war organization in Canada with a near all-weather aviation capability. The bush pilot mentality of civil aviation had not survived the war, due to the ever-increasing reliance on aviation and the international demand for safety in the transport of passengers. Risk management for more dangerous missions was left to military organizations. As a result, the RCAF was concerned that its resources would be overused in a mission type that was not a federal responsibility.[354]

Fortunately, the RCMP agreed that humanitarian requests for RCAF assistance needed to be limited. Requests from individuals or provincial authorities would be filtered by the police and referred to civilian agencies

---

[352] Robert F. Futrell, *The United States Air Force in Korea: 1950–1953*, rev. ed. (Washington, D.C.: Office of Air Force History, USAF, 1983), 572.

[353] LAC, RG24-E-1-c, Vol. 18117, 15 July 1960 "Responsibility for SAR."

[354] DHH 181.009 (D5200), Department of National Defence for Air 1945–1946, AMA Directorate, "Annual Report." This document describes SAR flying conditions with significant risk of a forced landing, yet all missions were successfully prosecuted, which is well beyond the limits set by ICAO for civilian flying.

when practicable.[355] Lost hunters, and similar matters, would be handled locally, while small northern communities with dire needs would receive timely RCAF support.[356] RCMP involvement ensured that only serious matters would require RCAF assistance because military airframes and aircrews were the only credible resources for urgent humanitarian aid in bad weather. Therefore, humanitarian missions should be viewed differently from the SAR marine and aviation mandates because this type of mission would likely have fallen upon military aircraft regardless of the organization responsible for SAR operations.

An aspect of humanitarian operations that is important to this discussion is ministerial involvement in ongoing rescue operations. On 10 November 1949, the Minister of DoT, Lionel Chevrier, contacted the Minister of National Defence, Brooke Claxton, and requested details of an RCAF mission to save someone named Father Dionne missing off of Eskimo Point in Hudson's Bay.[357] The mission for Father Dionne was a routine operation as a result of an RCMP request for help, but clearly Father Dionne had connections that made the search for him worthy of high-level attention. Although he was never found, RCAF assistance in matters important to ministers was directly supporting Claxton's 1947 stated desire for an RCAF integrated within society and undoubtedly made the Minister amenable to RCAF aims in Cabinet discussions. In the late 1940s, the small SAR community provided the RCAF with important leverage in an era when the RCAF desired large funding increases to provide defences against a Soviet threat.[358]

By 1949, the SAR organization had been completely established. There

---

[355] LAC, RG24-E-1-c, Vol. 18113, Search and Rescue Policy, File 766-1 SAR Policy, Letter with Report Enclosure to DND for Air from AOC WAC A/V/M J. L. Plant, 1 May 1946, "ASR Organization Conference in WAC, held on 15 April 1946."

[356] DHH 181.009 (D5200), Department of National Defence for Air 1945–1946, AMA Directorate, "Annual Report."

[357] LAC, RG24-E-1-c, Vol. 18117, SAR – Operations, 976-5 Vol. 1, Missing Persons Cases, Letter from Brooke Claxton to Lionel Chevrier, 10 November 1949, "Search for Father Dionne and Party."

[358] Ray Stouffer, *Swords, Clunks & Widowmakers: The Tumultuous Life of the RCAF's Original 1 Canadian Air Division* (Trenton, ON: DND, 2015), 7 and 17.

were 29 aircraft and 5 helicopters assigned to the rescue role, supported by 28 parachute-rescue personnel, all at the nine locations previously identified.[359] The RCAF had 12 ground search teams, which were augmented by Canadian Army personnel, as ordered by the Chief of the General Staff, Lieutenant-General Foulkes.[360] The ground search teams were essential to SAR success because aircraft often crashed in the vicinity of their operating airport, making a local response quicker and more effective than waiting for search aircraft from rescue locations.[361] Although the RCAF was the lead organization, the RCN, Canadian Army, RCMP, and others were deeply involved in the delivery of rescue services.

One can conclude that the SAR system that was developed, immediately following the 1947 decision to assign SAR to the RCAF, responded to many missions that would very likely have been assigned to the RCAF regardless of the organization responsible for domestic SAR. There were expectations of support from the American military to help recover their aircrew, and there were national-defence concerns associated with some military aircraft crashes. The lack of desire by the Air Force to take on responsibility for the SAR role did not reflect daily reality in the immediate post-war world. The RCAF may not have had a clear understanding of its inescapable roles within domestic-rescue missions.

SUMMARY OF CANADIAN ASR TO SAR TRANSITION

The RCAF did not view ASR or SAR as a military responsibility, largely because sovereignty was not a major factor in rescue-system development for Canada in the first years after the war. The RCAF organized and led SAR operations in a manner that satisfied American rescue requirements and limited the number of vessels and aircraft assigned by American military forces over Canada to search for their own downed personnel. Although it was not a major factor in this time period, sovereignty was

---

[359] LAC, RG24-E-1-c, Vol. 18128 File No. 978-7-3, SAR – Crash Rescue Assistance by Others, "RCAF SAR Facilities 1949."

[360] DHH, 112-32M2 (D340), Report of Interdepartmental Committee on Air Sea Rescue, Policy, letter to CA formations from CGS, LGen Foulkes, 5 July 1949, "Search and Rescue – Army Participation."

[361] Ibid.

an important outcome of the military's rescue systems to meet ICAO demands, and it is likely that the RCAF underplayed its importance.

In the first few years after the war, ICAO became a considerable force in civil-aviation regulation, and a SAR capability provided by ICAO's signatory nations was a clear expectation. Canada, the UK, and the US chose similar paths to the SAR mandate, assigning domestic aviation crash response to their national Air Force. That a SAR system was needed was not disputed, and the transition to a military-led SAR system by the three allies showed that they shared post-war realities of tight budgets and little appetite for new organizations.

Cost was critically important to the decision to assign aviation SAR to the RCAF instead of the RCMP. However, the burden of this new role was not entirely on the Air Force. The RCMP maintained responsibility for missing persons over land and ensured that RCAF resources were only called out for urgent requirements. The RCN provided personnel and built the necessary communications facilities needed for the system to become effective, and the Canadian Army provided personnel for ground search teams. The RCAF paid for most of the increase in expenses to provide a domestic SAR capability, but it did have some access to government resources to assist it in this new mandate. SAR costs were manageable in those early days, even without DoT financial assistance.

The Air Force was ordered by government to take on responsibility for aviation SAR because it was cost-effective; it was desired that the RCAF was integrated into society with at least one domestic role, and some of the personnel, vessels, and aircraft were already equipped and ready for the role. The RCAF may not have understood the positive implications of leading the SAR service, but it did not delay in recreating a rescue organization. The cost to the RCAF was an increase of 142 personnel and $1,762,000, which was authorized by the government.

In hindsight, progress towards today's SAR system was considerable, but with some key limitations. A national rescue system was created, but only for aviation rescue. Maritime rescue was still an incidental activity volunteered by the RCAF out of goodwill. Assigned aircraft and vessels were the resources used for rescue, and although they were leftover equipment from the Second World War, they were largely sufficient for the requirement of that time.

Table 5 shows that policy and resources had improved, but it was strictly to meet the civilian-aviation mandate. Even though the system was formalized for civilian-aviation requirements and the process was similar, the combat component of rescue was inexplicably overlooked and would remain so treated throughout the 1950s. In conclusion, the RCAF became the lead organization for aviation rescue in Canada during 1947, and the following chapter will demonstrate how the RCAF rescue system found itself expanded to include maritime-rescue responsibilities three years later.

Characteristic	Aviation	Maritime
National Standards	Aviation rescues. Required by ICAO, ordered by the government, and maintained by the RCAF	Maritime rescues. None
Available Resources	Aircraft. RCAF aircrew had training and procedures in nine locations across the country	Vessels. Six RCAF vessels and assistance available from the RCN provided coastal coverage only
Formalized Policy	Military rescues. RCCs had been established to investigate and respond to air incidents	Civilian rescues. The RCAF included policy to assist when requested, but this was not advertised to the public

Table 5. The RCAF's SAR System in 1948

Photo: DND

Taken early in the Second World War, this picture of a German U-boat was later confiscated from the German Navy archives. The threat from submarines like this one was the main impetus for creating an RCAF ASR system in 1942.

Photo: DND

The RCAF's Nootka was one of six high-speed rescue vessels built in 1941 for the war effort, and the vessels were the mainstay of RCAF maritime rescue throughout the Second World War and until 1954. The other vessels were the Abnaki, Huron, Malecite, Montagnais, and Takuli.

Photo: DND

The Walrus amphibious aircraft was an important asset for ASR after
the Battle of Britain in the UK. It also served the RCAF from 1943 to
1947 and was used for liaison work and domestic SAR in Canada.

Photo: DND

Taken on 14 January 1943, Lysanders, like this one, were used for
army-cooperation support flying and aircrew training in Canada,
but it is also famous for its role during the Battle of Britain
assisting the RAF with spotting aircrew downed at sea.

Photo: DND

The legendary Dakota served in the RCAF from 1943 to 1989. Throughout the 1950s, it was an important asset that was often used for SAR work as well as target towing and training. Most importantly, it was a versatile transport aircraft that could be used for a SAR mission one day and a transport one the next.

Photo: DND

An Avro Lancaster of 404 Squadron, which almost became the first and only Canadian ASR squadron, flies over the Scilly Isles. This iconic aircraft was manufactured by Victory Aircraft Ltd. in Malton, Ontario, and 430 Mk 10 versions were built. In post-war use, the Canadian-built Lancasters went on to serve in highly useful roles such as SAR, photographic reconnaissance, and maritime patrol.

Photo: DND

This photo of an Anson aircraft was taken near the end of its service life in 1952. A multi-role aircraft, it served primarily as a trainer, but it was also used for anti-submarine and ASR work during the war. After the war, it served in Canada primarily as a transport aircraft.

Photo: DND

Wilfrid "Wop" May circa 1920 well after his encounter with the "Red Baron." May remains a legend in the RCAF SAR community for his bravery, compassion, and his role in creating the parachute rescue specialist trade back in 1944. He and his friend, Group Captain Z. L. Leigh, can be considered the godfathers of ASR and SAR in Canada.

Photo: DND

This photo was taken during a training exercise at the rescue specialists' course in Edmonton. The parachute rescue specialists are now known as SAR technicians (more commonly as SAR Techs), and they have a long and brave history of saving Canadian lives *That Others May Live* (the SAR Tech motto).

Photo: Wikipedia

The Honourable Brian Brooke Claxton saw service in the Great War on the Western Front and became a lawyer after that war. He was first elected to the House of Commons in 1940 and served as Minister of National Defence from 1946 to 1954, playing an important role in the creation the domestic SAR service in Canada.

Photo: DND

Two RCAF nursing sisters converse with Master Sergeant Cecil D. Gray, in charge of Para Rescue personnel of 44th Air Rescue Squadron at Lowry Air Force Base Denver Colorado, during Operation Pike Peak. Rescue specialists used the Dakota aircraft–like the one in the background–for SAR training and operations throughout the 1950s.

Photo: DND

One of seven nursing sisters who trained as a parachute rescue specialist in the mid-1950s, Nursing Sister Marion L. Macdonald of Vancouver, BC, proved that women are just as capable as men in one of the most physically demanding trades in the RCAF. Nursing Sister Macdonald logged 25 parachute jumps and, as a former staff member of the RCAF's Survival School, served at both Edmonton and Mcleod River Bush Camp, Alberta. This photo was taken in Trenton, Ontario, in October 1952. Partly because women could not continue to serve after they were married and partly because the training affected their primary work in medical care, volunteer nursing sisters as rescue specialists were phased out in 1956.

Photo: DND

The Piasecki H-21 helicopter is shown hovering over a sports field at RCAF Station Trenton. The RCAF flew similar Piasecki helicopters at composite flights in the SAR role during the late 1940s and throughout the 1950s.

Photo: DND

This air-to-air view near the Lions Gate Bridge in Vancouver is of an RCAF Canso aircraft used in the SAR role. The Canso was a very successful anti-submarine patrol bomber during the Second World War, and it continued to serve the RCAF in roles like SAR until 1962.

Photo: DND

There were 10 Albatross seaplanes brought into RCAF service in 1960 specifically for the SAR role. They were replaced fewer than ten years later by a mix of helicopters and fixed-wing aircraft that operated from runways; to this day, the SAR fleet remains a mix of helicopters and fixed-wing aircraft.

Photo: DND

HMCS Saguenay passes HMCS Bonaventure during a sail past. This RCN vessel was one of several involved in the infamous Ferngulf incident that finally spurred the Canadian government to create the Canadian Coast Guard.

Photo: DND

The Labrador helicopter was the workhorse of RCAF SAR from its purchase in 1963 until its retirement in 2004. There are innumerable stories of RCAF aircrew who bravely used this aircraft to its full potential and beyond to save lives for over forty years.

Photo: Canadian Coast Guard

The Moorhen, an RCAF crash boat built in 1952 that was transferred to DoT in 1964 as part of the build-up of vessels for the new Canadian Coast Guard. The creation of the Canadian Coast Guard rescued the RCAF from its role as the sole agency responsible for rescue and together, these two organizations helped make Canada's SAR service into the internationally renowned system it is today.

ORGANIZATION

It is pretty clear from these cartoons how RCAF SAR personnel saw their organization and their role within it. These cartoons were found in the RCAF Searchmaster's Handbook, which was compiled by the Eastern Area Rescue Co-ordination Centre circa 1958, and it is a fascinating combination of satire and useful SAR information.

THE SEARCHMASTER

Chapter 6: A Gamble with Maritime Rescue in 1950

The RCAF established an aviation SAR system to meet ICAO requirements in 1947, but it will become evident that the RCAF's goal was to hand over the SAR mandate to any other agency. The RCAF was concerned about its SAR role because maritime rescue was about to become a mandated national activity, and the RCAF was the obvious candidate to lead the maritime-rescue function. Confirming RCAF concerns, developing civilian-transportation safety requirements led the United Nations to create the IMCO in 1948, as a maritime version of ICAO. During the first conference in 1948, IMCO formally agreed that signatory nations should provide a SAR capability to maritime vessels operating in their territorial waters.

As with the aviation mandate, the Canadian government intended to provide this requirement with the least amount of money and resources, so it scrutinized a growing call for a Canadian coast guard and considered adding the maritime-rescue component to the aviation mandate already assigned to the RCAF. The RCAF took a gamble on maritime-rescue, offering a limited rescue responsibility in the maritime domain on the assumption that a Canadian coast guard was inevitable in the immediate future. The machinations between Canadian organizations left mariners in a precarious state, as no one wanted ownership of this new responsibility.

THE MARITIME SAR MANDATE

The SAR service developed in 1947 for ICAO requirements was required to have surface marine craft to provide rescue resources for commercial aircraft that ditched at sea.[362] The RCAF had considerable expertise in the delivery of maritime rescue, as it had been the only wartime organization operating rescue craft within 200 miles of shore. Although the Navy would appear to be a more logical choice for rescue response at sea, the RCN had made it clear during the initial SAR deliberations that their ships required four hours to depart the dock, thus making RCAF resources far more responsive and attractive for SAR vessel requirements.[363] Both organizations would provide existing vessels on an as-available basis for the primary mandate of aviation rescue, and neither organization shied away from assisting with maritime emergencies.

It should be made clear that the only requirements for surface rescue vessels in Canada before 1948 were ICAO requirements for aviation rescue from seas and the Great Lakes, and not for the rescue of maritime vessels. ICSAR in 1946 had debated the available government resources that were the most effective for the aviation requirement and concluded that RCAF resources would take on primary responsibility for ocean-based rescues.[364] Any other government vessel, including RCN or Canadian Army vessels, could be considered a secondary resource for SAR operations. One can see that the RCAF already had a limited role in maritime rescue, but it was assisted in maritime-rescue missions by the other military services with ships at sea.

Support to aviation rescue for oceanic areas in 1947 had appeared effective using RCAF vessels and aircraft, but the trouble was how to respond to shipping emergencies in the Great Lakes. The RCAF had the two

---

[362] LAC, RG24-D-1-c, Vol. 8164 File Part 1 – 2, 1700-27 SUB 1, Organization and Administration – Interdepartmental Committee on Search and Rescue, Minutes Prepared by Secretary of ICSAR W/C A. M. Cameron, 7 June 1946, "Minutes of the Fourth Meeting of ICSAR."

[363] LAC, RG24-D-1-c, Vol. 8164 File Part 1 – 2, 1700-27 SUB 1, Organization and Administration – Interdepartmental Committee on Search and Rescue, Message to Naval Secretary DND from the CO Atlantic Coast, 12 December 1945, "ASR Naval Assistance."

[364] LAC, RG24-D-1-c, Vol. 8164, File Part 1 – 2, 1700-27 SUB 1, Organization and Administration – Interdepartmental Committee on Search and Rescue, Minutes Prepared by Secretary of ICSAR W/C A. M. Cameron, 22 March 1946, "Minutes of the Third Meeting of ICSAR."

high-speed rescue vessels in Trenton, but those only provided assistance for vessels in Lake Ontario. ICSAR agreed that the number of existing RCAF resources in the Great Lakes was insufficient, so other agencies would need to provide marine-vessel coverage for aircraft downed in those waters.[365] It was expected that the RCMP and DoT would have more marine resources available in the near future, so the RCAF was not expected to increase vessel resources in that area.[366] As the SAR discussions progressed in 1947, it was clear that the RCAF, RCN, RCMP, and DoT were all going to be expected to provide maritime resources for aviation rescue.[367]

Although maritime rescue was not yet mandated, rescue from vessels at sea would not be ignored. ICSAR recommended that the new SAR organization could provide assistance to mariners "wherever possible, particularly to shipping in distress in Canadian coastal waters."[368] The RCAF was even clearer in its direction to those responsible for the delivery of the SAR service: "every effort will be made to use aircraft where desirable to extend aid to surface craft lost or in difficulty."[369] Therefore, immediately after the formation of the SAR organization, it was already determined that the RCAF would have a role in maritime rescue.

In January 1948, the government of Canada was invited to a meeting in Geneva to discuss the establishment of the United Nation's IMCO, an organization created to formalize international maritime transport and safety standards.[370] The DoT was assigned sole responsibility for the meeting, and it was to determine how the growth in maritime rescue was going

---

[365] LAC, RG24-D-1-c, Vol. 8164, 7 June 1946, "Minutes of the Fourth Meeting of ICSAR."

[366] LAC, RG24-D-1-c, Vol. 8164, 22 March 1946, "Minutes of the Third Meeting of ICSAR."

[367] Ibid.

[368] LAC, RG24-D-1-c, Vol. 8164, 25 January 1946, "First Meeting of the Revised ICSAR."

[369] LAC, RG24-E-1-c, Vol. 18112 Search and Rescue – Organization and Administration 1945–1954, order to all commands from AFHQ, 4 September 1947, "Interim Plan for Search and Rescue."

[370] LAC, RG2, Cabinet Documents Vol. 66, Doc. No. 593, 22 January 1948, "United Nations Maritime Conference."

to affect SAR policy in Canada.[371] It is curious that the RCAF did not attend, because it regularly sent SAR experts to ICAO meetings to provide input for SAR standards.[372] Indeed, the RCAF had a full-time member assigned to work with ICAO, and other RCAF and RCN officers would attend any meetings where military interests were involved.[373] It is possible that the RCAF turned down an offer to attend IMCO, as soon-to-be CAS A/V/M Curtis "stated a preference of the RCAF that their representative on SAR be an advisor rather than the national representative since the subject matter has implications of primary importance to civilian departments."[374] Curtis preferred to keep SAR matters at arm's length, and DoT sent a representative, so the Geneva meeting took place without an RCAF presence. An RCAF lack of enthusiasm for marine SAR would become a theme for a long time following the initial IMCO meetings.

Following the Geneva meeting, a subsequent International Convention for the Safety of Life at Sea was held in London, June 1948. The convention built upon IMCO desires to improve the safety of marine transportation, and Regulation 15 of the subsequent documentation required contracting governments "to ensure that any necessary arrangements [were] made for coast watching and for the rescue of persons in distress at sea round its coasts."[375] There were no minimum rescue services required, similar to the approach that ICAO had taken a few years prior, but it did set the stage for future SAR resource monitoring, as it stated "each contracting government undertakes to make available information concerning its existing rescue

---

[371] Ibid.

[372] LAC, RG24-D-1-c, Vol. 33825 File Part 1, 1700-27, Organization and Administration – Air Sea Rescue Services, untitled memorandum to DSD from Director of Naval Plans and Intelligence, Captain H. N. Lay, 13 January 1947, on the second meeting of PICAO.

[373] W/C W. P. Pleasance, "I.C.A.O.," *The Roundel* 3, no. 8 (July–August 1951), 7 and 10.

[374] LAC, RG24-D-1-c, Vol. 33825 File Part 1, 1700-27, Organization and Administration – Air Sea Rescue Services, 27 November 1946, "Minutes from the 1st Meeting of the Canadian PICAO Advisory Committee."

[375] IMO, *International Convention for the Safety of Life at Sea* (London: 10 June 1948), 206.

facilities and plans for changes therein, if any."[376] It was reasonable to assume that minimum requirements for maritime SAR facilities would be mandated eventually, which suggests that the maritime mandate would be resisted by the RCAF for fear it would need to purchase more vessels.

Additional pressure to purchase more vessels was a possibility if IMCO developed along the lines of ICAO. IMCO was an organization with a similar agenda to ICAO, and ICAO had completed the transition from an agency that documented nation's best practices to an agency that set the standards for aviation-rescue facilities.[377] There were indications that IMCO was on the same path. Therefore, Canada needed to consider options not just for the immediate rescue requirements on the coasts but also for future requirements on the assumption that IMCO might grow in authority much as ICAO had already by 1949. One possible response to IMCO's requirement for maritime rescue in Canada was the creation of a Canadian coast guard, an option that was favoured by the sea-going Canadian public because the few military and RCMP resources that were able to assist with maritime rescue were often too far away to be of much use in a desperate emergency.[378] In order to identify the potential benefits of an additional organization for maritime rescue against expected high set-up costs, on 17 February 1949, Cabinet ordered ICSAR to study possible options for a rescue capability to meet immediate and perceived future IMCO requirements.[379]

ICSAR included the Canadian Maritime Commission, Mines and Resources, the Ministry of Justice, the Ministry of Fisheries, the Ministry of Finance, National Health and Welfare, DND, and DoT.[380] The majority of these representatives believed that "the present arrangements in

---

[376] Ibid.

[377] LAC, RG24-D-1-c, Vol. 33825 File Part 1, 1700-27, Organization and Administration – Air Sea Rescue Services, 23 August 1946, "PICAO SAR Division Second Session."

[378] LAC, RG24-D-1-c, Vol. 8164, Multiple Newspaper Clippings Supporting a Canadian Coast Guard, 1949. Dates and authors were not available on most of the clippings.

[379] LAC, Cabinet Conclusions, RG-2, Privy Council Office, Series A-5-a, Vol. 2643, No. 8464, 17 February 1949, "Search and Rescue Coast Guard Service."

[380] Ibid.

which the RCAF coordinated the search and rescue activities of the other government departments [were] quite satisfactory."[381] Unsurprisingly, the new marine-rescue requirement needed to be met with minimal new resources, and the RCAF rescue organization was believed to already meet the basic needs of IMCO. Therefore, there appeared to be no incentive to spend the extra money on a new organization that amalgamated sea-rescue services. A/V/M Roy Slemon, speaking on behalf of the RCAF, stated that "operating experience indicated that the present disposition of search and rescue facilities was satisfactory."[382] There was no general support for a coast guard in Canada in 1949, so the matter was shelved.[383]

The so-called satisfactory SAR service in question was composed of 6 high-speed launches, 28 aircraft that were still in the same locations as in 1947, and 5 RCCs operated by the RCAF, which had emergency authority over available government maritime vessels capable of rescue efforts.[384] Satisfactory was a relative term, as the RCN was not happy with the lack of support for a coast guard and the fact that tasking authority for Navy ships could come from an Air Force RCC without any maritime expertise.[385] The Naval Officers Association of British Columbia had been one of the applicants in 1949 for the immediate formation of a coast guard, and their stated desire was for an organization that "would direct existing vessels to the scene of the trouble."[386] The Naval Officers Association, with good reason, believed that experienced mariners should be the ones to direct maritime vessels to rescue situations at sea, rather than aviation experts. In

---

[381] LAC, RG24-D-1-c, Vol. 8164, File Part 1-2, 1700-27 SUB 1, Interdepartmental Committee on SAR, Vol. 1, Minutes of meeting prepared by W/C A. H. Newsome of the PCO, 30 March 1949, "Interdepartmental Committee on Search and Rescue."

[382] Ibid.

[383] A coast guard is not discussed in Cabinet, after February 1949, until after the Canadian Coast Guard is formed in 1962.

[384] LAC, RG24-D-1-c, Vol. 8164, 30 March 1949, "Interdepartmental Committee on Search and Rescue."

[385] LAC, RG2, Cabinet Documents Vol. 124, Doc. No. 147–50, 22 May 1950, "Re: Search and Rescue Service."

[386] LAC, RG24-D-1-c, Vol. 8164, File Part 1 – 2, 1700-27 SUB 1, Organization and Administration – Interdepartmental Committee on Search and Rescue, February 1949, "Aide Memoire on a Canadian Coast Guard."

British Columbia, the SAR area extended "700 miles out into the Pacific Ocean," as the SAR area still does today, so the area to be covered west of Vancouver Island was vast and treacherous for vessels.[387]

The RCAF was less concerned about the addition of maritime rescue to the SAR mandate than the RCN because the RCAF did not have the marine resources or knowledge for maritime SAR, unlike the RCN. When the matter of maritime rescue was discussed again in 1950, the RCAF expressed willingness to coordinate maritime rescue, but "it [was] not prepared to assume and direct responsibility for operational control of the ships of other government departments on the ground of lack of technical knowledge of seafaring matters."[388] The RCN, by contrast, likely saw itself as a target for similar incremental increases from IMCO that the RCAF was dealing with from ICAO in aviation rescue. Even if the RCN was going to increase resources for SAR, it most likely did not want to have those resources fall under the direct control of the RCAF.

One other concern of the Naval Officers Association was that the loss of one vessel, the US Army's *Clarksdale Victory*, resulted in a SAR response that consisted solely of US Coast Guard resources in Canadian waters.[389] The incident took place off of Haida Gwaii, British Columbia, in November 1947, and there was no record of RCAF aircraft assisting in this rescue.[390] The most likely explanation for the lack of RCAF searching is that a formal process for handling maritime emergencies did not exist, so the vessel's foreign operator would not have known whom in Canada to notify of the potential emergency. With no policy on marine rescue in Canadian waters, foreign authorities would have to expect to provide their own rescue efforts. Therefore, Canadian sovereignty could be perceived as at risk because Canada did not always respond to maritime distresses in its area, forcing the Americans to respond to emergencies in Canadian

---

[387] Gilliam, "Rescue Co-ordination Centre, Vancouver," 18.

[388] LAC, RG2, Cabinet Documents Vol. 124, Doc. No. 147–50, 22 May 1950, "Re: Search and Rescue Service."

[389] LAC, RG24-D-1-c, Vol. 8164, February 1949, "Aide Memoire on a Canadian Coast Guard."

[390] Associated Press, "Fear 47 Died in Shipwreck," *The Milwaukee Journal*, 27 November 1947. Haida Gwaii was previously known as Queen Charlotte Islands.

waters. It is quite possible that the RCN believed that additional American involvement of maritime rescue within the Canadian oceanic area could directly lead to more rescue requirements for the RCN. The RCN had consistently stated its lack of suitability for SAR work, so the Naval Officers Association supported the Canadian coast guard proposal, as likely relief from the possibility of routine SAR operations in the future.[391]

From the RCAF perspective, the main concern in maritime SAR discussions was the number of Air Force personnel required to meet the new need.[392] Priorities at the time were the development of a fighter force to protect vital areas from the communist threat, an antisubmarine capability to protect sea lines of communication, a tactical force to support the Army in the event Canada was invaded, a small bomber element, and a transport organization to support all elements. A personnel ceiling was potentially limiting the approved growth within those areas of concern and was threatening to limit Canadian assistance with the planned American air defence network. Rescue efforts were not a priority at all, so as long as the proposed maritime mandate did not require additional personnel, the RCAF would remain uninterested.

As ICSAR finalized the recommendation for maritime SAR as anticipated, expanding the existing aviation SAR mandate of the RCAF to include maritime SAR, the RCN formalized concerns about its role within the Air Force's SAR service. The proposal for maritime SAR gave the RCAF's RCCs direct tasking authority over any government vessel for marine emergencies, but the RCN demanded chain of command involvement before the RCAF could task an RCN vessel.[393] The chairman of ICSAR, J. V. Clyne, advised the government not to listen to the RCN because the involvement of shore-based command centres might delay an urgently needed RCN ship response to a maritime emergency.[394]

---

[391] LAC, RG24-D-1-c, Vol. 8164, February 1949, "Aide Memoire on a Canadian Coast Guard."

[392] DHH, 96/24, Air Force Headquarters fonds, Box 9, RCAF Plan F, 1949, 1–2. All information for this paragraph is taken from these two pages.

[393] LAC, RG2, Cabinet Documents Vol. 124, Doc. No. 147–50, 22 May 1950, "Re: Search and Rescue Service."

[394] Ibid.

All other government agencies had agreed to abandon their own on-going ship missions when the RCAF RCCs called for urgent assistance, so the RCN's concern was not considered very important in light of the cost savings that could be achieved by simply expanding the mandate of the RCAF. Subsequent to these discussions, the Cabinet ignored the RCN's concern of tasking authority and made the RCAF responsible for maritime SAR in Canada on 26 June 1950, as the most cost-effective solution.[395]

The SAR expansion into maritime rescue was announced to the public on 21 July 1950, and the announcement gave the RCAF's RCCs in Halifax, Trenton, and Vancouver full tasking authority over 234 government-owned vessels, for maritime SAR purposes only.[396] This announcement was nothing but sleight of hand, as nothing practical had changed. As previously discussed, the RCCs already had authority to task vessels from other government departments to a SAR mission. The announcement just formalized the process and made it public knowledge.

The official nature of the announcement, however, irked the RCN because they believed the RCAF was given too much authority over their vessels. The RCN continued to raise its concerns until 12 July 1951, when the Cabinet changed the wording slightly on the SAR directive to mollify the RCN.[397] Aside from the RCN problem with direct tasking authority, all members of ICSAR agreed that the RCAF approach to SAR was the most cost-effective response to the international requirements.[398] With much less discussion than aviation SAR, and no other options really considered, maritime SAR was made the responsibility of the RCAF.

It is difficult to understand the apparent lack of RCAF effort to avoid the maritime SAR mandate, given its past support for an amalgamated organization to conduct maritime SAR. Indeed, the official RCAF

[395] LAC, Cabinet Conclusions, Vol. 2645, No. 9983, 26 June 1950, "Search and Rescue Service."
[396] LAC, RG24-D-1-c, Vol. 8164, Newspaper Clipping, Canadian Press, Ottawa, 21 July 1950; and LAC, RG2, Cabinet Documents Vol. 124, Doc. No. 147–50, 22 May 1950, "Re: Search and Rescue Service."
[397] CJOC, SAR Historical File, 12 July 1951, "Cabinet Directive Circular No. 22."
[398] LAC, RG2, Cabinet Documents Vol. 124, Doc. No. 147–50, 22 May 1950, "Re: Search and Rescue Service."

policy on SAR, and other civilian commitments, was "to reduce these non-combatant commitments to the minimum acceptable and while they must be provided for, they should not be permitted to assume priority or scale of effort which would detract from combat efficiency."[399] The document further outlines, specifically with regard to the SAR role, that "restricted peacetime appropriations together with the obvious fact that these activities do not contribute to operational efficiency, clearly shows the desirability of being rid of them."[400]

Arguably, the RCAF might have believed that an amalgamated aviation and maritime SAR service would have been easier to pass on to another organization, for the time when the RCN succeeded in its quest for a Canadian coast guard. Continuing this line of argument, if aviation and maritime SAR were all part of one system, then it could be a fair assumption that the transfer of SAR to another organization would likely have included both components, and the RCAF would have rid itself of all aspects of SAR. The obvious hole in this logic is that the RCAF had seamless integration into the flying-control system in Canada that any other organization would have to duplicate, and the RCAF would still have had to provide for humanitarian missions and military-aircraft rescues. The RCAF, however, made no recognition that these facets were important military contributions. The RCAF had already demonstrated a lack of appreciation for the military benefits to SAR involvement, so leadership may have ignored gaps in the logic.

The idea that the RCAF agreed to the maritime mandate in 1950, in order to facilitate a complete handover in the future of all aspects of the SAR mandate, bears further scrutiny. It should be recalled that the RCAF supported an amalgamated marine-rescue service in both 1944 and 1946, but not in 1949. The RCAF expected that any growth in the SAR service by the Air Force was to be as a direct result of increased military SAR missions and not expanding civilian domestic requirements.[401] The

---

[399] DHH, 96/24, Air Force Headquarters fonds, Box 9, RCAF Plan G, 1 Sep 50 Revision, 4.

[400] Ibid., 8. This statement is in specific reference to the SAR organization and the NWSR.

[401] DHH, 96/24, Air Force Headquarters fonds, Box 9, RCAF Plan F, 1949, 8.

RCAF Plan G, 1 September 1950 Revision provided the future direction of the RCAF and stated that the RCAF wished to be rid of SAR and other "non-operational commitments," but it also stated "the aim at present will be to seek a method of being relieved of as many non-combatant commitments as possible."[402] Amalgamating aviation and maritime SAR into one organization available to be transferred to another organization was one possible way of being relieved of the SAR service. It was a risky gamble.

The personnel and equipment provided by the RCAF in 1951 were satisfactory for the air mission, but limited for maritime rescue. There were two RCCs, Halifax and Vancouver, that were manned 24/7 due to ICAO commitments, with three other RCCs at Trenton, Winnipeg, and Edmonton.[403] The types of airframe resources available for SAR missions were the Lancaster, Canso, Dakota, Norseman, and helicopters. High-speed rescue launches were at Pat Bay and Dartmouth, crash boats were at Pat Bay, Goose Bay, and Trenton.

The oceanic area of coverage extended a thousand miles out to sea over the Pacific, and on the eastern seaboard, Canadian coverage extended halfway to the British Isles.[404] Of the five Great Lakes, only Lake Ontario had any coverage at all. Four locations to cover the entire oceanic and Great Lakes of Canada were clearly insufficient.

THE LOW PRIORITY OF MARITIME RESCUE

Once the maritime mandate was formally assigned to the RCAF, actions were taken by the RCAF to limit its allocation of non-aircraft resources to this new role. During the 1949 ICSAR discussion on maritime SAR, A/V/M Slemon hinted at the RCAF's future actions towards SAR when he said "there was some doubt as to whether a substantial extension to the present [RCAF SAR] service could be achieved unless the public were

---

[402] DHH, 96/24, Air Force Headquarters fonds, Box 9, RCAF Plan G, 1 September 1950 Revision, 3.

[403] Miller, "Search and Rescue," 27. This source is used for all facts contained in this paragraph.

[404] Ed., "ICAO and the RCAF" *The Roundel* 8, no. 9 (November 1956), 26.

prepared to support a separate organization."[405] Slemon's statement can be seen as a warning to other government departments that the RCAF was not going to grow the SAR organization and that the RCAF subtly supported a coast guard. Whether the substantial expansion he mentioned could not be achieved due to lack of government priority or RCAF funding limitations, a domestic SAR service was clearly not an RCAF funding priority.[406]

The best example of the low funding priority for the SAR service was the subsequent actions regarding the high-speed rescue vessels. It may be recalled that G/C Leigh had been the officer who had convinced the CAS to acquire the parachute-rescue capability for the RCAF in 1944, and he had coordinated efforts for Op Attaché in 1948. His previous support of SAR was still evident in late 1950, when he was again part of AFHQ. Upon finding out that the RCAF was to become responsible for marine SAR, Leigh sent a letter to a superior officer proposing the purchase of replacement high-speed rescue vessels dedicated to the SAR role in order to carry out the maritime SAR responsibility effectively.[407] He wished to avoid complications of trying to task marine vessels from the RCMP, RCN, or DoT during emergencies.[408] His concern was logical, as the existing high-speed vessels were in a poor state and tasking other government departments could take valuable time, but his suggestion was not popular. The response from the superior officer was crystal clear: "we will not make the RCAF into a coast guard—nor will we take on the seaborne aspects of SAR."[409] Another superior-officer minute on the document echoed this

---

[405] LAC, RG24-D-1-c, Vol. 8164, 30 March 1949, "Interdepartmental Committee on Search and Rescue."

[406] DHH, 96/24, Air Force Headquarters fonds, Box 9, RCAF Plan H, 1 June 1951, 3.

[407] LAC, RG24-E-1-c, Vol. 18112, Search and Rescue – Organization and Administration 1945–1954, Letter to AMOT from DAO G/C Leigh, 3 November 1950, "Search and Rescue – Marine Distress Policy." The superior's name and position is illegible on the document.

[408] Ibid.

[409] LAC, RG24-E-1-c, Vol. 18112, 3 November 1950, "Search and Rescue – Marine Distress Policy." The signatures of the officers who responded are illegible and positions are not indicated. Emphasis included is exactly that from the document.

policy, which advised G/C Leigh that the RCAF would only coordinate maritime SAR operations rather than providing maritime resources.

The RCAF refusal to provide marine vessels to SAR operations was demonstrated shortly after G/C Leigh's letter. Plan H, 1951, included a plan to purchase 15 Sikorsky, Bell, and Piasecki helicopters for SAR duties to supplement the helicopter purchases that had already been completed for SAR, and these resources were planned as the RCAF response to aviation and maritime rescue.[410] Helicopters were able to conduct rescue work over land and the ocean, and as they were modern aviation resources capable of other RCAF missions, it was good sense to have them as part of the RCAF inventory. The Sikorsky and Bell helicopter deliveries were underway in 1951 and expected delivery completion was 31 March 1953. So, with helicopters arriving at rescue squadrons, the RCAF announced the disbandment of the two coastal marine squadrons in April 1952.[411]

The disbandment of the marine squadrons was part of "a new policy in regard to marine operations, which envisages the reduction of our marine branch to the status of range patrol and local crash duty only."[412] The RCAF followed protocol and advised ICAO of its intention to replace the rescue vessels with helicopters. ICAO, with growing authority and newly developed standards for maritime vessels involved in aviation rescue, responded that the reduction of vessel support was unacceptable and quoted the following US Coast Guard research:

> By no means will the helicopter entirely eliminate the present methods and equipment used in the saving of life and property at sea. Rather, it will serve as an indispensable assistant to (a) the surface vessel and its boats, (b) the shore lifeboat station, and (c) the conventional fixed

[410] DHH, 96/24, Air Force Headquarters fonds, Box 9, RCAF Plan H, 1 June 1951, 3.
[411] LAC, RG24-E-1-c, Vol. 18113, SAR – Policy, File 976-1, Letter to ICAO from Deputy Minister for Air, C. M. Drury, 1 April 1952, "Disbandment of Marine Squadrons."
[412] Ibid.

wing aircraft. It possesses certain inherent limitations that restrict its use under all conditions.[413]

The rebuke from ICAO went uncontested, but the RCAF still concluded that it should provide airborne equipment and not surface vessels.

The basic disagreement between ICAO and the Air Force stemmed from a stance on military forces conducting SAR that was vastly different from the RCAF's view of the SAR service. The ICAO Draft SAR Manual from 1951 clarifies that "many states have vested primary responsibility for search and rescue in a military service" and provided a list of the most beneficial military services, primarily communications.[414] It appeared standard for military forces worldwide to provide SAR services, and ICAO was sold on the benefits that military forces brought to this capability. By contrast, RCAF policy aimed at transferring the capability to a civil organization at the earliest opportunity. If that was not possible, then it would focus on minimizing resources for the SAR role.

The Air Force had made it very clear in 1949, before the decision was made to assign maritime SAR to the RCAF, that it had no intention of providing resources specifically for the maritime mission.[415] Even for aircraft emergencies in the water, the rationale behind RCAF decisions on maritime rescue was that "the effectiveness of rescue in ocean areas is primarily dependent upon whatever ships may be within reach of the distressed aircraft and good communications between them rather than upon small high-speed craft whose value is purely local."[416] The RCAF proceeded with the disbandment of marine squadrons, continued to pursue the purchase of helicopters, and formally requested the RCN to provide

---

[413] LAC, RG24-E-1-c, Vol. 18113, SAR – Policy, File 976-1, Letter to CNS from CAS, 17 February 1952, "SAR – Provision of Surface Rescue Vessels."

[414] LAC, RG24-E-1-c, Vol. 17554, Co-operation and Liaison with ICAO – SAR, 1945–1953, File 004-4 SAR Vol. 1, 19 July 1951, "ICAO Draft SAR Manual."

[415] LAC, RG2, Cabinet Documents Vol. 124, Doc. No. 147–50, 22 May 1950, "Re: Search and Rescue Service."

[416] LAC, RG24-E-1-c, Vol. 18113, 1 April 1952, "Disbandment of Marine Squadrons."

offshore surface vessels for rescue work.[417] To assist the RCN in rescue work, the RCAF gave the RCN the six high-speed rescue vessels, and the RCN finally agreed to a rescue role.[418]

The motivation of the RCN to assist with marine SAR, however, is not evident. One possible interpretation is that the RCN won a minor inter-service victory by claiming additional operational area from the maritime domain abandoned by the RCAF after Air Force vessels were limited to close proximity to air stations. Another possible interpretation is that the lack of a clear organization responsible for marine SAR could hasten the creation of a coast guard. Perhaps the RCN understood the RCAF's desire to get out of the marine environment and focus on aeronautical interests. Whatever the motivation, the RCN agreed to provide maritime SAR assistance as a temporary measure until fully replaced by RCAF helicopters.[419]

Although the RCN agreed in 1952 to a role in SAR, the RCN and RCAF had differences in views that worked towards the same results. The RCN did not feel it necessary to maintain the high-speed rescue vessels for rescue work, as "RCN or other government departments would provide suitable vessels for that purpose," subject to availability.[420] The RCAF interpretation was that "as the search and rescue commitment on the West Coast is being handed over to the Royal Canadian Navy, there is no longer a requirement for an auxiliary marine squadron."[421] With both military services assuming the other had the lead for maritime emergency response, the end result was a reduction of small high-speed rescue craft to assist Canadians in distress at sea.

The RCAF completely divested itself of any rescue vessels that could be

---

[417] LAC, RG24-E-1-c, Vol. 18113, SAR – Policy, File 976-1, Cover Page and Minutes to Chairman of ASR Facilities W/C J. Woolfenden, from D/Dir RCN Plans and Operations Commander R. C. Chenowith, 15 April 1952, "Minutes of ASR Meeting."

[418] DHH 74/438, "Former RCAF Air/Sea Rescue Launches."

[419] It is not known if the RCN was aware that ICAO would not accept helicopters-only for maritime rescue.

[420] LAC, RG24-E-1-c, Vol. 18113, 15 April 1952, "Minutes of ASR Meeting."

[421] DHH, 79/98, RCAF Organization Order 46/52, 24 June 1952, "Disbandment of 1 Marine Sqn (Aux) RCAF Patricia Bay, BC."

used outside of the immediate area of the air station, and at some point the RCN realized that its provision of maritime SAR resources was no longer a temporary requirement as the RCN "found itself with a moral obligation to supply rescue facilities" due to the resulting gap in rescue capability.[422] However, the RCN still had a four-hour response time; it refused to use the old RCAF vessels for rescue, and the state of maritime-rescue capability was in worse shape than when the RCAF was first given the responsibility for maritime SAR.[423] Maritime rescue was the equivalent of a hot potato that no one wanted to hold.

THE AVIATION AND MARITIME SAR SYSTEM

A complication for the RCAF was that aviation and maritime rescue were frequently interrelated. Moving back in time a little to illustrate some of the aviation complications that affected subsequent RCAF policy towards maritime rescue, we return to the new Province of Newfoundland in 1949. The RCAF had established a SAR capability in Goose Bay, Labrador, but the Canadian government had not supported permanent SAR resources to Newfoundland.[424] The inclusion of Newfoundland into Canada, however, resulted in concerns that the "necessity for using USAF aircraft for relatively minor and simple SAR incidents and initially in more serious cases, could be detrimental to Canadian prestige in the new Province of Newfoundland."[425] As a direct result, two RCAF aircraft were temporarily deployed from Greenwood, Nova Scotia, to Torbay, Newfoundland, on

---

[422] LAC, RG24-E-1-c, Vol. 18128, File No. 978-7-3, SAR – Crash Rescue Assistance by Others, SAR – Liaison between RCAF and Others, Civilian Organizations, Minutes prepared by Chairman S/L K. B. Handley, 17 February 1953, "Local ICSAR (Pacific Area), 8th Meeting."

[423] Ibid.

[424] Figure 6 showed that the RCAF had planned on an RCC and squadron in Torbay, but for reasons unclear, the system authorized in 1947 did not include resources in Newfoundland.

[425] LAC, RG24-E-1-c, Vol. 18112, Search and Rescue – Organization and Administration 1945–1954, Letter to CAS from AOC TC, 19 May 1949, "SAR – Commitments, Newfoundland."

1 November 1949.[426] The SAR aircraft deployed to Torbay were intended to decrease American involvement in Canadian SAR; although, the few number of aircraft would later prove insufficient.[427] The movement of existing aircraft to Torbay was a partial resolution to American involvement in Canadian SAR missions and was obtained at negligible cost to the RCAF.

The Americans did not appear to resent requests for rescue assistance, and perhaps that was because the RCAF response to American requests for SAR response over Canadian territory was exemplary. As an example, Op Mike was an RCAF and USAF search for a missing USAF C-54 Skymaster aircraft that disappeared between Alaska and Great Falls, Montana, in January 1950. The RCAF assisted in what is still believed to be the largest single search in Canada. The RCAF flew 3,056 hours with 32 other agencies covering 1,214,115 square miles.[428] Tragically, the month-long search for the missing 7 aircrew and 34 passengers proved fruitless. However, the time spent searching met American expectations for a solid effort to try and find missing aviators.[429] Although USAF policy was to provide a search coordinator, the RCAF was the lead agency in all of the aircraft crash investigations because the RCAF produced a large and effective response in all of the incidents where USAF aircraft crashed in Canada.[430] The close relationship between the RCAF and USAF certainly minimized friction over who would respond to which rescue mission over Canada. The relationship is very likely why the Americans did not complain about assisting in minor SAR missions in and around Newfoundland.

If the RCAF had to respond often to American aircraft crashes, there was no noted concern. In fact, the RCAF appeared to view support to the Americans as a necessary chore. As an example, ICAO SAR policy in 1952

---

[426] Smith, *Seek and Save*, 25.

[427] Ibid.

[428] S. R. Miller, "Search and Rescue in the R.C.A.F.," *The Roundel* 3, no. 2 (January 1951): 20.

[429] DHH, 79/631, RCAF SAR Operations 1947–1970, DIS Files 1–14, SAR Ops 1951, File 5, February 1951, "Directorate of Public Relations Release No. 7813."

[430] CJOC, Treaty Series, 1949 No. 2, Exchange of Notes between Canada and United States of America, effective 31 January 1949, "Constituting an Agreement Relating to Air Search and Rescue Operations Along the Common Boundary of the Two Countries."

examined a proposal that would require neighbouring countries to pay for SAR missions in foreign territory, and Canada initially supported the proposal.[431] One would think that cost recovery would have been appealing to Canada, considering that 12.9 per cent of SAR missions in the early 1950s were for foreign aircraft, and the majority of foreign aircraft SAR missions were American crashes in Canadian territory.[432] As well, SAR operations were increasing every year, and funding support was still not available to the RCAF for the SAR service. However, when the RCAF was requested to comment, it strongly recommended that Canada avoid cost-recovery options and that the RCAF should continue to foot the bill for SAR operations for Americans.[433]

External Affairs in Canada was confused about the RCAF reluctance to accept American funding. The RCAF explained that the US paid for its own SAR resources used in Canadian missions, but if the US had to pay for their own resources and pay Canada a fee, the Americans could reasonably demand a greater level of authority in how those resources were used.[434] "If the United States were paying part of the cost, control of some large-scale operations over Canadian territory would pass to the USAF. Air Commodore [Henry] Carscallen is of the opinion that the preservation of Canadian sovereignty in this type of operation is worth the additional cost to Canada."[435] The RCAF was content to strictly limit the number of resources in the delivery of SAR but not at the expense of having the Americans conduct a Canadian mandate. External Affairs supported the

---

[431] LAC, RG25-A-3-b, Vol. 8012, File Part 1, ICAO – Standards and Recommended Practices for SAR, 72-ADU-39-40 Pt 1, Letter to External Affairs from Air Transport Board, 6 May 1952, "Cost of SAR."

[432] Ibid.

[433] LAC, RG25-A-3-b, Vol. 8012, File Part 1, ICAO – Standards and Recommended Practices for SAR, 72-ADU-39-40 Pt 1, Memorandum for Economic Division from Mr. Wershof, 29 May 1952, "Costs of SAR Operations by Air."

[434] LAC, RG25-A-3-b, Vol. 8012, File Part 1, ICAO – Standards and Recommended Practices for SAR, 72-ADU-39-40 Pt 1, Unnamed Letter to Secretary Air Transport Board from Under-Secretary of State for External Affairs, 30 May 1952, "File 72-ADU-39-40."

[435] LAC, RG25-A-3-b, Vol. 8012, File Part 1, ICAO – Standards and Recommended Practices for SAR, 72-ADU-39-40 Pt 1, Memorandum for Mr. Wershof from R. A. J. Phillips, 28 May 1952, "Costs of SAR Operations by Air."

RCAF proposal and cost recovery was not pursued, nor did ICAO ever implement cost recovery.[436] Cost recovery was overly complicated for rescue activities, and it raised the uncomfortable possibility of requiring an international standard for a national service set by foreign neighbours.

The RCAF was correct in its assumption that the Americans were becoming concerned by the cost of ICAO, as the US economic burden was far greater than any other member.[437] This burden was further increased by the weather ships stationed in the Atlantic to provide transatlantic aircraft with accurate weather information. Although the US was the major contributor to the cost of these 10 ships monitoring the Atlantic weather, other nations regularly used their services but offered no payment. In 1953, the US threatened to walk away from the agreement altogether.[438] The RCAF proved to be in tune with American sensitivity to the high cost of ICAO, and the RCAF was unwilling to recommend a higher burden on the Americans that could potentially cause the RCAF to give up control of some SAR operations.

The following year, ICAO produced a progress report on SAR facilities worldwide that identified a continuing shortage of Canadian SAR facilities in Newfoundland.[439] The progress report was a formal and public declaration that some nations, like Canada, still had considerable work to do to meet ICAO standards. The report identified that USAF had to supplement Canadian SAR facilities in order to ensure that sufficient SAR resources were available on the airway approaches to North American from Europe, which was deeply undesirable for Canadian sovereignty interests.[440] The ICAO report identified that Canadian SAR expansion would not require much in the way of additional resources, but notwithstanding the criticism, the RCAF would reduce SAR resources, not expand them. Nine stations with rescue aircraft had been deemed essential in 1949, but early

---

[436] LAC, RG25-A-3-b, Vol. 8012, 30 May 1952, "File 72-ADU-39-40."

[437] David Mackenzie, *ICAO: A History of the International Civil Aviation Organization* (Toronto: University of Toronto Press, 2010), 167.

[438] Ibid., 182.

[439] LAC, RG24-E-1-c, Vol. 17554, Co-operation and Liaison with ICAO – SAR 1945–1953, File 004-4 SAR Vol. 1, 1 February 1952, "ICAO Second North Atlantic Regional Air Navigation Meeting, May 48, Progress Report No. 1A."

[440] Ibid.

in the 1950s the northern stations would be reduced.[441] Five stations with rescue aircraft and helicopters—harking back to the RCAF's original proposal for the SAR organization—were deemed sufficient in an era when the Air Force had other higher-priority military missions to maintain.

Perhaps because of the limited resources made available, the RCAF had become quite efficient in its use of personnel for the SAR mandate in order to prevent growth of the SAR organization. As an example, RCC personnel were not even required to be at the office all the time. An officer was in the RCC during normal working hours, but after hours and on weekends and holidays, a non-commissioned member would be on call at home.[442] RCC personnel could be called to work by flying-control personnel any time an emergency was reported, and this procedure minimized the number of people required on shift at any given time and yet still provided necessary resources to coordinate rescues. By all accounts, the RCAF personnel involved in the SAR service were completely dedicated to the mission, and they worked through low levels of manning and old equipment to save lives.

Canada was following standard international expectations for the SAR organization by using the RCAF, but the RCAF used the least amount of resources possible to the extent that even sovereignty concerns did not result in more resources assigned to SAR. The lack of movement on the Canadian Coast Guard project had called the RCAF on its bluff, and it was left responsible for the coordination of the maritime-rescue role. Without adequate resources for maritime rescue, tough times were ahead.

SUMMARY OF CANADIAN SAR EXPANSION

The RCAF had a difficult time coming to terms with the provision of SAR in Canada. From the RCAF's perspective, it believed it should be expected to provide aircraft and helicopters for SAR, if it had to provide for SAR at all, but it was not about to provide maritime vessels in the

---

[441] DHH, 81/224, CAP 342, *Orders for Aircraft Control and Services for the RCAF*, April 1956.
[442] LAC, RG24-E-1-c, Vol. 17870, Orders, Instructions, Directives – SAR, Command Instruction SOAT/10 signed by AOC Training Command, A/V/M C. R. Slemon, 15 May 1951, "TC Search and Rescue Organization."

delivery of that service. However, the RCAF belief that helicopters alone were sufficient for maritime rescue did not stand up to ICAO scrutiny. The RCAF was balancing a requirement to perform rescue activities at an acceptable level to international and national agencies with the minimum cost possible, because financial support was not made available for the expanding service. The reality was that minimal marine-rescue resources increased risk to mariners, and that reality appeared to be ignored by the RCAF and all other Canadian government organizations involved.

The risk to Canadian sovereignty sometimes came from unexpected quarters, as External Affairs had considered negotiations with ICAO to make foreign nations responsible for the cost of SAR when aircraft of their nation crashed in another country. The RCAF believed that demanding money from the Americans meant giving up control over rescue activities within Canada. As this demand could be a step towards loss of control over one's territory, the RCAF suggested that it needed to absorb the cost of all searches within Canada, regardless of the nationality of anyone requiring rescue. Sovereignty was occasionally an RCAF priority, but with American rescue assistance, sometimes sovereignty was insufficient justification for more funding allocated to the domestic-rescue service.

Canada's SAR service provided barely adequate safety measures for international visitors travelling by ship or aircraft, largely due to amenable American assistance, so there was international pressure on the RCAF to provide better maritime-rescue efforts. The RCAF saw little-to-no military value to SAR, which made it difficult for the Air Force to understand the ICAO pressure to provide dedicated rescue vessels. Although Canada was providing very limited amounts of resources, which sometimes required American support in the new Province of Newfoundland and Labrador, the strong relationship between USAF and the RCAF prevented international pressure from becoming a serious concern for the government.

Within Canada, the addition of the maritime-rescue requirement came with no additional funding. The government was quite content to use existing resources under the authority of the RCAF, so increased calls for a Canadian coast guard were ignored. Conspicuously absent in the discussions on maritime rescue was DoT, which would eventually have to own up to its responsibility for a service that was a civilian domestic mandate and had been deemed by the RCAF to have little-to-no military value. In short, the lowest cost for SAR had been achieved, but it was with little real interest from an RCAF that min-imized maritime resources in the broader hope that the entire SAR mandate could later be transferred to another governmental organization.

In light of the decreases from the system set up in 1948, progress was decidedly mixed. In a major step forward, a national standard was con-ceptually developed in 1950 for both aviation and maritime emergencies in Canada; although, the location of resources had yet to match the new standards as depicted in Table 6. Marine resources, however, took a large step backward as the high-speed rescue vessels were retired without replace-ment. Helicopters had been expected to be a better alternative to vessels, but that expectation failed scrutiny. This chapter outlined the growth of the SAR service into a national aviation and maritime system but demonstrated significant maritime-resource problems with the Air Force's organization. It will now be seen how the problem became even worse throughout the 1950s.

Characteristic	Aviation	Maritime
National Standards	Aviation rescues. Required by ICAO, ordered by the govern-ment, and maintained by the RCAF	Maritime rescues. Required by IMCO, or-dered by the government, and coordinated by the RCAF
Available Resources	Aircraft. The RCAF was reducing to five rescue locations across the country, despite the increase in mandate	Vessels. No RCAF vessels, four-hour notice-to-move assistance from the RCN, and helicopters that were limited in range
Formalized Policy	Military rescues. RCCs investigated and responded to all air incidents	Civilian rescues. The RCAF was mandated to in-vestigate and task resources, but there was no organi-zation formally tasked to respond to emergencies

Table 6. The RCAF's SAR System in 1954

Chapter 7: A Decade of Hardship

The maritime-rescue role had ended up an RCAF responsibility but without new funding or much support from other organizations. This would immediately become a problem, as the number of maritime emergencies soared after 1950. It is likely that no one involved in the decision making understood the ramifications of announcing to the public that the Air Force RCCs would respond to all maritime emergencies. After the announcement, there was someone who would answer the call for help and who was required to send resources to mariners in distress. Although there was little real change to previous rescue policies, the sea-going public made· full use of the newly available service. The RCCs and the rescue flights responded admirably, but the RCAF was in for a tough time in the 1950s.

The 1950s also saw the departure of key figures from the air-sea-rescue past. Sadly, in 1952, "Wop" May had a stroke and died during a hike in Utah. In June of 1957, G/C Leigh retired from the RCAF and became the director of operations for air shows in Toronto. The loss of both of these men from the RCAF had no practical impact on the RCAF's SAR organization, but it did leave a symbolic void of dedicated champions for the SAR service at a time when champions were desperately needed. Without the guidance and support of people like May and Leigh, emerging problems in the SAR system were not avoided.

Developments in 1958 will show how the RCAF dealt with some of the problems, even while DoT continued to evade responsibility in maritime rescue. AFHQ developed standards to ensure services were provided in a more consistent manner throughout the country, and it lengthened the time for aircraft to launch on SAR missions as one method to reduce the strain on the system. The RCAF also considered a separate helicopter-rescue capability for support solely to fighter operations in order to ensure that Air

Force crews had a rescue capability even when the SAR organization was busy with domestic missions. However, with decreased resources available to the SAR service and a massive increase in rescue missions, the changes were insufficient to reduce the hours RCAF aircraft had to put towards domestic-rescue missions, both aviation and maritime. It will become clear that the attempts at solving the problems were largely ineffective despite significant efforts by the RCAF to manage the SAR responsibility without maritime-rescue assistance from other national organizations.

THE STRUGGLE TO KEEP UP WITH SAR DEMAND

The 1950s would culminate in a turning point for SAR in Canada, with the RCAF fears of becoming a domestic-rescue agency in danger of being realized during that decade.[443] It has already been outlined that in the first year of SAR operations in 1947, there had only been 50 missions and that this amount of SAR activity was an insignificant drain on RCAF resources at that time. However, after the maritime SAR mandate had been added to RCAF SAR duties and with a growing overall public expectation of rescue services, the number of missions in 1950 increased to 252 with a resulting 4,667 hours flown by RCAF aircraft.[444] That increase was only the beginning, as the number of hours flown by SAR aircraft rose dramatically and the inadequacies of the system became obvious.

One of the most significant problems was finding enough medically trained personnel to keep SAR aircraft flying with enough medical expertise to save lives after crashes in remote locations. Parachute-rescue professionals would eventually receive this training and reduce the need for support from hospital staff, but in the 1950s, the system relied on volunteers from the RCAF medical personnel at stations with rescue flights. Doctors and medical assistants made up the majority of volunteers, but in 1951 and 1952, seven nursing sisters received specialty training and

---

[443] LAC, RG24-E-1-c, Vol. 18112, 3 November 1950, "Search and Rescue – Marine Distress Policy."

[444] Smith, *Seek and Save*, 23. The hours flown for SAR in 1950 may have been even higher as the RCAF had demonstrated inconsistency in how it accounted for all flying hours in the late 1940s and early 1950s.

became parachute-rescue professionals.[445] These seven women, known as para-belles, provided much-needed assistance to ease the tight manning of SAR flights in the early 1950s. These women are fascinating, as they were successful parachute-rescue professionals in one of the most physically demanding and specialized roles in the RCAF *decades before* women had the ability to enrol in the combat trades of the Canadian Armed Forces. It was not until 1989 that all military occupations were open to women, but the RCAF was well aware during and after the Second World War that women were highly capable of physically-demanding parachute rescues.[446] As there was no extra pay for the doctors or nurses who took on the intense training and dangerous operations of parachute-rescue, one can imagine the incredible sense of adventure and strength of character evident in these men and women who took on these dangers for no extra pay.

The first operational jump of a nursing sister took place on 5 July 1952 to aid an injured geologist in a remote and mountainous area east of Pitt Lake in British Columbia.[447] Nursing Sister Grace Woodman jumped out of a Dakota aircraft with S/L Dick Wynne, a volunteer doctor, and jumpmaster Sgt Red Jamieson. Woodman was smaller than the other two parachutists, and she drifted into an isolated valley and got stuck in a large tree. In her own words:

> I became entangled in branches about 125 feet above ground and because my harness was a little large for me, I slipped out of it and found myself hanging upside down by one leg! ... I gradually eased myself out of my awkward position. With the aid of a 100 ft length of nylon rope, carried for this purpose, I began the slow descent to the ground. Unfortunately, my gloves had fallen to the

[445] The Para Rescue Association, *That Others May Live*, 66.
[446] National Defence and the Canadian Armed Forces, "Women in the Canadian Armed Forces," 6 March 2014, http://www.forces.gc.ca/en/news/article.page?doc=-women-in-the-canadian-armed-forces/hie8w7rm (accessed 25 April 2018). Note that women were not able to join the submarine service until 2000.
[447] The Para Rescue Association, *That Others May Live*, 52–53. All information for this paragraph is taken from this source.

ground and during the slippery descent, I suffered severe
rope burns to my hands.

Woodman did not let the burns get the best of her though; she carried
her 60 pounds of gear up the mountainside and reunited with the team
the next morning and provided care to her patient.

Woodman's was but one example of the hardship these women en-
dured and the bravery they showed. Although the programme was dis-
continued in favour of adding positions for rescue professionals to rescue
flights, it was a good example of the kind of outside-the-box thinking used
by the SAR service to manage real-world problems.[448] The other practical
problem for the continued use of nursing sisters was the regulation, bi-
zarre in hindsight, that nurses had to leave the RCAF once they became
married.[449] Woodman left the RCAF due to marriage in 1955 and the last
para-belle, F/O Marion Neily, left the RCAF in 1956. The SAR service
needed all the help they could get, and by all accounts, the para-belles
provided outstanding support.

By 1953, the amount of rescue activity was overwhelming. One of
the units, 103 Rescue Unit, reported nearly 10 rescue missions a month
"with nearly 300 hours per month on operations alone."[450] Sadly, the
intense operations took their toll. One aircraft from 103 Rescue Unit,
which had been participating in a SAR mission, did not make it back to
base. On 20 April 1953, the Lancaster crashed 30 miles from its base in
Greenwood, Nova Scotia, and claimed six lives onboard.[451] "Amazingly
enough, one man survived. The radio officer, F/O K. A. Benson, was
found in a semi-conscious condition leaning against a tree near the wreckage. How he escaped from the broken and charred wreckage remains a

---

[448] The Para Rescue Association, *That Others May Live*, 66.

[449] Royal Canadian Air Force, "An Air Force Pioneer: Grace MacEachern, para-belle,"
http://www.rcaf-arc.forces.gc.ca/en/article-template-standard.page?doc=an-air-force-
pioneer-grace-maceachern-para-belle/izkjr5ic (accessed 25 April 2018). Her maiden
name was Woodman.

[450] Smith, *Seek and Save*, 48.

[451] Ibid., 45.

mystery."[452] This tragedy highlighted that long hours and high operational demand could take a costly toll on the personnel responsible for SAR missions and their families.

Despite the pressures, there was a great deal that the RCAF did well to maximize resources for rescue and ensure the SAR missions were prosecuted to the best of its abilities. From a coordination perspective, major searches were made considerably easier by the Air Defence Command Centre, which would deploy a fighter controller to work with search personnel during large missions to control aircraft and to deconflict the SAR aircraft from Canada's fighter aircraft that sometimes operated nearby.[453] Providing non-SAR military personnel to specific SAR missions was a highly effective way to achieve efficiency and highlights the benefit to having a pool of trained aircrew that could assist with searches, even if they did not have the training to assist in the rescue phase of the mission.

Despite the strain on the limited number of personnel assigned to SAR, it is worth noting that RCAF SAR aircraft were only responsible for 2.66 per cent of total annual RCAF flying by 1951.[454] After the new aviation and maritime SAR system became established, the size of the SAR community grew to 947 personnel—including aircrew, mechanics, and communicators—out of an establishment of 53,700 RCAF personnel in 1956.[455] This represented the high mark for the SAR community within the RCAF, and yet still it was only 1.8 per cent of the RCAF strength, which included all aircrew trained for SAR duties, even if they were often

[452] Ibid.

[453] LAC, RG24-E-1-c, Vol. 18113, Search and Rescue – Policy, File 976-1 Vol. 4, letter to AOC Maritime Group from CAS, signed by F/L L. B. Pearson, 26 May 1953, "SAR – ADCC-RCC Co-ordination."

[454] LAC, RG24, Vol. 20617, AFHQ Director of Flight Safety Statistics, 1942 to 1952, September 1950, "Flight Safety Report, Hours Flown per type of Accident."

[455] DHH, 181.004 (D28), "RCAF Programme of Activities, 1957–1960" (although it actually covers 1955–56), 16.

involved in other RCAF missions.[456] The overall small size of the community helps explain why it could get saturated with operational rescue activity, as only a few concurrent missions across the country could deplete the available resources.

Available resources became more of a challenge because even as the SAR organization grew in personnel, it was consolidated to fewer locations. By 1956, all four of the northern SAR units had been disbanded, and the growth of SAR personnel numbers had resulted from the higher aircrew and parachute-rescue specialist personnel requirements of the remaining four flights and two units that performed rescues.[457] Those SAR aircraft flights that remained were embedded within composite units, meaning the unit performed communications flights, flew short transport missions, provided platforms for general officers to maintain flying skills, as well as conducted SAR activities.[458] The composite units that survived the SAR downsizing were 102 in Trenton, Ontario; 105 in Namao, Alberta; 111 in Winnipeg, Manitoba; and 121 in Vancouver, British Columbia.[459] In addition to the composite units, there were two rescue units: 107 in Torbay, Newfoundland, and 103 in Greenwood, Nova Scotia. 107 Rescue Unit had become a formal unit in March 1954; for years prior to that date, it had been a detachment from 103 Rescue Unit.

The SAR organization was smaller, but the capabilities had been enhanced somewhat to provide better search capability. The RCAF purchased 14 Otter aircraft for the SAR role to augment the existing and ageing

---

[456] LAC, RG24-E-1-c, Vol. 18114, SAR – Policy, 976-2, details were not available, 10 February 1959, "DoT – RCAF Meeting on SAR Operations in Canada." There is a 1958 document that suggests there may have been a few more personnel allocated to SAR between 1956 and 1958, but a detailed count was not conducted before reductions took place. The RCAF used SAR personnel for air transport and communications flights, as well as other duties, throughout the 1950s; LAC, RG24-E-1-c, Vol. 18114, SAR – Policy, 976-2, Letter to CAS from AOC TC G/C Z. L. Leigh, 9 October 1959, "SAR Aircraft – 111KU Winnipeg, Utilization on Other than SAR Missions."
[457] DHH, DND, *Report of the Department of National Defence for the Fiscal Year 1954–55* (Ottawa: Edmond Cloutier, 1956). It appears that the report for 1955–56 is in the wrong cover.
[458] DHH, 181.004 (D26), RCAF Programme of Activities, 1955–56.
[459] Ibid.

fleets specifically for searching and deploying parachute-rescue personnel, but they had the same range and speed issues as the other, older, aircraft that they flew alongside.[460] Therefore, the sheer volume of aviation and maritime emergencies, the slow speed of available aircraft, and the limited range of the old aircraft and seaplanes remained serious challenges to prosecute lengthy missions in remote locations. That said, the newer airframes and more personnel on board to conduct the visual searches were improvements.

Despite the difficulties the RCAF had in maintaining operational effectiveness with decreasing numbers of units and resources available for SAR missions, Canada still had a comparatively effective SAR system in the international context. In fact, RCAF officers attending ICAO meetings in 1956 noted that the "Brazilians were so impressed by the RCAF manual [on SAR] that it patterned its SAR programme on the Canadian system. Since that time, RCAF officers have assisted in producing a search and rescue manual for the use of all ICAO member nations."[461] It is useful to keep in mind that the new requirement for SAR services to support both aeronautical and maritime emergencies was still in its infancy.

Marine emergencies were a large part of the increase of rescue activity, but after 1950, aviation rescue requirements had been on the rise as well. ICAO produced a report in 1953 that showed that air traffic worldwide had increased since 1947 by 148 per cent, with increasing numbers of civilian aircraft plying domestic aviation routes. The increase in air traffic was partly responsible for more aircraft hours flown on SAR, as the hours used for aviation rescue missions nearly doubled from just two years earlier.[462]

The number of hours flown is meaningless without context, and to-day's SAR system can provide us with important insight into the expansion of SAR throughout the 1950s. Recently available SAR numbers are 655

[460] Mowbray, "Lessons Forgotten?" 50.

[461] Ed., "ICAO and the RCAF," *The Roundel* 8, no. 9 (November 1956), 27.

[462] DHH, 79/631, RCAF Search and Rescue Operations 1947–1970, DIS Files 1–14, SAR Ops 1955, File 7, 8 September 1953, "Royal Canadian Air Force Release No. 8275"; and LAC, RG25-A-3-b, Vol. 8012, File Part 1, ICAO – Standards and Recommended Practices for SAR, File 72-ADU-38-40- Pt. 1, 1953, "ICAO Report on Development of Civil Air Transport."

missions and 2,499 hours flown by RCAF SAR aircraft in 2014, and the number of flying hours flown in 2014 is a rough and generally consistent expectation of yearly RCAF aircraft hours for SAR.[463]

In stark contrast to SAR activity today, SAR operations in 1956 had risen to 8,737 hours flown for 223 missions.[464] The difference in activity is that in 2014, each SAR operation averaged 3.8 hours of aircraft flight time; in 1956, each operation averaged 39.2 hours of flight time. Put another way, SAR missions have become ten times more efficient in how they are resolved with available resources. The lack of efficiency in the 1950's search procedures and the lack of accurate flight information from missing aircraft compounded the difficulties encountered by the rise in the number of missions. An inefficient use of resources could not be sustained indefinitely.

Throughout the mid-1950s, the hours remained around 8,000 hours flown per year with an annual cost to the RCAF of $6 million for SAR missions.[465] Even the well-known supporter of the SAR organization, G/C Leigh, before he retired, had had enough of the ever-increasing impact to other RCAF missions and complained to AFHQ about the ability of RCCs to task aircraft resources directly.[466] His concern was that the

---

[463] Canadian Armed Forces and Canadian Coast Guard, *Annual Report 2014*, 22; and email from Senior Staff Officer SAR for 1 Cdn Air Div, LCol Bryn Elliott, on 20 November 2015. The actual number of flying hours on SAR missions is higher as missions flown by CH-124 Sea Kings and CP-140 Aurora aircraft were not captured in the SAR reporting, but those flying hours typically do not exceed 200 hours in any given year, based on the author's experience at an RCC. The data consistency was determined by looking at the data available to Maj Gillian Parker, J3 SAR-2, at CJOC during a visit 23 September 2015.

[464] DHH, DND, *Report of the Department of National Defence for the Fiscal Year 1954–55* (Ottawa: Edmond Cloutier, 1956), 56. It appears that the report for 1955–56 is in the wrong cover.

[465] LAC, RG24-E-1-c, Vol. 18114, SAR – Policy, File 976-2, DoT and RCAF Meeting headed by A/V/M de Niverville, the Director of Air Services for the RCAF, and R. W Godwin, the Assistant Director General of Air Services, for DoT, 10 February 1959, "SAR Operations in Canada."

[466] LAC, RG24-E-1-c, Vol. 18112, SAR – Organization and Administration 1945–1954, 976-0 Vol. 7, Letter to CAS from AOC TC, G/C Leigh, 29 December 1953, "Operations Policy SAR – Emergency Operations."

RCCs did not require chain of command involvement to pull aircraft from other missions to SAR operations, much as had been the case prior to 1943. However, restricting aircraft from participating in searches at RCC request was politically sensitive and no changes were made. In 1956, RCAF aircraft utilization for SAR missions appeared limitless, as the SAR mandate doubled in hours flown from 1950 to 1956, and with no end to the increase in sight.

Sympathy for the RCAF, however, should be tempered by the fact that very little work appears to have been conducted to limit the size of search areas that RCAF aircraft had to cover for survivors. The RCAF had a few tools it could have employed to limit search activity. Namely, the RCAF could have purchased modern aircraft to search farther and faster; it could have used historical data to limit the size of search areas, or it could have hired maritime experts to coordinate focused searches over water. None of these options was used.

The first option was the potential to purchase new aircraft to search large areas more efficiently. However, it has clearly been outlined that the RCAF had no interest in expensive resources for a mandate it did not wish to retain. The RCAF had no plans in 1956 to replace the ageing Dakota, Canso, or Lancaster aircraft used for SAR operations, so the option of purchasing more aircraft would not be pursued until the late 1950s.[467]

Another of the possible methods to control the usage of resources was the size of search areas for aircraft lost over land areas. One may recall that the 1944 procedure had been to assign a 100 nautical mile by 100 nautical mile square search area to aircraft until the search object was found. In 1948, the guiding document on SAR had refined the procedure based on 8 per cent of the distance flown since the last known position of the missing aircraft, but the division of the search area was "divided into blocks of 300 square miles."[468] The 1948 procedure produced an overall smaller area than the 1944 procedure, but not by much. In 1956, the area had been further refined to "possibility areas" extending as far as 20 nautical miles off the

---

[467] DHH, 181.004 (D27), "RCAF Programme of Activities, 1956–1957" (although it actually covers 1954–55).

[468] DHH, 89/288, CAP 342, *RCAF Flying Control and Search and Rescue Orders*, 1948, paras 160 and 163.

planned flight route for the missing aircraft, but with increases of 10 per cent of the off-track distance added to each additional turning point, that still left the search areas very large for longer planned flights of missing aircraft.[469]

The 1956 changes to search area limited the size for smaller searches, but for missing aircraft with long flight paths and many turning points, the areas were still massive. Practically, the downsizing of the search areas through procedural changes proved to be marginal. However, it was not just incumbent on the RCAF to determine search areas. Flight planning and aviation reporting policy were the responsibility of the DoT, so it appears that DoT could have done considerably more to assist the RCAF by forcing pilots to improve reporting procedures or in requiring pilots to provide more accurate flight information before departure. Additionally, DoT could have managed rescue expectations through pilot licensing programmes; however, such a programme does not appear to have been used.

The evolution of search procedures was on the right path, but the only known research to improve SAR procedures in this era, a 1949 report, focused only on the probability of detection of search objects by aircrews.[470] The report did nothing to limit the resource requirements for the RCAF, but it made searches more effective. Finding crashes was indeed a challenge, and the RCAF occasionally passed on requests for policy changes to DoT to make it easier for RCAF search operations, such as requesting that specific bright colours be used in the paint scheme of "all light aircraft operating in bush country."[471] The suggestions that were made in the 1949 report were important, but it would not be until 1974, when detailed research reports were produced, that statistics were used to refine search areas to an area based on sound historical experience.[472]

The procedures developed strongly suggest that changes to search

---

[469] DHH, 81/224, CAP 342, *Orders for Aircraft Control and Services for the RCAF*, April 1956.

[470] Mowbray, "Lessons Forgotten?" 39.

[471] LAC RG24-E-1-c, Vol. 18114, Search and Rescue – Policy, 976-1 Vol. 5 SAR Policy, letter to CAS from AOC TC, G/C J. G. Stevenson, 7 July 1955, "Colouring of Helicopters – Search and Rescue Operations."

[472] Mowbray, "Lessons Forgotten?" 98.

procedures in 1948 and 1956 were the professional opinion of RCC personnel, without much statistical support that could have further refined procedures. Later search procedures were based upon the historical odds of aircraft crashes residing in the given search area, but this technique is not present in any of this era's documentation. Given the large increase in flying hours that was seen in the 1950s, it is very surprising that operational research was not conducted earlier to limit the large search areas, based on the available data provided by found crash locations.

Similarly, there exists no known research to make marine searches in the 1950s more effective. The RCN had not increased its assistance to the RCAF SAR system, and in fact, it sold the six ageing RCAF high-speed rescue vessels in 1956–57, declaring them surplus to naval requirements.[473] The lack of apparent effort in the maritime-rescue domain is perhaps surprising, as 38 per cent of the SAR workload in 1955 (almost triple the number of aircraft crashes prosecuted by RCCs) was for maritime SAR operations.[474] The RCAF's purchase of new helicopters, notably the Piasecki H21A, was completed in 1955, and this more capable helicopter had to shoulder much of the load for the increased maritime work.[475] Maritime-rescue activity provided by RCAF aircraft and helicopters was a significant source of hours flown.

The number of aircraft hours flown on marine SAR was very likely a result of RCC inexperience in the maritime domain. As an Air Force agency, the RCC had little knowledge of the sea with which to limit the search areas for missing vessels. The RCC lacked expertise in maritime searches throughout the 1950s, and that contrasts starkly with the RCAF's earlier experience in maritime rescue. Throughout the Second World War, integration with the RCN staff accounted for effective search procedures for enemy submarines and for RCAF searches. RCN expertise was immediately available in the control headquarters for advice on search matters, but the RCCs no longer maintained a daily interaction with RCN personnel with

[473] DHH 74/438, "Former RCAF Air/Sea Rescue Launches."
[474] DHH 79/631, RCAF SAR Operations 1947–1970, DIS Files 1–14, SAR Ops 1955, File 9, 15 February 1956, "RCAF Press Release No. 8634."
[475] DHH, 181.004 (D28), "RCAF Programme of Activities, 1957–1960" (although it actually covers 1955–56), 16.

which to maintain that level of effective planning.[476] It was disappointing that the RCAF failed to resolve maritime-search planning matters earlier.

The importance of maritime knowledge in search planning over water cannot be overstressed because of complicated movements of search objects in water based on tides and the amount of freeboard of an object drifting in the water due to wind.[477] Without detailed knowledge of the maritime environment, a search coordinator has to bound the area in the widest possible manner, potentially leading to very large search areas.[478] An obvious way of providing expertise in marine SAR was to employ maritime experts in the RCCs. However, evidence suggests that maritime personnel in RCCs were not hired until 1959, leaving the RCCs with large search areas in the maritime domain until that time.[479]

The large search areas for both aviation- and maritime-search missions led to an ever-increasing workload for the SAR service, and there were repercussions. The overall increase in activity led to a surprising reversal of RCAF policy towards American SAR forces in Newfoundland by 1955. No longer was it discouraged to utilize American resources; in fact, the public in Atlantic Canada was informed that the Halifax RCC relied on American SAR forces as *primary resources* for SAR operations in Canada.[480] A reliance on American resources meant, shockingly, that Americans were often the first responders on routine rescue missions in the new Province of Newfoundland rather than Canadian rescue resources. An RCC and permanent aircraft resources had been assigned to Torbay, Newfoundland, in 1954, but these resources were officially supplemented by American

---

[476] Douglas, *Official History of the Royal Canadian Air Force*, 548.

[477] National Defence and Fisheries and Oceans Canada, *CAMSAR II*, Appendix C.

[478] Canada now uses a computer program called Canadian Search and Rescue Planning to model the search area based on actual measurements of wind and water currents, reducing what is otherwise complicated manual calculations to limit search areas.

[479] LAC, RG24-E-1-c, Vol. 18114, SAR Operations – Marine and Aircraft Cases, File 976-4, Letter to W/C Showler from DoT, 13 July 1960, "Report from Marine Coordinators." Mowbray, ("Lessons Forgotten?" 30) suggests that maritime coordinators may have been employed in at least one RCC as early as 1954, but his statement comes from another secondary source and is not corroborated by primary sources, nor JRCC Halifax history.

[480] DHH 73/1194, *SAR in Atlantic Area*, April 1955, 2.

SAR facilities in the Newfoundland cities of Stephenville, Harmon, and Argentia as well as Goose Bay in Labrador.[481] The RCAF proved willing to use any available resources to offset the huge increase in SAR demand, even at the risk to sovereignty as viewed by the public and the government.

A factor that perhaps limited the sovereignty concerns for the RCAF was the inclusion of SAR in North Atlantic Treaty Organization (NATO) policy. It is difficult to outline how much impact NATO had on SAR policy in Canada because the documents remain classified, but there were meetings throughout the 1950s for coordination specifically between Canada, the UK, and the US.[482] The regular interaction with NATO strongly suggests that the RCAF had to expect a continued role in at least aviation SAR to meet American expectations, if not those of any NATO country flying aircraft in Canada. NATO SAR policy required nations to use existing resources to help out Allied aircraft in the vicinity, so it must not have been a large stretch for American SAR forces to assist with Canadian civilian-rescue requirements, as American SAR forces were already poised to effect a rescue of any American, NATO, or RCAF military aircraft in the vicinity that needed assistance.[483]

Military jet aircraft were a particular concern in this time period because crashes occurred often as a result of Canadian pilots transitioning to a very advanced single-seat fighter. In Chatham, New Brunswick, the need to rescue F-86 jet aircrew from nearby crashes had been assessed as critically necessary, and the need was met by a helicopter detachment of

---

[481] Ibid.; Smith, *Seek and Save*, 48; and DHH, 79/631 RCAF SASR Operations 1947–1970, DIS Files 1–14, SAR Ops 1954, File 8, 28 July 1954, "RCAF Press Release No. 8395."

[482] LAC, RG24-E-1-c, Vol. 32687 contains UK, US, and Canada military discussions of SAR that are classified. Vols. 41591 and 32651 contain NATO SAR documents, all classified. Vol. 18118 contains Canadian–American information on SAR for the Distant Early Warning Line, again, classified.

[483] LAC, RG24-E-1-c, Vol. 18113, SAR – Policy, File 976-0, Vol. 8, Minutes prepared by G/C N. S. Anderson, 20 September 1954, "Minutes of a Meeting between RCN/RCAF Personnel of Maritime Headquarters." This is the only document found that contained unclassified details about Canadian SAR policy integration with NATO.

103 Rescue Unit from Greenwood.[484] It was within the capabilities of the unit to meet both the SAR mandate and the rescue needs of Chatham, but it meant considerable extra work for busy SAR personnel. Chatham suggested that helicopters based permanently at fighter jet stations were a necessity to reduce the workload for rescue units, but this concept would not be revisited until 1958. Despite the number of crashes, it appeared that aircrew were rescued in a timely enough manner.

Another source of potential aid was the RCN's Air Section. Unfortunately, it is not clear how often RCN aircraft were used to support SAR missions. The documentation rarely mentions the service, so it can perhaps be assumed that the RCN did not provide assistance often, but that is conjecture. There is one clear case, however, where the Navy's air section came to the rescue in very dramatic circumstances.

A Liberian freighter, *Kismet II*, lost power on 25 November 1955 and was pushed up against a cliff of Cape Breton, Nova Scotia.[485] The 21 people on board were in dire straits, as the wind and waves were breaking up the ship against the cliff. As the RCAF did not have a helicopter available at that time, the RCC in Halifax requested that the RCN send a helicopter to rescue the personnel from the distressed vessel. The account of the rescue that occurred on 26 November is frightening, as the winds were howling and the helicopter needed to manoeuvre very close to the cliff in order to load the passengers onto their helicopter. In pilot Lieutenant Commander J. H. Beeman's own words, the "turbulence would increase to such an extent that the helicopter was almost uncontrollable, alternately gaining and losing five hundred feet, with the airspeed fluctuating between ten and sixty knots."[486] Flying in these conditions was exceptionally dangerous and exhausting. Beeman and fellow pilot Lieutenant Commander F. R. Fink alternated flights to the vessel to prevent both of them from becoming exhausted, and they safely extracted all 21 souls on board the freighter, earning them both George Medals for acts of great bravery. The Navy's

---

[484] LAC, RG24-E-1-c, Vol. 18113, SAR – Policy, File 976-0, Vol. 8, letter to CAS from AOC ADC, signed by A/C C. L. Annis, 7 June 1954.

[485] DHH 79/631, RCAF Search and Rescue Operation 1947–1970, DIS Files 1–14, SAR Ops 1955, File 9, 16 December 1955, "The Rescue of the Crew of Kismet II."

[486] Ibid.

air section may not have conducted many rescues, but this one was highly successful despite outrageously treacherous conditions.

The RCAF had recruited assistance from the Canadian Army as well. On the East Coast, this assistance is well documented in the form of ground search teams that were solely provided by the Canadian Army. Specifically, personnel from various East Coast Army units would assist the RCAF with ground search teams when they requested extra help.[487] It is not clear if the Army assisted as much or as often in the rest of Canada, but standing guidance from the Chief of the General Staff stated that the Army needed to provide this form of ground-search-team assistance.[488] Military interoperability allowed the SAR service to obtain assistance for distress situations from other military services quickly and effectively. Such help was required to reduce the strain caused by tragic fatalities, such as the loss of two pilots to the crash of a No.121 Communications and Rescue Flight Canso operating near Vancouver in July 1955.[489] To meet rising operations and expectations, the RCAF needed all the assistance they could obtain.

The SAR system was operating full-out, and this fact was very evident in the response to the TCA flight 810 distress on 9 December 1956, one of the worst airline crashes in the world at that time.[490] The flight had departed Vancouver for Calgary at 6:10 pm Pacific Standard Time, and one hour later, it had turned around with one engine out, on its way back to Vancouver. The weather had been awful, and combined with the onboard emergency, the pilots lost track of their position and thundered into Mount Slesse, near Chilliwack, British Columbia. Until the crash location was determined months later, RCC Vancouver and the RCAF led an intense and ultimately fruitless air search for the aircraft with 62 souls on board.

---

[487] DHH, 323.009 (D240), Eastern Command, Operations, SAR, May 1955 to January 1958, various memos on air/land search parties.

[488] DHH, 112-32M2 (D340), Report of Interdepartmental Committee on Air Sea Rescue, Policy, letter to CA formations from CGS, LGen Foulkes, 5 July 1949, "Search and Rescue – Army Participation."

[489] Larry Milberry, *Air Transport in Canada, Volume 2* (Toronto: CANAV Books, 1997), 925.

[490] Betty O'Keefe and Ian Macdonald, *Disaster on Mount Slesse: The Story of Western Canada's Worst Air Crash* (Halfmoon Bay, BC: Caitlin Press, 2006), 15.

The initial aircraft sent to search that night were three aircraft from the composite flight in Vancouver and an Air Force Lancaster aircraft from Comox, British Columbia. Even with very little notice, RCAF aircraft outside of the SAR organization were immediately available to assist in emergencies.[491] That night, S/L George Sheahan, the CO of No. 121 composite flight, took charge of search efforts and organized a staggering 50 aircraft that would start searching the following morning; 14 of them were provided by the RCAF.[492] As it was normal to launch just a few aircraft for any given emergency, the quick and plentiful RCAF response shows just how dedicated the military aircrews were when an emergency arose.

The searching took place with heightened urgency for possible survivors who could be overcome by the terrible weather conditions in the days to come. As related in *Disaster on Mount Slesse*, the effort to find and save any survivors was intense:

> On December, 11, 1956, the second full day of the most extensive air search in Canadian history, sixty planes took to the air. ...
>
> The armada followed a prescribed search pattern mapped out by headquarters and included twenty RCAF planes from Sea Island [Vancouver], three Lancasters from Comox, three RCMP craft, two TCA DC-3s, and one DC-3 from Canadian Pacific Airlines. There were also three helicopters from the Department of Transport and more than twenty-five light aircraft from assorted companies and flying clubs. ...
>
> There was next to no visibility, and cloud-shrouded peaks posed a hazard for everyone.[493]

The air search went on for six days, and even the last day of searching

---

[491] Ibid., 57.
[492] Ibid., 58 and 64.
[493] Ibid., 68 and 69.

used 18 military aircraft.[494] The efforts described above fully demonstrate the deep commitment that RCAF personnel made to respond to emergencies and that the SAR organization was only the beginning of the commitment the RCAF was willing to make when tragedy struck. Although civilians participated in the search, they were limited by rules and regulations designed to keep aviators safe. Military aircrew, however, could accept considerably more risk and took on the more dangerous search areas in the mountains.

In summary, the increase of SAR missions and the lack of effective search-area policy resulted in a significant, and unwelcome, increase in the number of aircraft hours for SAR activity provided by the RCAF. The RCAF was attempting to find help from any quarter, even though they were not taking steps to help themselves by containing searches. The Air Force was forced to rob aircraft from other mission requirements to assist in the SAR mandate.[495] In fact, between 1956 and 1958, the use of other RCAF aircraft for SAR missions was so prevalent that aircraft assigned to primary SAR duties accounted for only half of the hours flown on SAR missions.[496] It is not clear how much of an impact SAR missions by non-SAR Air Force aircraft were having on overall RCAF operations, but the growth of aircraft SAR requirements had to be contained. Something had to change.

INCONSISTENCY IN 1958

The RCAF explored options for change in 1958 to reduce the workload, and one positive change was the standardization of SAR operations across the country. The most important of the standards changes was the aircraft launch times. The time required to launch SAR aircraft had varied from air station to air station across the country, from stations able to launch on 30-minutes notice at all times, to a station that had routinely

---

[494] Ibid., 80.

[495] LAC, RG24-E-1-c, Vol. 18114, SAR – Policy, 976-2, Letter to CAS from AOC TC G/C Z. L. Leigh, 9 October 1959, "SAR Aircraft – 111KU Winnipeg, Utilization on Other than SAR Missions."

[496] LAC, RG24-E-1-c, Vol. 18114, 10 February 1959, "DoT – RCAF Meeting on SAR Operations in Canada."

required two hours to become airborne.[497] The 1958 version of the CAP 342 document aimed to resolve the inconsistency, and it called for SAR aircraft "to be maintained on a thirty-minute standby basis during normal working hours and are to be on a one-hour standby basis during off-duty hours and holidays."[498] This new standard, however, raised significant concerns from commanders across the country.

In Winnipeg, Manitoba, the concern was that 111 Communications and Rescue Flight did not have the personnel to meet a one-hour launch after normal working hours; indeed, the flight suggested either an increase in personnel establishment or a reduction from a one-hour launch, after hours, to a two-hour launch.[499] In Torbay, Newfoundland, the rescue aircraft of 107 Rescue Unit maintained a continuous 30-minute standby posture, but commanders were concerned about the implications of the SAR launch times while they were tasked with other non-SAR commitments that occasionally left the unit without a SAR capability.[500] In Vancouver, British Columbia, there was deep concern that slower aircraft launch times for 121 Communications and Rescue Flight did "not meet the requirement" for marine rescue due to approximately "50,000 pleasure craft in the area."[501] The concerns were a wide-ranging mix that required AFHQ-directed operational research to determine a common solution to the various problems.[502]

---

[497] This statement is based on comments within multiple 1958 reports from RCCs across the country that discussed the normality of aircraft launch times varying from 30 minutes to two hours.

[498] LAC, RG24-E-1-c, Vol. 18114, SAR – Policy, File 976-1 Vol. 5, Memorandum to COps from A/DTRO W/C J. G. Showler, 28 May 1958, "SAR – Standby Policy."

[499] LAC, RG24-E-1-c, Vol. 18114, SAR – Policy, File 976-1 Vol. 5, Letter to AOC TC from A/Group Cdr, W/C J. L. Berven, 1 April 1958, "SAR – Standby Basis."

[500] LAC, RG24-E-1-c, Vol. 18114, SAR – Policy, File 976-1 Vol. 5, Letter to CAS from A/AOC MAC, G/C J. H. Roberts, 14 July 1958, "SAR – Standby Commitment."

[501] LAC, RG24-E-1-c, Vol. 18114, SAR – Policy, File 976-1 Vol. 5, Letter to CAS from 5 AD Vancouver, W/C F. W. Hillock, 11 June 1958, "SAR – Standby Commitment."

[502] Trenton did not have the same manning issues, as they provided SAR training for all units, meaning there were extra personnel who could assist with rescue standby when not engaged in training duties.

AFHQ followed up with an in-depth report on how many personnel were actually needed to perform the SAR mandate with the new launch times. It was discovered that the composite flights and rescue units across the country were badly undermanned, and to standardize launch times, AFHQ would need to establish 100 new positions for SAR or add another hour to the launch time regulation to match the existing personnel establishment.[503] The units had been launching aircraft as quickly as possible but at unsustainable demands of the aircrew.[504] In line with the existing 1950 policy to minimize resources for SAR, CAS chose to reduce the SAR launch times, after hours and on holidays, to two hours.[505] The CAS decision eliminated the need to expand the SAR organization and reduced the workload at some of the stations.

The rationale used by CAS for limiting the launch times of SAR aircraft, thereby avoiding personnel increases, deserves to be quoted at length for its relevance to RCAF policy.

> It will be noted that the protection of Air Traffic is the only RCAF SAR responsibility calling for the establishment and maintenance of primary facilities at Rescue Units. It is on the basis of the air requirement that unit equipment is scaled and personnel establishments determined. The responsibility with respect to Marine Cases is primarily one of coordination. It follows from the considerations noted above that the state of readiness maintained at Rescue Units is dictated by the air situation. The protection afforded to Marine Craft is, in a sense, a by-product of this arrangement.[506]

---

[503] LAC, RG24-E-1-c, Vol. 18114, 28 May 1958, "SAR – Standby Policy."

[504] LAC, RG24-E-1-c, Vol. 18114, 1 April 1958, "SAR – Standby Basis."

[505] LAC, RG24-E-1-c, Vol. 18114, SAR – Policy, File 976-1 Vol. 5, Letter to MAC, TC, TAC, and ADC from CAS, signed by W/C J. G. Showler, 11 June 1958, "SAR – Standby Commitment."

[506] LAC, RG24-E-1-c, Vol. 18114, SAR – Policy, File 976-2, Letter to 5 AD from CAS, signed by W/C J. G. Showler, 24 June 1958, "SAR – Standby Commitment."

The CAS policy quoted above is critical to any discussion on 1950s rescue because it shows that the stresses created by ever-increasing aircraft hours flown on SAR operations in the 1950s had finally resulted in limits set by AFHQ on SAR response capabilities. The quote also makes it clear that a division between aviation and maritime SAR had developed. The RCAF had assumed full responsibility for aviation rescue, but maritime rescue was still not a priority and could not become so while the RCAF sought to limit growth in the SAR organization.

One explanation for a division between air and marine SAR is that maritime SAR in the RCAF had expanded beyond the intended limits set by Cabinet, certainly well beyond the zero funding provided by government for the additional mandate. Mission creep, used to describe a phenomenon where military forces allow actual resources and effort to exceed the original mission intent, had developed within the maritime SAR mandate of the RCAF.[507] In the 1950s, mission creep was demonstrated by the fact that hundreds of hours were used by RCAF helicopter and aircraft for marine missions, when the 1950 government intent had been for the RCAF to simply coordinate nearby vessels to respond.[508] From a practitioner's perspective, mission creep was completely understandable, as there was a job to be done that was saving many lives. From an HQ perspective, the SAR mandate was one of many commitments that had to be balanced. AFHQ remained adamant that the RCAF was not to be turned into a coast guard, so if SAR was to be kept from using limited resources outside the SAR service, there had to be a reduction in the hours flown by RCAF aircraft on maritime-rescue missions. A line in the water, so to speak, was drawn. The RCAF would not allow the maritime mandate to expand further within its organization despite the constant yearly increase in the number of maritime emergencies.

The overall sorry state of maritime rescue had received high-level attention by late 1955. The Deputy Minister of Transport, J. R. Baldwin, reported on the state of maritime rescue in British Columbia. His conclusions

---

[507] A useful definition of mission creep can be found on the Wikipedia website; "Mission Creep," https://en.wikipedia.org/wiki/Mission_creep (accessed 25 April 2018).

[508] DHH 79/631, RCAF SAR Operations 1947–1970, DIS Files 1–14, SAR Ops 1955, File 9, 15 February 1956, "RCAF Press Release No. 8634."

were that there was a need for an improved helicopter service, RCN vessels took too long to set sail, RCMP and Fisheries vessels were too small and slow, and DoT ships were too slow and otherwise engaged.[509] It is fair to say that these conditions were mirrored on the East Coast and the Great Lakes, leaving maritime rescue as a growing national problem. However, there is no indication that DoT or any other government agency responded to the problem or offered greater assistance to the RCAF for SAR improvements. Once again, the RCAF was left to fund and fly rescue missions without help.

One aspect of the CAS's policy, quoted earlier on the amount of time needed to launch aircraft for SAR emergencies, needs clarification. RCCs launched aircraft when they had reason to believe that a distress existed.[510] For many maritime distresses, a radio call would be received that would make it immediately clear that rescue was required. In the case of aircraft, however, the lack of communication was usually the first indication of distress. Once an aircraft was overdue at its intended destination, the RCC could start the aircraft launching process while concurrently obtaining all the information needed to assign a search area, meaning a 30-minute launch window was often not needed to still respond in a timely manner for aviation emergencies. Therefore, the change from a 30-minute launch time to a two-hour launch time had fewer repercussions on aviation rescues as might appear. Without question, however, service to maritime rescue was reduced on both coasts.

Along with standardized launch times, the location of rescue resources had to be considered. As helicopters had proven immensely useful in rescue work, a study was conducted in 1958 to determine where these limited resources should be stationed. The study concluded that helicopters were required for rescue work from the stations in Greenwood,

---

[509] Charles D. Maginley, *The Canadian Coast Guard 1962–2002* (St. Catherines: Vanwell Publishing Ltd., 2003), 29.

[510] DHH, 81/224, CAP 342, *Orders for Aircraft Control and Services for the RCAF*, April 1956, 7 and 17. This document outlines the procedures that the RCC took between investigation, launching aircraft, and assigning searches. This document is the source for the entire following paragraph.

Trenton, Winnipeg, and Vancouver.[511] However, the study was focused only on providing SAR resources for the domestic rescues and did not take into account the need to rescue aircrew from crashed RCAF jet aircraft, which was also part of the SAR mandate. There were fighter operations in provinces without SAR helicopters, which meant that crashes could predictably occur at long distances from existing SAR stations and result in an avoidable loss of life.

A separate study was completed, concurrently, to determine the rescue needs of the fighter aircraft community. The study concluded that 35 new helicopters should be purchased to form a base-rescue capability at locations where the RCAF flew jet aircraft.[512] The intriguing nature of this proposal is that these helicopters were separated from the SAR system, recommended as a stand-alone capability at each station.[513] This sounds suspiciously like a return to 1939, when stations were responsible for their own rescue requirements. However, one can see the logic. In 1958, there was a rescue system in place in Canada, unlike 1939, and the civilian-rescue requirements were met through the SAR system provided by the RCAF. Therefore, the RCAF needed to ensure that military aircrew received adequate rescue coverage, and if that meant a separation in rescue systems, then organization costs would not increase because existing station processes could control the base-rescue services.[514]

Where the logic fails is in the personnel establishment. It is not known how many personnel would have been required to man 35 helicopters, but it was fact that 947 personnel were manning 44 SAR aircraft across the

[511] LAC, RG24-E-1-c, Vol. 18128, File No. 978-7-3, SAR – Crash Rescue Assistance by Others, SAR – Techniques and Procedures – Crash Rescue – Helicopters, Memorandum to VCAS from COps, A/C M. Lipton, 11 August 1958, "SAR Helicopters – Location."
[512] LAC, RG24-E-1-c, Vol. 18128, File No. 978-7-3, SAR – Crash Rescue Assistance by Others, SAR – Techniques and Procedures – Crash Rescue – Helicopters, 7 May 1958, "Report for Base Rescue – Ambulance Helicopters."
[513] LAC, RG24-E-1-c, Vol. 18128, File No. 978-7-3, SAR – Crash Rescue Assistance by Others, SAR – Techniques and Procedures – Crash Rescue – Helicopters, 18 June 1958, "Extract from the Minutes of the 22/58 Air Council Meeting."
[514] Ibid.

country.[515] One can reasonably conclude that 35 new helicopters would require more than the 100 personnel identified to establish a nationwide 30-minute posture that, arguably, could have been augmented to achieve an acceptable rescue service for jet aircrew. Rather than augmenting the civilian SAR system any further, the Air Force seemed intent on the separation of military and domestic-rescue systems.

This separation was certainly not planned with any ill will; it was a simple way to solve a growing problem. The base-flight concept actually started in 1954, with Cold Lake acquiring a Beechcraft Expeditor for a communications link with Edmonton, both locations in Alberta.[516] It appears that the base-flight concept spread, and a rescue role was added circa 1957 if a helicopter was based at the station.[517] The concept solved a growing problem for RCAF fighter operations.

It should be noted that the RCAF did not purchase the 35 helicopters in the proposed time frame of 1959–1961. Single or multiple helicopters, when available at the applicable fighter station, would be used to function as a rescue flight in the late 1950s and throughout the 1960s. It was not until the Iroquois helicopter was brought into service in 1968 that the base-rescue role was formalized with one aircraft type to set a common standard.[518] Just for the curious, there are three base-rescue units remaining today in Goose Bay, Labrador; Bagotville, Quebec; and Cold Lake, Alberta.[519] The importance of the base-rescue helicopters was that the

---

[515] LAC, RG24-E-1-c, Vol. 18114, 10 February 1959, "DoT – RCAF Meeting on SAR Operations in Canada."

[516] Royal Canadian Air Force, "Wings and Squadrons," *417 Combat Support*, http://www.rcaf-arc.forces.gc.ca/en/4-wing/417-squadron.page (accessed 25 April 2018).

[517] LAC, RG24-E-1-c, Vol. 18128, File No. 978-7-3, SAR – Crash Rescue Assistance by Others, SAR – Techniques and Procedures – Crash Rescue – Helicopters, 18 June 1958, "Air Council Minutes."

[518] National Air Force Museum of Canada, "Iroquois," *http://airforcemuseum.ca/engl/?page_id=577* (accessed 25 April 2018).

[519] Royal Canadian Air Force, "Wings and Squadrons," *444 Combat Support Squadron*, and *417 Combat Support Squadron*, http://www.rcaf-arc.forces.gc.ca/en/4-wing/417-squadron.page http://www.rcaf-arc.forces.gc.ca/en/5-wing/444-squadron.page (accessed 25 April 2018). 439 Squadron in Bagotville has the same mission, but that fact is not clear on the website.

RCAF proceeded with a separation between military- and domestic-rescue systems. One can only assume that this project was pursued so that there were RCAF rescue helicopters that could not be hijacked by civilian domestic-rescue needs.

Both the discussion surrounding base-rescue helicopters and the decision to allow slower aircraft launch times displays the conundrum of rescue for the RCAF. Since the beginning of the Second World War, the lack of a domestic-rescue system in Canada meant that the RCAF was left with providing for its own needs as well as those of the civilian aviation and maritime communities. The maritime-rescue effort, however, was clearly being sidelined by AFHQ, and help was needed to ensure that Canadians at sea received adequate rescue support. The 1950s proved deeply challenging for the SAR organization within the RCAF.

SUMMARY FOR A DIFFICULT DECADE

The dramatic increase of SAR activity in the 1950s was hard. There was RCN and Canadian Army assistance in many SAR missions that alleviated some strain, but the vast majority of the increase needed to be managed by the Air Force. Recall that today there are 66 Canadian Coast Guard stations responding to four times the number of SAR missions than the RCAF in 2014, and imagine the difficulties of the 1950s when none of that existed. The RCAF had to shoulder a massive and growing burden.

The Americans also helped offset some of the strain from the RCAF. Sovereignty, however, was reduced by the RCAF's reliance on American SAR forces in Newfoundland and Labrador. As demonstrated, the RCAF had to request assistance from other military services in Canada as well as the Americans, to ensure that rising rescue expectations were met. The lack of adequate marine craft to assist with rescues at sea and the lack of maritime expertise in the RCCs were likely factors at the root of the maritime problems encountered in the 1950s. A tight relationship between Canadian and American SAR forces certainly helped.

International pressure on the SAR organization had eased by this time, as ICAO and IMCO were well established and the deficiencies within the Canadian SAR framework were documented and known by international partners. NATO, however, can be assumed to be a driving force that would eventually lead to SAR acceptance by the RCAF. Military involvement in domestic SAR was becoming an international expectation, even if the military aspects cannot be quantified due to the continued classification of key documents.

Cost factors were an implicit burden in the reduction of nine rescue locations down to five, which appeared to be part of a longer-term plan by the RCAF to revert the SAR organization back to the size it had claimed it could sustain during the initial discussion in 1946. However, the small number of rescue resources and the fact that lives were on the line meant that the RCAF had to employ aircraft from other stations and other roles in order to meet the daily life-and-death challenges across the nation. While newer helicopters helped meet rising challenges in the 1950s, the number of helicopters was still insufficient to the stated requirement by the jet fighter community. The burden increased to the point that in 1958, the AFHQ lowered standards for the time required to launch aircraft in order to prevent further growth of the SAR organization. While there are no examples of SAR mission requirements going unmet, the daily struggle of the SAR organization was real.

As depicted in Table 7, the mid-1950s saw an overall backward progress for the SAR service. The aircraft used for SAR were still the leftovers from the Second World War, and they were proving inadequate for the requirements as the number of locations dropped from nine to five. Whether the problems with the aircraft were range, maintenance, or slow speed, together those factors transferred much rescue responsibility to other, non-SAR, aircraft types within the Air Force. The next chapter will demonstrate how the RCAF reacted to the growing crisis, who rectified the resource problems, and why the RCAF came to accept a permanent leadership role with the Canadian national SAR organization.

Characteristic	Aviation	Maritime
National Standards	**Aviation rescues.** Required by ICAO, ordered by the government, and maintained by the RCAF	**Maritime rescues.** Required by IMCO, ordered by the government, and coordinated by the RCAF
Available Resources	**Aircraft.** The RCAF aircrew had reduced to five locations across the country, despite the increasing number of missions	**Vessels.** No RCAF vessels, four-hour notice-to-move assistance from the RCN, and helicopters that were limited in range
Formalized Policy	**Military rescues.** Military aircraft crashes were delinked from the RCC response, although the RCCs were kept informed of military missions	**Civilian rescues.** The RCAF was mandated to investigate and task resources, but there was no organization formally tasked to respond to emergencies

Table 7. The RCAF's SAR System in 1958

Chapter 8: A Developing Partnership

As no organization was clearly accepting responsibility for maritime rescue, there was considerable risk to the successful prosecution of maritime emergencies. Air force personnel could investigate the maritime incident improperly due to a lack of specialized knowledge, there could be a lack of effective vessels available for searches, or the rescue effort could be poorly communicated among the various agencies involved. At some point, a SAR mission would occur that would highlight the problems with maritime rescue in contrast with the well-publicized Air Force leadership of aviation rescue. Improvement was desperately needed.

After the election of a Progressive Conservative Government in 1957 that campaigned on a promise of a Canadian coast guard, among many other promises, it appeared that winds of change were blowing and a resolution to maritime rescue was finally possible. The RCAF, in keeping with the 1950 policy "to seek a method of being relieved of this non-operational commitment," attempted to hand the SAR mandate over to DoT in 1959 as part of the discussion on the new organization for marine-rescue services.[520] It should not come as a surprise by now that DoT refused to take on all aspects of SAR; although, it is apparent that a major shift had occurred by the government towards SAR policy and changes came rapidly.

CHANGE BEGINS IN 1959

Publicly, the government was still dragging its feet well into 1959 over maritime rescue, even though the Conservatives had been advocates

---

[520] DHH, 96/24, Air Force Headquarters fonds, Box 9, RCAF Plan G, 1950, 3.

of a coast guard when in opposition.[521] On 1 April 1959, the Minister of Transport, George Hees, explained that no action had been taken to date, as "a fleet of special vessels solely for Search and Rescue would require a very expensive organization."[522] Privately, however, discussions had already taken place.

It is unclear whether the government had already internally committed to a coast guard or if options were requested from the organizations involved, but the RCAF clearly knew that a coast guard was finally on the table as a real possibility, and it took immediate action. Air Commodore Maurice Lipton, the Chief of RCAF Operations, called an informal meeting with DoT in February 1959 to discuss the "possible passing of this [SAR] role to the DoT from the RCAF."[523] The RCAF wanted to know if "there was some part of the search and rescue operation which could be taken over by the Department of Transport, and to determine what would be involved if the [DoT] were called upon to take over the whole search and rescue responsibility."[524] The meeting was the culmination of Air Force strategy to be rid of the role, which had taken on a new level of meaning with the massive expansion of SAR activity in the years since RCAF Plan G's inception in 1950.

During the meeting, DoT argued that it would take several years to expand its organization enough to take on SAR responsibility and that 80 per cent of all searches in 1958 were conducted for lost civilian aircraft, a role that the RCAF performed quite well.[525] The RCAF contingent, led by A/V/M Albert de Niverville, countered that they could provide a nucleus of trained personnel and that civilian aircraft searches would be less frequent and more successful if DoT would strictly enforce existing

---

[521] Maginley, *Canadian Coast Guard*, 29.

[522] Ibid., 30.

[523] LAC, RG24-E-1-c, Vol. 18114, SAR – Policy, File 976-1 Vol. 5, SAR Policy, DoT and RCAF Meeting headed by A/V/M de Niverville, the Director of Air Services for the RCAF, and R. W Godwin, the Assistant Director General of Air Services, for DoT, 10 February 1959, "SAR Operations in Canada."

[524] LAC, RG24-E-1-c, Vol. 18114, 10 February 1959, "DoT – RCAF Meeting on SAR Operations in Canada."

[525] Ibid.

air regulations "to avoid poorly equipped small civil aircraft taking off on flights beyond the capability of the aircraft, and in a good many cases, beyond the capability of the pilots."[526] The DoT representatives, led by J. R. K. Main, Director of Civil Aviation, "did not feel that the take-over of this responsibility could be justified as the RCAF already have an organization set up for search and rescue purposes, and have personnel highly skilled in the special techniques required to carry out this function, and have well established bases at strategic locations throughout Canada."[527] The RCAF officers did not even bother to point out that DoT was legally responsible for civil-aviation matters in Canada.

The argument from DoT must have been very frustrating for the Air Force, as civil aviation was unquestionably a DoT responsibility and the crux of DoT's argument seemed to be that the Air Force performed SAR very well, so they should retain aviation rescue no matter that the DoT was the ultimate responsibility for civil aviation. Obviously, the DoT did not agree to take on aviation rescue. Interestingly, there was absolutely no mention of marine rescue in the meeting.[528] This is highly suggestive that the decision to create a Canadian coast guard had already been made and the point of the meeting had been to have the soon-to-be-created Canadian Coast Guard take over aviation rescue from the Air Force.

With the RCAF aim in mind, one can perhaps understand the reluctance of DoT to agree to aviation rescue. DoT had remained on the fringe of rescue operations for years, and in 1959, it likely knew it was going to have to take on the growing maritime-rescue role and build a maritime-rescue capability from very little already in existence. By 1959, aviation SAR was a large responsibility on top of a critically important maritime-rescue role, and if it could be avoided, DoT was setting itself up to focus only on the growing importance of maritime rescue within the existing rescue framework provided, unwittingly, by the Air Force. The time had finally come for maritime rescue to receive the same level of effort that had become standard in aviation.

---

[526] Ibid.

[527] Ibid.

[528] Ibid.

Although the link has not been made elsewhere, it seems evident that new support for a coast guard was directly related to increased shipping. Maritime rescue as a growing important role in Canada was almost certainly spurred on by the opening of the St. Lawrence Seaway on 29 April 1959, which opened the Great Lakes to oceanic shipping vessels.[529] The magnitude of the shipping made available by the seaway is highlighted by the fact that 2.5 billion metric tons have been moved through the seaway in the first 50 years of use, "with an estimated value of more than $375 billion."[530] The expected revenue from the additional vessels in Canadian waters would have been solid justification for increased maritime-rescue services.

In the context of commercial shipping, if a coast guard had not already been firmly decided upon in early 1959, a maritime incident was about to solidify government interest in improving maritime rescue to satisfy concerns about maritime safety in Canada.

> On 1 May at 4:23 p.m. the Norwegian freighter *Ferngulf,* when off Port Atkinson in the approaches to Vancouver, reported that she was on fire with injured on board. The first help did not arrive until 5:00 p.m., when an RCAF helicopter put a doctor on board. The Vancouver fireboat was not able to respond—later giving the reason, much criticized, that its activities were restricted to the harbour. Fortunately, two Canadian destroyers and a USN submarine were in port. Fire-fighting crews from HMCS *Saguenay* and *Assiniboine* and USS *Cavallo*, led by RCN Commander Ken Lewis, reached the *Ferngulf* at 6:00 p.m. and succeeded in bringing the fire under control. There were casualties among the freighter's crew, however, one of whom died in hospital. This event resulted in much publicity and further demands for action. From this time

---

[529] Maginley, *Canadian Coast Guard*, 35.

[530] The St. Lawrence Seaway Management Corporation, "The Seaway," Great Lakes St. Lawrence Seaway System, http://www.greatlakes-seaway.com/en/seaway/vital/index.html (accessed 25 April 2018).

on, it is clear from internal correspondence that a Coast Guard would only be a matter of time.[531]

The incident above strongly suggested that luck, with RCN and American Navy vessels in the immediate vicinity, could not be relied upon for future rescues. The Canadian Coast Guard's time had come.

The *Ferngulf* incident does not convey the coordination efforts that took place behind the scenes, and marine emergency coordination was an important component of the rescue organization that needed immediate improvement. In this case, the incident would certainly have been communicated to RCC Vancouver, which would have been responsible for tasking the helicopter to bring the doctor onboard, and the RCC might have assisted with arranging for assistance from the Navy vessels. Once again, it would have been noted that only Air Force personnel, who may not have been aware of the urgency necessitated by a fire onboard a vessel, manned the RCCs. Whether the RCC personnel acted appropriately or not was likely irrelevant; the expertise needed to improve marine emergency coordination was not part of the existing RCC manning. Maritime expertise had long been needed within the RCCs, and it appeared that the incident above provoked a DoT response.

In what must have been a very welcome change for the Air Force, experienced mariners were hired by DoT in the summer of 1959 to provide one marine coordinator for RCCs in Halifax, Trenton, and Vancouver: the three RCCs with significant maritime responsibilities.[532] These coordinators were administered by DoT, but operationally, they reported to the RCAF officer in command of the RCC. One of the reasons for the subordinate relationship was that commercial maritime operators had long deferred to RCAF expertise for rescue matters and regulatory support, obviously due to the Air Force's extensive and lonely experience managing the SAR organization for Canada.[533] The relationship worked because the

---

[531] Maginley, *Canadian Coast Guard*, 30.

[532] LAC, RG24-E-1-c, Vol. 18114, 13 July 1960, "Report from Marine Coordinators."

[533] LAC, RG24-E-1-c, Vol. 18128, File No. 978-7-3, SAR – Crash Rescue Assistance by Others. Multiple documents in this file make it clear that commercial operators relied on RCAF regulatory assistance.

DoT maritime coordinators were given the authority to run searches over water using their expertise with wind and tides in the maritime domain, and they had the ability to obtain aircraft support from their Air Force colleague prosecuting aviation rescue missions in the same workspace.[534]

Marine coordinators proved to be a major step forward in the successful prosecution of SAR incidents. In a clear correlation, hours on maritime SAR missions conducted by RCAF aircraft as a percentage of overall yearly effort dropped from a high of 38 per cent in 1955 to 9.5 per cent in 1961.[535] As most of the DoT vessels had not come into service by then, most of the drop in RCAF aircraft activity appears to have been a result of trained professional mariners coordinating rescues from the RCCs and the gradual increase of DoT rescue vessels.

Concurrently, the RCAF improved the training of SAR personnel by consolidating most major SAR training programs at Trenton, Ontario, "to promote efficiency and standardization in the proven methods and procedures used by each unit across the country."[536] Marine and aeronautical coordinators, as well as the personnel responsible for large search missions and even personnel flying daily SAR missions, would have benefited from these courses. Therefore, the professionalization of SAR was occurring concurrently in both aviation and maritime rescue.

For maritime rescue, multiple SAR vessels had been ordered by DoT in 1958 to provide an expanded surface-vessel rescue fleet on both coasts. Additionally, by 1960, SAR cutters were planned to augment rescue resources on both coasts and on the Great Lakes.[537] These cutters would operate from locations where there was a known high incidence of maritime-rescue needs, to fill in the gaps formed by government vessels that were repositioning

---

[534] This statement is based on the author's eight years of experience working in RCCs.

[535] LAC, RG24-E-1-c, Vol. 18117, 4 October 1961, "Supporting Data for Air Council Meeting."

[536] Smith, *Seek and Save*, 63.

[537] LAC, RG12, Vol 8906-81, "SAR Vessel for British Columbia 1957–1965;" LAC, RG12, Vol 8906-78, "SAR Vessel for East Coast 1957–1964;" and LAC, RG12, Vol 8906-109, "Proposed Patrol Cutter for SAR 1960–1967."

daily for their mandated missions requirements.[538] Establishing marine stations in predetermined locations was essential because each government organization tasked their ships according to their own mandate, which may not have matched the high-activity periods of commercial fishing or recreational mariners. To illustrate, government vessels moved from one assignment to another, and that could result in the departure of the only ship near a lobster fishing opening during a time when it was known that SAR incidents were more likely to occur.[539] Therefore, government vessels in the 1950s were by no means guaranteed to be anywhere near where they were needed most for rescues. The new SAR patrol cutters would operate from shore locations where a rescue requirement had been identified, thus resolving many of the concerns of the existing system for maritime rescue.[540] Specifically, this would resolve the main problem identified in the *Ferngulf* incident as a SAR cutter was planned for the Vancouver area.

Matching the DoT commitment, the RCAF planned a long-overdue modernization of resources and capability with new aircraft and helicopters. At the beginning of 1950, there had been 5 RCCs and 9 air stations operating a total of 34 aircraft and helicopters as well as 6 high-speed rescue vessels at 2 marine stations.[541] At the end of the 1950s, there were 4 RCCs, 5 air stations operating a total of 25 aircraft and helicopters, and no rescue vessels capable of missions at any distance from the stations to which they belonged.[542] In order to maximize the capability of the few resources assigned to SAR, the 1959 RCAF acquisition plan included the purchase of ten SA-16B Albatross amphibious seaplanes and six CH-113

---

[538] LAC, RG24-D-1-c, Vol. 8164, 30 March 1949, "Interdepartmental Committee on Search and Rescue."

[539] Ibid.

[540] Thomas Appleton, *Usque Ad Mare: A History of the Canadian Coast Guard and Marine Services* (Ottawa: DoT, 1968), section on shore-based lifeboats.

[541] DHH, 79/631, RCAF SAR Operations 1947–1970, DIS Files 1–14, SAR Ops 1940, File 3, circa early 1950, "RCAF Press Release No.7615."

[542] E. D. Bryson and N. D. Bray, "An Evaluation of the Future RCAF Search and Rescue Requirement," *Department of National Defence, Chief of Operational Requirements, DRDC CORA* (Ottawa: February 1964), page N/A.

Labrador helicopters that were to be used solely for SAR purposes.[543] These aircraft had much improved range and overall capabilities, meaning that the long distances between the five rescue locations were less of a problem due to the airframe's increased transit speeds and fewer required fuel stops.[544] The range of the Albatross was 2,500 nautical miles in contrast with the Canso's 1,500 nautical mile range, and the Labrador was a similar improvement for the helicopter role.[545] While the range and speed of these new assets still left gaps in coverage nationwide, plans were being formulated to increase the numbers of aircraft resources within the next decade. The five locations were made more acceptable by reducing the time it took to get aircraft and helicopters to distress locations by using modern equipment.

All of these changes and improvements were good news for the RCAF. The overall number of SAR incidents in 1959 reduced to 2,735 total, the first time the number of SAR missions in a year had dropped, and the number of RCAF flying hours were recorded as 5,527, down from a three-year average of approximately 8,000 hours.[546] Potentially better news was that, also for the first time, every aircraft that had gone missing in that year had been found during the subsequent search. SAR personnel always hoped for survivors, but if there were none, then a located crash site provided the limited satisfaction of closure to grieving families. 1959 had been the first kind year to the SAR organization as a direct result of funding and interest from all levels of government.

543 DHH, 181.004 (D23), RCAF Programme of Activities, 1963–1968 with Amendments, page numbers N/A; LAC, RG24-E-1-c, Vol. 18149, STOL Transport/SAR 1959–1961, 24 November 1959, "Standard of Preparation – Vertol 107 Model II-1 Helicopter"; and 24 July 1959, "Operational Characteristics for a Short Range, STOL, Transport/SAR Aircraft."
544 The Albatross had greatly improved range, but its speed was slow by other transport aircraft standards in the 1960s. Recognizing this reality, the Albatross was replaced with the CC-115 Buffalo in 1971.
545 Flight Cadet D. A. McIsaac "SAR: New Look," *The Roundel* 3, no. 2 (January 1951), 8.
546 Smith, *Seek and Save*, 63.

A NEW APPROACH

The early 1960s saw even more changes that fundamentally altered the outlook of RCAF leadership on the SAR role. The most significant change was the creation of the Canadian Coast Guard, but there were other changes that were captured in various reports that, combined, show a very different AFHQ approach to the SAR organization. Of great importance is that the reports that will be discussed show a new and surprisingly big-picture view by AFHQ of the rescue role within Canadian society, which was not a perspective evident in earlier documentation. Partly, the new approach was brought on by the unpredictable nature of SAR operations, as 1960 resumed the hectic operational requirement, with 6,800 flying hours expended in 48 major searches, which does not count all the single-flight missions.[547] The first area of SAR to receive a new look and policy confirmation was the humanitarian mission.

Although humanitarian missions had increased in numbers since the early 1950s, a 1961 report identified that the procedures between the RCAF and the RCMP were largely effective and that there had been a gradual reduction of demand in the late 1950s.[548] The report included insightful observations that humanitarian missions provided a great deal of public goodwill and that cost recovery was not worth the hassle it would require, due to the fact that the provinces that used the system the most were the least capable of paying back the federal government. The report concluded that the process developed with provincial authorities needed to be followed scrupulously to avoid abuse of the system, so the report recommended that the "current [humanitarian] policy remain in effect." Humanitarian missions ceased to be an area of growth for the RCAF, and AFHQ was able to scrutinize other aspects of domestic SAR in more detail.

Detail was provided by a review of overall SAR policy in 1961. The Air Council had requested a review of the SAR organization, and one of the options considered in the review had been to split the SAR service into military and civilian organizations with a view to, potentially, handing off

---

[547] McIsaac, "SAR: New Look," 8.
[548] LAC, RG24-E-1-c, Vol. 18117, 23 October 1961, "A Paper on the Prevalence of Mercy Flights 1953–1961." This document is the source for the rest of this paragraph.

the civilian part to the DoT.[549] The expectation of a potential handoff of SAR responsibility is odd, considering the outcome of the meeting with DoT two years before, but the conclusion of this report identified that the RCAF could save some resources if it provided just the military SAR service. The RCAF, if it did not have to provide for domestic SAR, would be able to eliminate 1 RCC and 14 aircraft from the SAR role, but "it would be very expensive indeed for some other agency of government to duplicate facilities which the RCAF already has at its disposal to deal with SAR incidents." The report goes on to identify that "there is no doubt that the RCAF would continue to receive requests for assistance on cases involving civilian interests. Such requests could hardly be ignored when RCAF resources are available and lives are at stake." This report appeared not only to have slowed the separation of the military- and civilian-rescue services but also suggested that the base-rescue flight concept should be kept integrated with the domestic SAR organization. Indeed, that is the case today.

The two reports identified above show a remarkable clarity by the RCAF leadership on its long-term role with the SAR mandate. The Air Force had refined procedures with the RCMP to control growth in humanitarian missions, and it understood that it was not cost-effective for anyone else to provide civil-aviation rescue. In addition to this clarity, the RCAF had also realized that there was a wartime role for SAR forces. The RCN brought the issue forward by requesting RCAF consideration to assigning SAR forces over the Atlantic to the RCN, as a way for the RCN to maintain more authority over the maritime domain.[550] The CAS, Air Marshal Hugh Campbell, informed the RCN that he was opposed to breaking up the command and control structure of the SAR organization because the SAR responsibility extended all over the country and commonality was critical for other government departments to work with the system.[551] However, subsequent discussion determined that the command and con-

---

[549] LAC, RG24-E-1-c, Vol. 18117, SAR – Operations, File 976-100, 4 October 1961, "Supporting Data for Air Council Meeting: Review of the SAR Organization." This document is the source for the rest of this paragraph.

[550] LAC, RG24-E-1-c, Vol. 18117, SAR – Operations, File 976-100, Memo to CAS from CNS, 25 April 1960, "Responsibility for SAR."

[551] Ibid.

trol could change during wartime, recognizing that the RCN would be the lead agency in oceanic areas.[552]

The discussion surrounding a wartime role for SAR forces was important because it showed that military authorities were again aware of the most basic reason that SAR was created in the first place: to recover aircrew downed at sea and keep as many aircrew as possible to defend Canada. One aspect of the wartime plans should be kept in mind: Canada only envisaged SAR forces rescuing personnel from Canadian waters and territory. Both the RAF and USAF had well-developed military roles for SAR forces that could and would be deployed overseas to provide rescue in wartime scenarios.[553] In fact, a 1961 J. F. Kennedy administration memorandum confirmed that the "loss or diminution of U.S. use of Canadian air space and real estate and the contributions of the Canadian military, particularly the RCAF and Royal Canadian Navy, would be intolerable in time of crisis."[554] The American view of access to Canadian airspace and territory must have been a factor in the consideration of military wartime SAR discussions to avoid unwanted American help. Canada continued to focus on SAR as a domestic service only; although, the inclusion of wartime command and control was a positive step forward for an integrated place for SAR forces within the RCAF.

By 1961, the changes to locations for SAR resources within the RCAF had stabilized. While there would be minor changes in the decades afterwards, for the most part, four RCCs and five rescue stations had become the standard. As depicted in Figure 7, there were four rescue regions, and each RCC had one collocated rescue unit except for Edmonton, which had no in-house resources at hand.[555] The Air Force SAR organization of only five rescue stations was made adequate given that the range and capabilities of the rescue aircraft and helicopters had been much improved with the new aircraft purchases.

---

[552] LAC, RG24-E-1-c, Vol. 18113, SAR – Policy, File 976-0, Vol. 8, 16 March 1961, "Report to the Chiefs of Staff Committee by the Joint Planning Committee on SAR."

[553] Galdorisi and Phillips, *Leave No Man Behind*, 213; and Sutherland and Canwell, *RAF Air Sea Rescue*, 145.

[554] Barry and Bratt, "Defence Against Help," 71.

[555] LAC, RG24-E-1-c, Vol. 18117, 4 October 1961, "Supporting Data for Air Council Meeting."

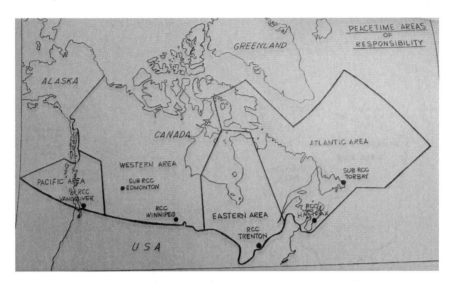

Figure 7. The RCAF's SAR Resources in 1961

Purchasing the Labrador helicopter to augment the earlier helicopter purchases and to provide more than one helicopter at each of the identified helicopter stations enhanced the capability at each rescue station. Greenwood, Trenton, Winnipeg, and Vancouver each received two Labrador helicopters so that aircrew did not have to rely on the serviceability of only one machine.[556] One helicopter at a station had been standard up until the 1960s, but only one helicopter asset was clearly insufficient for 24/7 SAR operations as every airframe needs downtime for maintenance. Until DoT high-speed vessels would be available in 1963, the RCAF helicopters were a critically important component of maritime rescue.[557]

The dramatic change from the challenged SAR system of 1958 to the relatively rosy situation in the early 1960s, with new and welcome assistance from DoT, changed the outlook of the RCAF on the SAR mission. Bearing in mind all of the changes between 1959 and 1961 and that the RCAF leadership knew about the upcoming formation of the Canadian Coast Guard, the Air Council held a review of the SAR organization on 4

---

[556] DHH, 181.004 (D23), RCAF Programme of Activities, 1963–1968 with amendments.

[557] Maginley, *Canadian Coast Guard*, 56.

October 1961. The Air Council agreed "that both civil and military SAR requirements in Canada and the seaward approaches should continue to be met by a single SAR organization; that the RCAF SAR organization is to be retained at its present level of establishment to meet Canadian SAR requirements."[558] The RCAF, with support from the DoT, had finally come to terms with its role with the SAR mandate.

DoT progress towards the formation of the Canadian Coast Guard was well underway in the early 1960s, and the Canada Shipping Act was amended in 1961 "to empower the Minister of Transport to designate marine coordinators [in three RCCs] to organize search and rescue work on the high seas and on the coast of Canada."[559] The amendment simply formalized the marine coordinator authority within the RCCs, but the legislation change was a major step forward in sharing rescue responsibility. In 1962, three 95-foot SAR vessels were completed for the East Coast, which provided the first dedicated SAR vessels in Canada since the RCAF high-speed rescue vessels were given to the RCN in April 1952.[560] The addition of these vessels was a very important milestone in the progress of SAR developments.

Undoubtedly, the most significant change to SAR organization in Canada since its inception was the formation of the Canadian Coast Guard. On 26 January 1962, Hon. Leon Balcer, the Minister of Transport in Prime Minister John Diefenbaker's Government, "rose in the House of Commons and announced that the government had decided that the Department of Transport fleet of ships would, in the future, be known as the Canadian Coast Guard."[561] The Canadian Coast Guard would also provide all components of the maritime-rescue system; although, the RCAF retained command and control of the overall SAR organization.

The Canadian Coast Guard relieved the RCAF of the need to coordinate the maritime missions and, more importantly, the eventual increase of marine-rescue vessels in Atlantic Canada appears to have relieved the

---

[558] LAC, RG24-E-1-c, Vol. 18117, 4 October 1961, "Air Council Meeting: Review of the SAR Organization."

[559] Appleton, *Usque Ad Mare*, section on Search and Rescue.

[560] LAC, RG12, Vol 8906-78, "SAR Vessel for East Coast 1957–1964."

[561] Maginley, *Canadian Coast Guard*, 12.

American forces from their deep involvement in 1950s domestic rescue.[562] SAR documentation no longer listed Americans forces as primary or secondary SAR resources, and American rescue resources gradually returned to the US.[563] The American military left St. John's, Newfoundland, in August 1961, and the USAF air-defence presence in Stephenville ended in 1966; although, the American naval base at Argentia did not close until 1994.[564] It took the addition of the Canadian Coast Guard to tip the scales to enough Canadian sovereignty in Newfoundland to ensure the American withdrawal.

With the addition of the Canadian Coast Guard, enough change had occurred that the RCAF commissioned a research report on the RCAF SAR establishment to ensure that the organization met the stated requirements for the RCAF portion of the overall organization. The Centre for Operational Research and Analysis released the report in February 1964, titled "An Evaluation of the Future RCAF Search and Rescue Requirement."[565] What is important about this report is not the myriad of changes it recommended, as interesting and necessary as they were, but the fact that all the changes were minor in nature and reinforced the basic structure of RCAF and Canadian Coast Guard cooperation that had recently developed. Equally important, it found that the SAR organization finally met the international obligations established by ICAO and IMCO.

This report marks a change from reports prior to the 1960s that recommended major structural changes to the SAR organization. In the period after 1964, only minor changes were recommended (such as adjusting locations of resources or RCCs, area coverage, and other policies). The recommendations from this 1964 report were nowhere near as significant

---

[562] LAC, RG24-D-10, Vol. 11608, RCNAS Shearwater – Ops and Plans – SAR 1955–60. In this file are multiple reports from RCC Torbay that show a significant reduction in American resources assigned to SAR missions in the late 1950s.

[563] DHH, 181.004 (D20), RCAF Programme of Activities, 1964–1969, Chapter 19 – Section 1, "Search and Rescue."

[564] Higgins, "American Presence in Newfoundland."

[565] E. D. Bryson and N. D. Bray, "An Evaluation of the Future RCAF Search and Rescue Requirement," Department of National Defence, Chief of Operational Requirements, DRDC CORA (Ottawa: February 1964).

as the changes that had occurred over the previous 25 years. One of those minor changes, noted here only for the SAR professionals who may be curious, was a proposal in May 1964 to have all the rescue units and composite flights with a rescue capability come under the command authority of Air Transport Command (ATC). This was proposed for "coordination and standardization for all SAR operations both within ATC and with other commands," and was a noteworthy change from SAR flights and units all coming under different masters, as had been the case since the units first became specialized in SAR.[566] The logic was to put all the SAR resources in one chain of command where it would be easier to develop and maintain rescue standards and avoid the previous challenges that had been evident in the regional approach to rescue resources. The choice of ATC as the command authority made a certain sense in that the specialized equipment could be removed from every SAR aircraft and used in a transport-aircraft role. The refinements had begun, and continue today.

SUMMARY OF CHANGES BETWEEN 1959 AND 1964

A maritime mission, the most likely point of failure throughout the 1950s, tragically demonstrated the problems with Canadian rescue at sea in May 1959—the *Ferngulf* incident. Fortunately, a multitude of Navy resources nearby prevented a bad situation from becoming a calamity. Canada took action before a worse tragedy could take place, and an expensive Canadian Coast Guard was finally accepted as necessary. Large challenges for the RCAF's SAR organization diminished in 1959 because the major changes in maritime resources and mission management lessened the expectations of the RCAF. Eventually, the Air Force accepted a permanent role in the delivery of aviation SAR services.

The RCAF's acceptance of SAR eased the Newfoundland sovereignty concerns from the previous decade and resulted in the gradual reduction of American forces from Newfoundland. With the Americans no longer being responsible for primary SAR missions in Canada, territorial

<hr>

[566] LAC, RG24-E-1-c, Vol. 18113, Search and Rescue Policy, SAR – Organization and Administration, 976-0, Vol. 9, details were not available on this memo from 21 May 1964 on the role of SAR within the RCAF.

integrity was better maintained. Despite the fact that the Americans did not appear concerned about assisting in Canadian SAR missions, it was in Canada's best interests to maintain its own internationally defined SAR responsibilities.

International pressure seemed largely absent in this time frame; although, there may have been implied pressure to improve maritime rescue with the opening of the St. Lawrence Seaway. Regardless, with the increase of DoT vessels assigned specifically to SAR, the Americans gradually reduced their role in Canadian rescue missions. Clearly, Canadian acceptance of a robust maritime-rescue capability in the early 1960s was enough to satisfy the international community that Canadian SAR capabilities had achieved the desired standard.

From a cost perspective, 1959 to 1964 was a major relief for the RCAF. Although the Air Force had to replace very old aircraft with new ones and add to the overall number of helicopters assigned to the rescue role, it did not have to absorb any cost for the development and growth of the Canadian Coast Guard or for the increase of capability to its RCCs (the addition of Canadian Coast Guard marine coordinators). The Canadian government opened its purse strings for the Canadian Coast Guard, likely to enable additional revenue generated by the opening of the St. Lawrence Seaway during the post-war economic growth period, and that source of revenue warranted new resources to ensure the safety of increased shipping.

The RCAF's 1959 meeting with DoT did not meet the initial RCAF aims of eliminating the expensive aviation SAR role, but in the long run, it did achieve an effective and dramatic lessening of the RCAF's maritime SAR commitment. In a critical change to the SAR organization, the establishment of the Canadian Coast Guard in 1962 reduced the RCAF's SAR responsibilities and made its remaining rescue commitments manageable. A detailed examination of SAR organization realities, based on assistance from DoT, resulted in the Air Council understanding that the RCAF was the right organization to lead SAR in Canada. The changes that were made in 1959 and afterwards resulted in a permanent shift from the resistance the RCAF had consistently shown towards the SAR mandate since 1944 to a new era when the RCAF embraced the SAR responsibility.

This chapter outlined key components of today's SAR system that were put in place by 1964, as depicted in Table 8. The effectiveness of the new system was confirmed that year by a report on the future of SAR within the RCAF, and it had two major findings. First, a national system for aviation and maritime rescue had been standardized across the country and found effective. Second, better RCAF aircraft and helicopter resources were planned for operational use in the early 1960s, and the Canadian Coast Guard provided a long-overdue maritime-rescue capability that had been missing since the Air Force had given up the high-speed rescue vessels. Finally, the SAR system in Canada was formalized for both military- and civilian-rescue missions. In a clear validation of the accomplishments from 1959 to 1964, the differences that exist between the SAR organization of the early 1960s and the SAR organization today are minor, so we now have a detailed understanding of the formation of Canada's SAR system.

Characteristic	Aviation	Maritime
National Standards	**Aviation rescues.** Required by ICAO, ordered by the government, and maintained by the RCAF	**Maritime rescues.** Required by IMCO, ordered by the government, and maintained by the Canadian Coast Guard
Available Resources	**Aircraft.** RCAF resources at five locations across the country were sufficient due to the increased helicopter and aircraft capabilities	**Vessels.** DoT vessels were under construction and rescue stations were created immediately after the Canadian Coast Guard was formed in 1962
Formalized Policy	**Military rescues.** Required by NATO, provided by the RCAF, and supported by all branches of the military	**Civilian rescues.** Required by ICAO/ IMO and provided by the RCAF and Canadian Coast Guard under RCAF leadership

Table 8. Canada's SAR System in 1964

Chapter 9: Conclusion

The SAR organization of the early 1960s is remarkably similar to the organization of today, after a very rough development process starting in the Second World War. Key components of the SAR system were developed gradually starting in 1942, and the final pieces were put in place quite late in the period of this study, as demonstrated by the initiation of national rescue standards in 1958 and the 1962 formation of the Canadian Coast Guard. It must be recalled, however, that the RCAF's creation of a rescue system had to start from scratch after 1939, which helps explain why it took so long to develop an effective aviation and maritime SAR system in Canada to support military- and civilian-rescue requirements. As discussed, the key components of the Canadian rescue system did not follow a linear process; they developed in fits and starts until 1964 and were dependent on the actions of other government departments. All things considered, 25 years taken to develop the basics of today's effective system does not seem as long when one measures the progress from zero national rescue capability to a fully standardized system that was functional in all parts of Canada.

The aims of this book were to identify, one, why the RCAF acquired operational responsibility for the aviation and maritime SAR system in Canada; and two, to show how the RCAF developed the system into a close approximation of the one that exists today. Contrary to the existing presumption that the RCAF volunteered for the rescue service after the RCMP proposal was turned down by government, the RCAF was reluctant to develop air- and sea-rescue systems until the 1960s, even though the Air Force knew as early as 1940 that ASR was an important requirement both during and after the war. This book has clarified why a SAR system is important, and it has offered detailed rationale for the importance of the military to SAR developments in Canada. Perhaps more importantly, we now have additional historical knowledge of the long and challenged path that rescue developments in Canada took on the road to the current effective system.

Wartime experiences led to the overarching Allied requirement for rescue systems to ensure aircrew were returned to the fight whenever possible. The RCAF initiated rescue-system development due to the proven importance of aircrew rescue during combat operations and the 1942 perception that Canada could become a theatre of intense air combat operations. After the war, SAR became the means to meet Canadian national and international post-war transportation safety requirements for trade and travel that helped spark the post-war economic boom. SAR developments internationally were critical to the overall growth of aviation and maritime transportation in Canada, which underlines the importance of research in the interconnected areas of military- and civilian-rescue development.

These pages offered new knowledge with which to judge the provision of Canadian rescue systems by military organizations. The ability of the RCAF to use additional non-rescue resources to surge for large search missions, the risk-management aspect of military aviation, and the RCAF's ability to absorb unexpected costs all combined to provide important historical reasons why the military continued to lead the SAR service throughout the period under study. Of equal importance, this study has partially closed a gap in current literature between the initial formation of an ASR system in 1942, including the decision to assign maritime rescue to the RCAF in 1950, and the formation of the Canadian Coast Guard in 1962. In conclusion, the three themes woven throughout this study will be re-examined, and the role of the RCAF will be scrutinized for some final insights into overall rescue-system developments in Canada.

A SUMMARY OF THEMES

The themes woven through Canadian government and RCAF decision making during the development of both wartime and peacetime rescue systems were: one, a national requirement to develop and maintain sovereignty; two, international pressure to develop rescue systems; and three, government preference to conduct SAR at the lowest cost. These themes were important by demonstrating the forces aligned against the RCAF's insistence on limiting rescue-system development within its organization due to the civilian nature of aviation and maritime SAR and the lack of funding support. Additionally, the themes provided a framework for analysing developments within the specific timelines of each chapter, and they will be useful here to provide closing analysis of the pressures that created and complicated rescue-system development in Canada. In each of these themes there exists significant findings that will assist in bringing clarity to the RCAF's tumultuous rescue-system history.

The most important finding of this book is that rescue systems support national sovereignty. Both the German and British air forces demonstrated that air combat could only be maintained effectively in a long war by recovering as many aircrew personnel from the sea as was possible. It was demonstrated that Canada agreed with the basic principle that a rescue system was essential to support combat operations within territorial areas. Following that principle, the RCAF loosely recreated the RAF's ASR example with a system for Canada's oceanic areas to respond to the threat posed by German U-boat and Japanese submarines approaching Canadian shores. The trigger for rescue-system development in Canada had been the threat of invasion, and the system created was ready to support Canadian sovereignty late in the Second World War. In short, the threat of air combat near Canada was the primary driver to create an RCAF ASR system in 1942. This finding can lead us to an additional conclusion in the contemporary environment: if the Canadian Armed Forces has any concern of possible invasion to this country by any other nation, a rescue system capable of operations in a military environment remains a critical capability. Any decision to remove the SAR role from the RCAF would have to consider that important aspect of national defence.

Less obvious than invasion, the military supports sovereignty by its very presence. The simple matter of troops based in locations across the country supports the assertion that Canadian territory belongs to Canadians. Rescue systems during and after the war supported Canadian sovereignty by limiting the development of American ASR bases in Canada, and that was only possible due to the rescue role being incorporated within the RCAF and the trust the Americans had that the RCAF would search to their high standards. The 1944 addition of parachute-rescue personnel into domestic-rescue operations was demonstrated as a factor that limited the

Americans from establishing an ASR presence in Northern Canada during the war. Unfortunately, as Canadian rescue-system developments in the late 1940s were slow and gaps developed in early 1950s maritime-rescue coverage, American forces in Newfoundland and Labrador became the primary rescue resources by 1955. The lesson of the rescue role and its link to sovereignty was lost.

The reliance on American rescue services must have been embarrassing, and even the addition of an RCC and a rescue flight of airframes and aircrew to the air station of Torbay in 1954 was insufficient to meet the increasing number of rescue operations in the new Province of Newfoundland. The RCAF found itself in an awkward dependence on American SAR forces over Canadian territory and waters. The RCAF's lack of willingness to modernize rescue services in the 1950s lessened Canadian sovereignty in the new Province of Newfoundland and Labrador and was the low point of the SAR service in Canada. As developments after 1964 were mostly outside of the scope of this study and the Americans no longer have air bases in Newfoundland or Labrador, one can only assume that the Canadian Coast Guard and the greater capabilities of the SA-16B Albatross and CH-113 Labrador aircraft were the final rescue enablers that allowed the American rescue forces to retreat from Canadian territory in the mid to late 1960s. One can criticize the RCAF for not putting more effort into SAR earlier, but the RCAF never let the civilian-rescue requirements fail.

The American presence in rescue operations in the 1950s leads to another key finding: that a rescue system, no matter which organization provides it, leads directly to greater control over foreign resources in one's territory. In Canada's case, the RCAF's robust response to Op Brix in 1950 was critically important to Canadian national interests due to the potential nuclear weapon onboard an American aircraft downed in Canada. Other missions demonstrated that a robust RCAF response to downed American aircraft resulted in the Americans ignoring their own guidelines to coordinate searches for American aircraft. The close relationship between the RCAF and USAF assisted in reducing an American rescue presence in Canada and limited the numbers of resources sent to participate over Canadian territory for specific rescue missions. One can reasonably conclude that a military role in SAR missions was necessary for integration with American forces, which makes one question the wisdom of the RCAF's 1950 goal of being rid of SAR. Given the number and types of military missions in the 1950s and the American expectation of RCAF involvement, the RCAF should have embraced the delivery of SAR earlier than it did due to the obvious benefit of increased ties to American forces.

The RCAF's close ties with USAF were one result of the Canadian shift from a close orbit of the UK and Commonwealth policies, to an orbit of influence based on the US. The physical proximity to the US, however, meant that expectations of Canadian organizations in areas like military-aviation rescue were elevated. Given the evidence of USAF and RCAF interactions after the war, one can surmise that Canada needed a higher standard of SAR capabilities than Canada might otherwise have held because our American neighbours had robust expectations for rescue responses that applied to American military aircraft crashed in Canada. Again, the RCAF did not appear to recognize the benefits of involvement in the SAR service and that its participation in American rescue missions inside Canada was an expectation.

Another key finding from this study was that rescue systems became an international requirement for aviation and maritime civil transportation safety between 1945 and 1948. In Canada, the international requirements for aviation and maritime rescue were problematic because Canada did not have a pre-existing domestic-rescue organization that could form the basis of a domestic aviation and maritime SAR system. The very limited Canadian Lifesaving Service for domestic maritime rescue from before the war did not survive the transition to a wartime capability, and it was not rebuilt by the RCN after the war.

The lack of any effective Canadian domestic-rescue system before the Second World War meant that the ASR system developed by the RCAF during the war was the only rescue capability in Canada that could meet growing international rescue requirements after the war. The fact that the only rescue system used for civilian aviation and maritime emergencies at war's end was that of the RCAF provided a solid, albeit unintended, argument against the robust RCMP proposal to provide a Canadian SAR service. Arguably, the international requirement for aviation- and maritime-rescue systems devolved to the RCAF in Canada because it was the only organization that had rescue experience, and the RCAF had even included civilian-rescue activities throughout and after the war. Because the RCAF had developed the rescue service, expertise ran deep in the Air Force personnel assigned to the role and that expertise led the politicians to ask why they would want to change rescue leadership when the RCAF already had an effective, if small, rescue organization.

International agreements did not specify that a national Air Force must provide the domestic response, but ICAO, the British, and the Americans all appeared to believe that a national Air Force was the most appropriate entity to lead some aspect of post-war SAR response. The communications required between the military flying-control organization, civilian air-traffic services, and any SAR organization made the selection of an Air Force for a SAR service a cost-effective and obvious option. However, the situation in Canada was complicated because Canada did not have a domestic service for the maritime component of rescue before 1947, as did both the British and Americans. Until the DoT provided sufficient personnel and vessels for the domestic maritime service, the RCAF was handicapped by a lack of maritime expertise and adequate vessel resources to perform to developing international rescue expectations. The RCAF tried to focus its rescue system on military requirements only, but the various pressures from allies, international organizations, and domestic partners made it a common expectation that the RCAF would remain involved in post-war rescue organizations. It is still common for air forces to lead SAR services because of the robust communications capabilities with other organizations and the long-proven ability to manage risky missions.

Another key finding, although an unsurprising one, was that cost concerns were critical to decisions relating to rescue-system development in Canada. Examples of cost concerns affecting rescue developments were the unwillingness to expand the Flying Control Organization and ASR in 1941, the American rescue vessels that were unsuccessfully considered for purchase in 1942, the lack of willingness of the government to support the $5.8 million RCMP SAR system proposal in 1946, and the RCAF's lack of willingness to provide any maritime-rescue vessels after 1950. It is not clear what factors were at work to delay the assistance of DoT in rescue matters, but it is certainly possible that cost was a factor in DoT's 1959 decision to not replace the RCAF as the lead organization for SAR services. As DoT had been poorly funded throughout the war, it is likely that insufficient post-war funding and manning pressures were at the root cause of DoT's lack of engagement in rescue. Research was not conducted into all of the responsibilities that DoT had to discharge or the funding it was given, so it is quite possible that there were legitimate reasons behind the DoT's failure to assist any earlier.

In general, Canada has historically taken a penny-pinching approach to government organizations, including the military, and this study provided evidence that Canada was unwilling to expend funds on any rescue system deemed greater than the minimum required by international standards. Cost for the rescue organization was a critical factor for the government that overrode the RCAF's unwillingness to take on responsibility for domestic civilian rescue. It was a good thing that the RCAF had a large budget to draw from to meet the responsibility.

Contrarily, cost concerns did not necessarily deter Canadian rescue-system development at first. In fact, those concerns appeared to drive cooperation among several government departments. Starting in 1944, the RCMP, RCN, and RCAF worked together to provide the best possible rescue service to the Canadian public given the wartime circumstances. These agencies were very proactive in planning for a post-war rescue service that recognized future international and national requirements for SAR services. The RCAF even responded to DoT requests to provide a standing maritime-rescue capability for civilians in the later years of the war. However, rescue development remained stunted and challenged until the DoT developed an appreciation for a civil maritime-rescue organization within the domestic SAR mandate. As the cost of the SAR service went up in the 1950s, the RCAF proved capable of absorbing the expense and using non-SAR resources to meet the needs, although grudgingly. It is highly likely that the long wait for DoT acceptance of rescue responsibility caused the RCAF to lower its expectation of the 1959 discussions to transfer SAR to DoT, and the RCAF subsequently accepted a shared role in SAR with relief.

The overdue acceptance of rescue responsibility by the DoT provides one last important finding of this study within the Canadian national context: resources and funding were difficult enough to obtain in the post-war environment that one organization alone could not reasonably be expected to develop the expertise and resources to support a national rescue system. Canadian military organizations are too small to maintain air, sea, and land capabilities within each branch of the military, as demonstrated by the RCAF's abandonment of maritime-rescue vessel use outside of the immediate vicinity of air stations. The RCAF simply did not have the depth of available resources to meet all aspects of SAR expectations within existing means, nor did the RCN or DoT. The RCMP wished to develop such a robust capability, but the government refused to support massive expansion within the police service. One can conclude that it was unreasonable to expect the RCAF to coordinate aviation- and maritime-rescue operations for Canadian sovereignty, and international requirements after 1950, without expertise from other government departments. When the DoT accepted responsibility for the maritime SAR role, the RCAF's reluctance to retain the SAR mandate was all but eliminated by the fact that it would no longer be solely responsible for failure in life-and-death rescue situations.

The interaction between DoT, RCMP, and RCAF demonstrated struggles with the legitimate concerns of who was responsible for what role and with what funding. These very real problems translated to the ability or inability of organizations to respond daily to life-and-death situations, so it was important for organizations to limit their responsibility in areas where they felt unable to fund the activity to a satisfactory level. As the RCMP found out, just because you have a great idea for an effective way to accomplish a mission such as SAR, there is no guarantee you will get the funding. Here, then, is a view of the RCAF from a government perspective: if money is tight and we have to provide a response with people, airframes, and funding regardless, why not assign extra roles to the military? The military is a large expenditure of government funds, it retains a standing capability to respond to crises, the government wanted it integrated with the public, and the military has other resources that can be called upon for surge operations. Unlike other countries that can afford to compartmentalize these different capabilities, Canada's limited number of resources for the size of the territory involved means that organizations are expected to maximize the effectiveness of all assigned resources.

INSIGHT INTO THE RCAF

This study demonstrated that after the 1947 decision to assign aviation SAR to the RCAF, the Air Force was left to coordinate a national rescue service with only limited assistance from other government departments until 1959. As the lead agency for Canada's rescue organizations since 1942, evidence from between 1942 and 1959 offers two insights into the RCAF. First, the RCAF proved very reluctant to adapt to post-war government direction to maintain "non-military" roles and serve the Canadian public in a rescue capacity during times of peace. Second, and all things considered, the RCAF proved quite adept at maintaining a minimally sized, and yet very effective, rescue system for many years and with little help from other government departments. The RCAF's ability to ensure that basic rescue requirements were treated as a no-fail mission was a fundamental aspect of the government's unwillingness to relieve the RCAF of SAR responsibility, and that finding is likely still relevant today.

The Canadian government made it clear in 1945 that it expected the RCAF to maintain roles the Air Force considered "non-military" as part of government direction to better serve the Canadian public in the post-war era. However, the RCAF developed its own policy in 1950 to be rid of "non-military" roles as soon as practicable. Indeed, it has been hypothesized in this study that the RCAF went even further and packaged the aviation and maritime SAR capability into one organization in order to handoff all aspects of the rescue system at a later date. This raises one final question: why was the RCAF reluctant to rescue? The answer is less clear than why it ceased to be reluctant after 1959, but we can come to reasonable conclusions.

First, there was never any doubt that the rescue mandate for civilian domestic requirements was one of the roles that the RCAF wanted to be rid of, as the RCAF did not see a combat connection with that mandate. The RCAF had significant defence priorities from the rising Soviet threat and a limited budget. The SAR service, at nearly $6 million a year to run, could be perceived to take away funding from missions the Air Force thought were more important. Essentially, the RCAF's actions to be rid of SAR, contrary to government direction, provides evidence that military organizations can be incredibly resistant to government-ordered change. It is likely that the RCAF policies were based on the recent and intense normative experiences of rescue during the war when the RCAF developed a rescue service solely for its own military requirements. It is even possible that the war experience fundamentally intensified the way the RCAF officer corps viewed its military role in Canada. Regardless, the RCAF did not view rescue activities for non-military personnel to be a desirable role for a military organization.

Second, the RCAF's actions to minimize the SAR mandate, its reluctance to rescue, were in many ways an understandable response to the incremental increases in rescue responsibility that the RCAF was required to accommodate between 1942 and 1950 without any financial, maritime-vessel, or personnel support. Civilian- and domestic-rescue responsibilities replaced the original military-rescue requirement without any clear government direction on a desired systemic end state of SAR in Canada. Even though the RCMP proposal for SAR was better and the RCAF did not have the maritime resources to conduct the maritime-rescue mandate effectively, the government proved unwilling to look past the RCAF's strengths in aviation SAR and assign rescue to both the RCAF and another organization with the necessary maritime-rescue expertise. As understandable as the RCAF response was to a government decision that left maritime rescue in a precarious state, it is still clear that the RCAF put up stiff resistance against the SAR role in the 1950s.

The biggest criticism of the RCAF is the action it took in the 1950–1955 era, when it eliminated the high-speed rescue vessels and reduced rescue air locations from nine down to five. The justification for these decisions was not found, nor is it likely available in remaining historical documentation. The Air Force resisted ICAO's standards of adequate services as a clear sign of rebellion against a government that refused to make funding available for an important domestic capability that it had assigned to the RCAF. The RCAF's actions are perhaps understandable, but it undeniably put lives at risk and strained SAR personnel resources. The counterargument to the military providing a SAR service is the lack of effort that military leadership may provide to the domestic-rescue role when other roles and responsibilities are internally assessed as a higher priority.

Despite the RCAF's resistance against a mandate the RCAF felt was a civil responsibility, the RCAF did prove equal to the task. As evidence, the small number of RCAF aircraft assigned to the SAR role did not limit the response to rescue missions, whether the mission was military or civilian. The RCAF owned up to its responsibilities and allowed the SAR mission to use many other RCAF aircraft as the RCCs required to save lives. Indeed, the RCAF offered to pay for SAR out of its own budget when it could have supported an ICAO discussion that would have resulted in the US paying a fee for American aircraft crashes in Canada that required RCAF responses for rescue. The actions described above are but two among a great number of actions that the RCAF took to ensure that basic national SAR objectives were met throughout the difficult 1950s. Once the RCAF had convinced the Canadian government that five rescue locations were acceptable in Canada, it never let resources drop below that threshold.

Ultimately, the RCAF conducted detailed studies of SAR and how Canadian rescue would best be served. In 1961, the RCAF determined that it was indeed the right organization to lead SAR in Canada. This determination was backed up with new aircraft specifically for domestic-rescue services, in order to keep the number of rescue stations at five across the nation, and the RCAF included wartime planning to complete the development of the SAR service as it is recognized today. Even though DoT personnel and resources were desperately required to make the overall system effective, it was RCAF actions that initiated that essential change. The RCAF went to great pains to ensure that the domestic SAR system was always in capable hands. Perhaps this is the most compelling argument for a military service to perform domestic-rescue responsibilities: military forces tend to take any assigned task and refuse to let the mission fail despite any challenges.

CONCLUDING THOUGHTS

This topic has interesting implications for the study of civil-military relations and bureaucratic politics in Canada. It appears that the Canadian government sought to demonstrate the RCAF's peacetime utility and make the most efficient use of resources to meet international obligations, despite the RCAF's determination to limit SAR efforts to military purposes only. The Air Force largely ignored the government's priority for SAR in order to maximize money and personnel for other missions it deemed of higher importance. The RCAF took a gamble by accepting the maritime SAR mandate in the hopes it could hand over all of SAR later, and clearly, the Air Force lost. By accepting the aviation role in SAR due to DoT assistance in maritime rescue, the RCAF managed to find balance between the government's and its own priorities.

Further research can shed light on the current role of the RCAF in the

SAR mandate. It certainly appears that Canadian allies have viewed SAR as both a domestic civilian role and an important military role, domestic and deployed. Now, however, the UK is trialing privatization of domestic SAR, suggesting that a fundamental change to the rationale for allocating domestic SAR to military forces may be taking place. If Canada wanted to take a similar approach and assign domestic SAR to another organization, it may have to determine if there is a bigger role for the RCAF's SAR organization within NATO and coalition rescue organizations for deployed operations, or it may risk losing military involvement in the rescue role altogether. The neglected importance of combat SAR may be part of the rationale for the RCAF to fight and keep the SAR mandate, and if not, maybe it should be.

From my perspective, biased though it may be, the military has a great deal to offer the SAR mandate in Canada. The number of aircraft and vessels in this vast country are simply too few and far between not to have immediate access to military resources for any large crisis. Swiss Air 111 was offered as a recent example, but Op Brix was another good example where a country with limited resources really needs to have a level of integration between rescue and military organizations that other countries, like the US and UK, may not need. Privatization may not be as suitable here as it is appearing to be in the UK, or even desirable. The underlying factors behind allocating SAR to the RCAF are, arguably, still very valid today.

The validity of the military conducting SAR is well understood by the Canadian government that was elected in 2015. Much as past governments have chosen, the Trudeau Government included SAR as one of the Canadian Armed Forces core missions.[567] SAR as a core mission makes sense because expeditionary operations, the most common non-North American Aerospace Defence Command (NORAD) use of RCAF assets, is a discretionary activity. Prioritization of the safety and security of Canadians at home, something SAR contributes to on a daily basis, is

---

[567] Canada, National Defence, *Strong, Secure, Engaged: Canada's Defence Policy* (9 June 2017), 17, http://dgpaapp.forces.gc.ca/en/canada-defence-policy/index.asp (accessed 25 April 2018).

an activity that requires the unlimited liability of military personnel and it provides visible benefit of an expensive military to the Canadian public. Until a new government is chosen, the RCAF is certain to remain responsible for this no-fail mission.

No matter which direction the SAR organization in Canada takes in the future, there should be a great deal of pride taken in the accomplishments of the RCAF along the rough and rocky road of SAR development in the 1940s and 1950s. The massive number of rescues that were conducted and the huge amount of hours that the RCAF allocated to save Canadian lives in the 1950s did not deter the RCAF from performing difficult missions while the DoT evaded its responsibilities in the life-saving SAR service. Despite the lack of funding and many other operational responsibilities, the RCAF developed an organization that did the job successfully until 1959 and subsequently worked with the DoT to build a national SAR system that is internationally renowned for excellence. Without question, SAR in Canada became a no-fail mission.

Epilogue

The historical evidence that was presented should prove useful to the ongoing debate surrounding the use of the RCAF in a domestic SAR role. There are two sides to the debate on military resources used for domestic rescue, and even though I have demonstrated a preference for one side, the development of the SAR organization in Canada offers substantial evidence for both sides. However, one aspect of the debate was not covered very well in the post-war development described earlier, and that is the desirability of providing Canadian rescue resources to deployed military operations and what that means to the Canadian SAR service. Canada's recent participation in Afghanistan made the deployed aspect of rescue services very topical, so I wanted to provide some personal context on rescue integration efforts between the RCAF's domestic SAR organization and the combat SAR mission. Rescue for deployed military personnel is an underdeveloped capability in Canada, even from a knowledge and policy standpoint, let alone the bridge too far of resources for deployed combat SAR, and I believe that discussion on deployed rescue services is important to the ongoing debate.

We have seen why deployed rescue is underdeveloped in Canada: the RCAF never had to provide a deployed capability during or after the Second World War, and even the wartime rescue organization created in Canada was used more for domestic requirements than military ones. Therefore, there is a long-standing tradition behind the lack of deployable rescue in Canada. The tradition was reinforced in the decades since the war because it never came up as a problem. Either the Americans or British provided rescue for a deployed operation, or Canada made ad hoc arrangements for deployed rescue situations.

There is a lot of literature on American and British combat-rescue activity, but Canadian rescue activity outside of Canada is really only one mission. Yes, Canada has special operations forces that can conduct hostage-recovery missions or other high-risk activities, but that capability is small and cannot be made available in all locations where RCAF resources may need assistance. So, despite the awesome capabilities of our special forces, there is still a need to discuss routine combat-rescue missions in a deployed context.

The Chief of Staff of a United Nations mission to the Congo in late 1963 and early 1964 was Canadian Brigadier-General Jacques Dextrase. He was a daring leader who was willing to take risks to save as many lives as possible during the violent confrontations between rival governments and United Nations troops. Maliciously, insurgents took missionaries and aid workers hostage in order to influence the situation. Dextrase formed a composite Canadian–Nigerian–Swedish airmobile rescue force with whatever was handy and boldly saved at least 100 people. Now, this crisis does not advance any part of the argument for Canada to have a second look at the military-rescue component. In fact, it does the opposite. The only real deployed rescue operation conducted by Canada was a successful mission using personnel and resources immediately available, so this example reinforced the Canadian outlook of a standing rescue capability as a domestic and civilian responsibility only.

Fast-forward to the post-9/11 conflict in Afghanistan, and the existing Canadian outlook on military rescue becomes very challenged. While I am not an expert in military rescue, I did spend seven months in Afghanistan as the chief of combat rescue in late 2008 and early 2009, so I have a solid understanding of the issues at play. First and foremost of the issues, the Americans have a "leave no one behind" philosophy that means combat rescue is a fundamental component of their combat operations. They are so shockingly adamant about bringing everyone home, that they lost a total of 18 soldiers in Somalia during the disastrous battle for Mogadishu on 3 and 4 October 1993 instead of consolidating forces and leaving the scene of the battle. Their philosophy is deeply embedded in their operational concepts, and it has been demonstrated in the years since Somalia by a very robust capability of HH-60G Blackhawk helicopters that provided combat-rescue services in Iraq and Afghanistan.

In Afghanistan, it was crystal clear that Americans take combat rescue of their troops very seriously, and the rest of us had to get on board with their philosophy. When I first deployed to Afghanistan, NATO and the

US had separate rescue systems, but that turned out to be deeply inefficient, and in April of 2009, the systems were merged. The merger set the
standard for an integrated rescue capability that was used for the rest of
the Afghanistan campaign, the Libya campaign in 2011, and the mission
a few years later against the Islamic State of Iraq and the Levant. Since
Afghanistan, NATO operations and any large coalition of the future that
involves US troops will have a deployed combat SAR capability of some
form. Combat SAR is an expectation of the Americans that cannot be
denied.

The obvious question arising from this quick march from the Second
World War to Afghanistan is: so what? Given that the Americans or
NATO will set up a combat SAR capability, how can that possibly affect
Canada's domestic SAR system? The answers will resonate with the his-
torical lessons of the past.

First, if Canada is going to participate in NATO or coalition operations, as has been the case since 9/11, it has to understand the terminology
and procedures that are used in combat SAR. Aviators are expected to
have survive/evade/resist/escape training and an evasion plan of action
in the event they are shot down over enemy territory. Soldiers must have
something called an isolated personnel report, which is used by combat
SAR forces to confirm they are communicating with the right person
and not an enemy imposter. All deployed personnel must have the right
survival equipment. All of these requirements to operate over enemy territory should sound vaguely familiar: the ASROs of the Second World War
were responsible for all of those aspects of combat operations, at home
and deployed. All of those lessons learned in the war to properly prepare
aircrew for combat operations are still relevant today, and the RCAF needs
to restore the ASRO capability to better interact with future coalitions.

Arguably, Canada still has a limited ASRO capability. Canada has
provided domestic SAR personnel to combat operations in Afghanistan
and Libya because domestic SAR personnel have a deep understanding
of the mechanics of investigating distress situations and tasking resources
for rescue missions. While combat SAR is much more complex, the fact
that the aviation domestic SAR service is run by military personnel in
Canada allows for those same military personnel to work in a deployed
coalition environment with other military personnel. Think back to the

B-36 Peacemaker incident in 1950 and how the cryptographic failure caused problems that military personnel in rescue centres were able to resolve. That same principle applies to deployed rescue: military personnel speak a common language and, with their security clearances, are able to discuss matters of distress with whatever rescue resource is assigned to the combat-rescue mission.

If the RCAF were to cease responsibility for SAR in Canada, would they then retain the investigative skills and embedded policies to understand coalition rescue mission? I cannot answer that question, but without the hundreds of operational rescue missions that RCAF crews perform every year and the thousands of distress situations investigated by military personnel, the expertise currently embedded in the RCAF on such matters would certainly be decreased. Based on the low level of combat-rescue knowledge among Canadian military personnel that I witnessed in Afghanistan, I believe a strong case can be made for the correlation between domestic SAR experience in military personnel and the deployed combat-rescue environment.

Another concern that could result from decreased RCAF experience in domestic SAR is this: would the Canadian Armed Forces become so reliant on other nations for deployable rescue that it would limit other nation's views of our operational desirability in coalitions? Perhaps not, but there is a risk that by decreasing the military's role in the domestic SAR service, the Canadian Armed Forces could be considered to have an undesirable knowledge-and-experience gap for combat operations. I believe that there needs to be more integration between domestic and combat SAR systems, not less.

Returning to domestic considerations, there are important capabilities inherent in the current SAR organization. Swiss Air 111 had a very quick and efficient response from the RCN, the Canadian Army, and the RCAF, but only because those linkages are practised every day. Swiss Air 111 has echoes from the past as well. Remember Op Attaché in 1948, where the Canadian Army, USAF, and RCAF all worked together at no notice to organize a large-scale search that saved five lives. The historical lessons suggest that the military interoperability experience gained since the beginning of SAR history in Canada is still very much relevant today.

Additionally, can Canada afford to have sufficient resources for the military and separate resources for the SAR service? Anyone who has followed the military's procurement woes for purchasing new aircraft over recent decades will know that we have to be prepared to use ageing equipment in few numbers. It is simply part of the Canadian experience.

The difficulty in the purchase of large and expensive airframes specifically for rescue may be a critically important point: the RCAF has an inherent ability to tap into other aircraft and helicopter resources when primary SAR resources encounter mechanical issues. The use of other non-SAR RCAF aircraft to hold standby happens on a regular basis, and that flexibility would be difficult to achieve in a smaller organization. Of all the organizations in Canada that could provide a rescue service, only the military has the depth of resources and personnel to surge as required for major aviation and maritime disasters.

So, how does deployed rescue affect domestic rescue in Canada? The Canadian military has a requirement to maintain interoperability with coalition and NATO partners, and that means developing more deployed-rescue knowledge than we have at present. The RCAF currently bridges the gap in deployed operations by using domestic SAR personnel in deployed combat-rescue coordination roles because of their extensive experience in the domestic role. Therefore, any decrease to RCAF involvement in domestic rescue may create unwelcome follow-on challenges for the military's deployed coalition requirements for any operation.

There are counterarguments to the points I have made above, but most of the arguments I have heard fail to take into consideration the importance and effort that the Americans put into rescue efforts. Indeed, we have seen how importantly they treated rescue throughout early SAR history, with massive searches and a complete willingness to respond to Canadian domestic SAR missions on a regular basis. As Canada occasionally considers the question of who should provide domestic rescue in Canada, consideration must be given to our American allies who have a deep interest in the safety of their citizens travelling through Canada. The international community drove rescue requirements in the post-war world, and it remains deeply interested in how we perform this mission today.

I expect that the RCAF leadership largely agrees with my assessments that the RCAF is good for SAR, and that SAR is good for the RCAF. I would be quite surprised if the RCAF did not continue to fight for the SAR mandate in the future, much as it did in 2011. The rationale for assigning SAR to the military in the first place is still relevant, and an objective view of the Canadian situation would find other options to be challenging from a cost perspective. Since 1942, the RCAF has been involved in domestic rescue, and it has handled its responsibility so well that Canada's SAR system is widely viewed as a high standard. The way rescue developed in Canada after the Second World War has simply embedded the domestic SAR role into the one organization that has the depth and expertise to treat SAR as the no-fail mission that it must always remain.

Bibliography

PRIMARY SOURCES

Library and Archives Canada

Records Group 2	Cabinet Conclusions
	Cabinet Documents
	Cabinet Defence Committee
Records Group 12	Department of Transport
Records Group 24	Department of National Defence
Records Group 25	Department of External Affairs
Manuscript Group 32, B6	Hon. Douglas Abbott

Directorate of History and Heritage

Air Force Headquarters Fonds.

Chief of the Air Staff, RCAF, *Roundel* (Ottawa: 1948–1964).

Document File System.

KARDEX File System.

R. L. Raymont Fonds.

Canadian Joint Operations Centre

SAR Historical Documents file.

International Civil Aviation Organization

"Convention on International Civil Aviation - Doc 7300." ICAO.

http://www.icao.int/publications/Pages/doc7300.aspx (accessed 25 April 2018).

Chicago Convention, 7 December 1944.

International Maritime Organization

"International Convention for the Safety of Life at Sea, 1948." http://www.imo.org/en/KnowledgeCentre/ReferencesAndArchives/HistoryofSOLAS/Documents/SOLAS 1948 UK Treaty Series.pdf (accessed 25 April 2018).

Safety of Life at Sea, 1929 Conference.

Safety of Life at Sea, 1948 Conference.

RCAF Operations Records Books

"Royal Canadian Air Force Operations Record Books." Library and Archives Canada (LAC). http://heritage.canadiana.ca/view/oocihm.lac_mikan_135766 (accessed 25 April 2018).

Reel ID C-12160, Western Air Command Headquarters, Daily Diary 6 March 1938 to 31 October 1942.

Reel ID C-12156, Eastern Air Command Headquarters, Daily Diary 1 May 1940 to 30 September 1944.

Official Histories and Other Primary-Source Materials

Appleton, Thomas. *Usque Ad Mare: A History of the Canadian Coast Guard and Marine Services.* Ottawa: Department of Transport, 1968. http://www.ccg-gcc.gc.ca/eng/CCG/USQUE_Table_Contents (accessed 25 April 2018).

Bryson, E. D., and Bray, N. D., "An Evaluation of the Future RCAF Search and Rescue Requirement." Department of National Defence,

Chief of Operational Requirements, DRDC CORA. Ottawa: February 1964.

Canadian Armed Forces and Canadian Coast Guard. *Federal Search and Rescue Operational Governance Committee Annual Report 2014*. Ottawa: Canadian Joint Operations Command, March 2015.

Chief of the Defence Staff. *Duty with Honour: The Profession of Arms in Canada*. Kingston: Canadian Defence Academy, 2003.

Chief of the Air Staff, RCAF, *The Roundel* (Ottawa: 1948–1964).

Douglas, W. A. B. *The Official History of the Royal Canadian Air Force*. Vol. 2, *The Creation of a National Air Force*. Canada: University of Toronto Press, 1980.

Ferguson, Michael. "Report of the Auditor General of Canada – Spring 2013." Office of the Auditor General, 2013. http://www.oag-bvg. gc.ca/internet/English/parl_oag_201304_07_e_38192.html (accessed 25 April 2018).

Forest History Society, *History of Smokejumping*, updated 12 September 2011, http://www.foresthistory.org/ASPNET/Publications/smoke-jumping/sec2.htm (last accessed December 16, 2015). This web page is no longer available.

Greenhous, Brereton, Harris, Stephen J., Johnston, William C., and Rawling, William G.P. *The Official History of the Royal Canadian Air Force*. Vol. 3, *The Crucible of War, 1939–1945*. Toronto: University of Toronto Press, 1994.

National Defence and Fisheries and Oceans Canada. *CAMSAR, Canadian Aeronautical and Maritime Search and Rescue Manual, Combined Edition – Volumes I, II, and III*, B-GA-209-001/FP-001. Effective date 30 September 2014.

Richards, Denis. *Royal Air Force 1939–45*. Vol. 1, *The Fight at Odds*. London: Her Majesty's Stationery Office, 1974.

Royal Canadian Air Force. *Canadian Forces Aerospace Move Doctrine*. Astra: Canadian Forces Aerospace Warfare Centre, 2011.

The United States Coast Guard, "The Coast Guard Along the North Atlantic Coast," *U.S. Coast Guard History*, December 1988, http://www.uscg.mil/history/h_index.asp (last accessed December 21, 2015). This web page is no longer available.

SECONDARY SOURCES

Associated Press. "Fear 47 Died in Shipwreck." *The Milwaukee Journal*, Wednesday, November 27, 1947.

Barry, Donald, and Bratt, Duane. "Defence Against Help: Explaining Canada–U.S. Security Relations." *American Review of Canadian Studies*, 2007: 63–89.

Campbell, Colin. "J. L. Ilsley and the Transition to the Post-war Tax System: 1943–1946." *Canadian Tax Journal* (2015), 1–52.

Christie, Carl A. *Ocean Bridge: The History of RAF Ferry Command*. Toronto: University of Toronto Press, 1995.

Creighton, Donald. *The Forked Road: Canada 1939–1957*. Toronto: McClelland and Stewart Limited, 1976.

Evans, Clayton. *Rescue at Sea: An International History of Lifesaving, Coastal Rescue Craft and Organisations*. London: Conway Maritime Press, 2003.

Futrell, Robert F. *The United States Air Force in Korea: 1950–1953*. Rev. ed. Washington, D.C.: Office of Air Force History, USAF, 1983.

Galdorisi, George, and Phillips, Tom. *Leave No Man Behind: The Saga of Combat Search and Rescue*. Minneapolis: Zenith Press, 2008.

Halliday, Hugh A. "The Role of the Boats: Air Force Part 46." *Legion Magazine*, 30 August 2011.

Higgins, Jenny. "The American Presence in Newfoundland and Labrador," *Heritage Newfoundland & Labrador*, 2006, http://www.heritage.nf.ca/articles/politics/american-presence-newfoundland-labrador.php (accessed 25 April 2018).

Leigh, Z. Lewis. *And I Shall Fly: The Flying Memoirs of Z. Lewis Leigh*. Toronto: Canav Books, 1985.

MacKenzie, David. *Canada and International Civil Aviation 1932–1948*. Toronto: University of Toronto Press, 1989.

———. *ICAO: A History of the International Civil Aviation Organization*. Toronto: University of Toronto Press, 2010.

Maginley, Charles D. *The Canadian Coast Guard 1962–2002*. St. Catherines, ON: Vanwell Publishing Limited, 2003.

May, Denny. "RCAF Rescue Service," *The Adventures of W. R. (Wop) May*, http://www.wopmay.com/current/adventures/rcafRescue.htm (accessed 25 April 2018).

Milberry, Larry. *Air Transport in Canada, Volume 1*. Toronto: CANAV Books, 1997.

———. *Air Transport in Canada, Volume 2*. Toronto: CANAV Books, 1997.

———. *Canada's Air Force: At War and At Peace, Volume 1*. Toronto: CANAV Books, 2000.

Mowbray, Clinton, LCol. "Lessons Forgotten? A Historical Examination of the RCAF Search and Rescue Organization." Directed Research Project. Canadian Forces College, Toronto, ON, 2010.

O'Keefe, Betty, and Macdonald, Ian. *Disaster on Mount Slesse: The Story of Western Canada's Worst Air Crash*. Halfmoon Bay, BC: Caitlin Press, 2006.

Ostram, Thomas P. *The United States Coast Guard in World War II: A History of Domestic and Overseas Actions*. North Carolina: McFarland & Co. Inc., 2009.

The Para Rescue Association of Canada. *That Others May Live: 50 Years of Para Rescue in Canada*. Astra: The Para Rescue Association of Canada, 1994.

Pilborough, Geoff D. *The Royal Canadian Air Force Marine Squadrons*. Vol. 1, *1935–1945*. Edmonton: Canimpex, 1996.

Pugliese, David. "Ottawa May Privatize Search-and-Rescue Projects." *Postmedia News*, July 21, 2011. http://news.nationalpost.com/news/canada/ottawa-may-privatize-search-and-rescue-projects (accessed 25 April 2018).

Smith, G. Y. *Seek and Save: The History of 103 Rescue Unit*. Erin, ON: The Boston Mills Press, 1990.

Stouffer, Ray. *Swords, Clunks & Widowmakers: The Tumultuous Life of the RCAF's Original 1 Canadian Air Division*. Trenton: Canadian Department of National Defence, 2015.

Strauss, Richard. "The Diplomatic Negotiations Leading to the Establishment of American Bases in Newfoundland: June 1940 – April 1941." Memorial University of Newfoundland, March 1972.

Sutherland, Jon, and Canwell, Diane. *The RAF Air Sea Rescue Service: 1918–1986*. Great Britain: Pen & Sword Books Ltd., 2005.

Taylor, L. B. Jr. *That Others May Live: The Aerospace Rescue and Recovery Service.* New York: E. P. Dutton & Co., Inc., 1967.

Vernon, J. E. "RCAF Marine Craft." *4th Annual Air Force Historical Conference: 80 Years of Maritime Aviation in Canada.* 12 Wing, Shearwater, NS, August 24–25, 1998.

Whittle, Peter, and Borissow, Michael. *Angels Without Wings: The Dramatic Inside Stories of the RAF's Search and Rescue Squadrons.* Great Britain: The Angley Book Company Ltd., 1966.

Index

Note: air sea rescue (ASR), Royal Canadian Air Force (RCAF), and search and rescue (SAR) have not been included in the index because those topics are the main subjects of this book and are embedded throughout.

Battle of Britain: 27-29, 31-35, 42, 57, 116, 122

BC Star: 52, 53

Beachcraft Expeditor aircraft: 175

Beeman, LCdr, J. H. (RCN): 166, 167

Bell helicopter, HTL-4: 143

Bolingbroke aircraft: 37

British Commonwealth Air Training Plan: 64

Cabinet Defence Committee: 5, 106

Campbell, A/M, Hugh (CAS): 188

Canadian Air Publication (CAP): 51, 170

Canadian Airways: 8, 11

Canadian Army: 6, 20, 72, 73, 119, 132, 167, 176, 212

Canadian Cabinet: 89, 90, 94, 95, 98-103, 105-107, 135, 139

Canadian Coast Guard: xiii, xv, 20, 21, 24, 26, 176 proposal of: 83, 84, 131, 135, 138, 140, 142, 150 creation of: 179-183, 187, 188, 190-196, 199

Canadian Joint Operations Command (CJOC): 5

Canadian Lifesaving Service: 7, 12, 15, 35, 200

Canadian security shift, concept of: 14, 84-87, 199, 200

Canso seaplane: 38, 76, 110, 127, 141, 161, 167, 186

Carscallen, A/C: 148

Cavallo, USS: 182

Chatham, New Brunswick: 166

Chevrier, Hon., Lionel (MoT): 117

Chicago Convention: 85-87

Chief of the Air Staff (CAS): 57, 97, 142, 171-173, 188

Churchill, Manitoba: 103, 109, 112

Civilian Public Service Program: 60

Clarksdale Victory: 137

Claxton, Hon., Brooke (MND): 102, 107, 117, 125

Clyne, J. V. (Chairman of ICSAR): 138

Combat rescue: 3, 69, 70, 75, 76, 78, 79, 89, 111, 116, 188, 189, 197, 198, 205, 209-213

Composite flights: 71, 91, 105, 109, 158, 190

Cost, theme of: 24-26, 48, 79, 80, 99, 100, 102, 105-108, 119, 148, 149, 151, 152, 160, 177, 194, 201-203

Costello, A/C, Martin: 112, 113

Curtis, A/V/M Wilfred: 134

Dakota aircraft, C-47: 123, 141, 155, 161

Dartmouth, Nova Scotia: 10, 88, 105, 110, 141

Defence against help concept: 14, 189, 191, 192, 198-200

Destroyers for bases: 36

De Niverville, A/V/M: 180

Department of External Affairs: 99, 148, 149

Department of Fisheries: 83, 135, 173

Department of Mines and Resources: 83, 135

Department of National Defence: 102, 135

Department of Transport (DoT): xviii, 62, 83, 87, 89, 91, 93, 99, 107, 119, 133, 135, 142, 151, 153, 162, 179-185, 188, 191, 194, 201-203, 208

Diefenbaker (John) Government: 191

Directorate of ASR: 32, 47

Doe, Sgt, Jones Francis: 11

Domestic rescue: 15, 16, 18, 20-23, 50, 52-56, 59-63, 65-67, 71, 78-80,

224

79, 118, 119, 151, 176, 179, 193, 194, 198-200

Soviet threat: 117, 138, 204

S.S. Northolm: 52, 53

Stephenville, Newfoundland: 165, 192

Strouts, F/L: 104

Submarines (see also U-boat): 41, 48, 53, 182, 198

Swiss Air 111: xiii-xv, 207, 212

Thompson, Scotty: 60

Tiger Moth aircraft: 38

Torbay (see St. John's)

Trans Canada Airlines: 11, 12, 61, 167-169

Transport Canada: 107

Trenton, Ontario: xiv, 10-12, 19, 76, 88, 91, 104, 109, 110, 133, 139, 141, 174, 183, 190

Trudeau (Justin) Government: 3, 207

U-boat submarine: 27, 35, 39, 41, 48, 54, 64, 121, 198

United Kingdom: 2, 16, 17, 27-32, 35, 36, 40, 41, 43, 44, 46, 56, 66, 78, 84-86, 108, 119

United Nations: 25, 131, 133, 211

United States: 12, 16, 17, 25, 33, 34, 53, 60, 82, 85, 86, 94, 103, 108, 112, 119, 137, 165, 189, 192, 200, 212

United States Air Force: 112-114, 116, 147, 149, 151, 199, 200, 212

United States Army: 137

United States Army Air Corps: 47, 74

United States Coast Guard: 33, 108, 114, 143

United States Navy: 112, 182

Vancouver, British Columbia: 77, 88, 109, 110, 114, 139, 141,

167, 168, 170, 174, 182, 183, 185, 190

Victoria, British Columbia: 18

Walrus seaplane: 32, 33, 122

Weather ships: 149

Western Air Command: 27, 35, 43, 44, 50-54, 56, 63, 65, 66, 69, 71, 73, 74, 80, 110

Whitehorse, Yukon: 103, 109

Wilson, J. A. (Controller of Civil Aviation): 8

Winnipeg, Manitoba: 141, 174, 190

Woodman, Nursing Sister Grace: 155, 156

Wynne, S/L Dick: 155